Grilling 1-2-3

Grilling 1-2-3®

Editor: Carrie E. Holcomb
Contributing Editor: Mary Williams
Contributing Writer: Don Gulbrandsen
Copy Chief: Terri Fredrickson
Publishing Operations Manager: Karen Schirm
Senior Editor, Asset and Information Manager: Phillip Morgan
Edit and Design Coordinator: Mary Lee Gavin
Editorial and Design Assistants: Cheryl Eckert, Renee E. McAtee
Book Production Managers: Pam Kvitne, Marjorie J. Schenkelberg,
   Rick von Holdt, Mark Weaver
Contributing Copy Editor: Amanda Knief
Contributing Proofreaders: Gretchen Kauffman, Mary Helen Schlitz,
   Donna Segal
Indexer: Elizabeth Parson
Additional Photography: Blain Moats

Additional Editorial and Design contributions from:
OEC Graphics IT
   Account Executive: Katherine Running
   Production Coordinator: Michael Kurtz
   Production: Chris Grathen
   Quality Control: Scott Wenzlau

Abramowitz Creative Studios
   Publishing Director/Designer: Tim Abramowitz
   Graphic Designers: Kelly Bailey, Joel Wires

Photography: Image Studios
   Account Executive: Lisa Egan
   Primary Photographers: Glen Hartjes, Bill Rein
   Contributing Photographers: Michael Leschisin, Jeff Lendrum,
      John von Dorn
   Food Stylists: Nancy Froncek, Karla Kaphaem, Russ Keller
   Assistant Food Stylist: Theresa Farris
   Stylists: Sara Privett, Vicki Sumwalt

Meredith® Books
Executive Director, Editorial: Gregory H. Kayko
Executive Director, Design: Matt Strelecki
Managing Editor: Amy Tincher-Durik
Executive Editor/Group Manager: Benjamin W. Allen
Senior Editor/Group Manager: Jan Miller
Senior Associate Design Director: Tom Wegner
Marketing Product Manager: Brent Wiersma
National Marketing Manager-Home Depot: Suzy Johnson

Publisher and Editor in Chief: James D. Blume
Editorial Director: Linda Raglan Cunningham
Executive Director, Marketing: Steve Malone
Executive Director, New Business Development: Todd M. Davis
Director, Sales-Home Depot: Robb Morris
Executive Director, Sales: Ken Zagor
Director, Operations: George A. Susral
Director, Production: Douglas M. Johnston
Director, Marketing: Amy Nichols
Business Director: Jim Leonard

Vice President and General Manager: Douglas J. Guendel

Meredith Publishing Group
President: Jack Griffin
Senior Vice President: Bob Mate

Meredith Corporation
Chairman and Chief Executive Officer: William T. Kerr
President and Chief Operating Officer: Stephen M. Lacy

In Memoriam: E.T. Meredith III (1933-2003)

How to use this book

People are turning their attention outdoors and adopting lifestyles that mean more quality time in the backyard with family and friends. Outdoor cooking—grilling—has long been popular with Americans, but in recent years it has started to change dramatically. There are new and improved grills, new outdoor-oriented cooking tools, and new techniques, all designed to keep up with this lifestyle shift outdoors.

Unfortunately too many people think that a grill is little more than a machine for quick-cooking a few burgers. How wrong they are! Grills, in fact, are full-featured cooking machines that can mimic almost everything your oven and cook top can do—and often they can do more than those kitchen appliances, plus deliver food that tastes fantastic. *Grilling 1-2-3* is your guide to unlocking the secrets of outdoor cooking and moving beyond burgers and steaks to a world of exciting grill foods. Along the way you are going to learn a lot about food and cooking and you are going to have a lot of fun. Your family and friends are going to be amazed at the entrées you prepare for them. Forget about fancy restaurants—backyard cooking is where it's at!

Getting started

Chapter 1 introduces you to outdoor cooking and helps you select the right grill for your needs. Additional sections discuss smokers and turkey fryers, other popular outdoor cookers. Detailed sections follow that cover all the basics you need for grilling success: setting up a grilling area, selecting fuel, starting a fire, controlling heat, and determining when food is done. Comprehensive charts tell you how long and at what temperature to cook just about any food you want to grill. The chapter wraps up with must-read sections on grill maintenance, grilling gadgets, and grill safety.

Learn as you cook

The rest of the book covers what we love most: great-tasting food and how to cook it. Each of the remaining chapters contains mouthwatering recipes featuring detailed instructions and informative photographs that will both tell you and show you how to prepare each entrée. Along the way you will learn a variety of great outdoor-cooking techniques, plus explore tools and ingredients that will make the job easier and the food tastier. Plus each recipe features a tip box—under headings such as Closer Look, Tool Savvy, Buyer's Guide, and more—that gives you essential information on grill food, tools, and techniques.

Direct versus indirect

Chapters 2 and 3 explain the differences between direct and indirect grilling. All other techniques are offshoots of these two basic strategies. A tremendous collection of recipes accompanies the how-to information. You'll be surprised by all the foods that are fit for the grill: pizza, lobster, potatoes, rib roast, and pork chops, just to name a few.

Chapters 4 and 5 offer popular variations on indirect grilling. Chapter 4 covers one of grilling's most popular tools, the rotisserie, while smoking is the focus of Chapter 5. You don't have a smoker? Don't worry; *Grilling 1-2-3* explains how to use your charcoal kettle or gas grill as a smoker.

From frying to mops

Turkey fryers are the latest outdoor-cooking craze, and Chapter 6 explains how to use them safely and effectively. You'll discover that these devices are great for cooking a lot more than turkeys.

Gadgets are fun and a great way to expand the cooking capabilities of your grill. Check out Chapter 7 for recipes and creative ideas for using skewers, grill woks, grill baskets, and hardwood planks.

Grilling is about a lot more than fire and tools—it's also about adding flavor to foods. Chapter 8 explores the little-known technique of brining, a form of marinating with a saltwater solution that helps meats stay juicy and tasty after cooking a long time. Sauces, marinades, rubs, and mops are the focus of Chapter 9. After reading this section and putting the recipes to work, you'll never have to worry about bland food again.

▼ **Sweet-Hot Barbecue Sauce (see recipe, page 216)**

Grilling 1-2-3®
Table of contents

Chapter 6
FRYING   152

Chapter 7
GRILL GADGETS   178

Chapter 8
BRINING   198

Chapter 9
SAUCES, MARINADES, RUBS & MOPS   210

Grilling Basics

 ooking food over fire seems like the simplest way to prepare a meal. Yet if you're one of those people who think that grilling consists of nothing more than slapping meat down over some coals—maybe embellished with some sauce out of a jar—you are barely scratching the surface. Cooking over fire offers countless variations resulting in a nearly infinite variety of dishes. In fact, if you explore grilling to its fullest, you can turn your deck or patio into a food-producing paradise whose output can easily rival the best-stocked gourmet kitchen.

Grilling or Barbecuing?

One of the keys to expanding your grill-side skills is to understand some of the important differences between different types of cooking. Though this book will use the term "grilling" generically when referring to all types of cooking over fire, there are significant differences between the two main categories of grill cooking—grilling and barbecuing.

Grilling refers to cooking food over high, direct—right under the food—heat for a short period of time. This is the traditional style of grill cooking that backyard chefs use to cook burgers, steaks, chicken breasts, and a variety of foods over their charcoal or gas grills. The intense heat sears the food surface and seals in the juices, and the fire's smoke imparts the mouthwatering flavor that makes this type of cooking so popular. Grilling is perfect for small or thin cuts of meat, or small pieces of vegetables. One advantage of direct grilling is that it can be done on an uncovered grill, though a cover is an indispensable tool, useful for speeding cooking time, adding flavor, and controlling flare-ups.

The term "barbecuing" is sometimes used interchangeably with grilling, but it is actually an entirely different method in which food is cooked for a longer time over a low-heat, smoldering wood fire. Barbecuing usually employs indirect heat—meaning that the fire is off to the side of the food, not under it—and requires the use of some type of

Chapter 1

covered cooker. This method is better used for larger cuts of meat like roasts, hams, or whole turkeys, or for tougher meats—for example, ribs or brisket—that benefit from the extra time to break down their stringy connective tissues. Whatever food you cook this way will end up with the distinctive savory, smoky flavor that makes barbecued dishes so delicious.

Foods Fit for the Grill

One of the problems with most grill chefs is that they get in a rut, cooking the same old foods using the same old methods. Well, it's time to graduate from burgers and steaks! Believe it or not, your grill is a versatile tool in which you can cook a variety of dishes that you might have never thought suited patio cuisine. Some of these foods might require specialized tools or techniques to adapt them to the grill, but the results are going to make you change your mind about what constitutes "grill food."

- Vegetables: Mom always told you to eat your vegetables, and today's dietitians are telling you she was right. The problem is that vegetables don't always have enough flavor—until you cook them on the grill. Cooked over an open fire—directly on the rack, on skewers, or even in a grill wok—vegetables will soon become a much-anticipated component of your meals, not something you have to eat.

- Seafood: Fish gets high marks from health professionals but low marks for bland flavor—or worse—"fishy" taste. Liven up your fish by grilling it—in fact, many people swear that grilled fish tastes better than traditional grilled beef, pork, and chicken entreés. Plus, think beyond fish—shrimp and other shellfish are also very grill-friendly foods.

- Pizza: No way—pizza on a grill? Why not—most of us have eaten at those fancy wood-fired pizza places; the concept isn't much different than using your grill. Once you experience the smoky goodness of your first grilled pizza, a standard pie in the oven may never again make the grade for you.

Choose Your Grill: Charcoal

The first step to outdoor cooking success is choosing the right grill. There are two main categories, based on their fuel type: charcoal and gas. Charcoal grills, which are fueled by charcoal briquettes (see "Feeding the Fire: Fuel" on pages 18 to 19), offer the traditional entry point for most grilling novices. They are less expensive than gas grills, easy to learn how to use, less prone to problems, and quite versatile. That said, you get what you pay for, and not all charcoal grills are equal.

The most basic type of charcoal grill is the open, portable type; Japanese-style versions are known as hibachi grills. These are fine if you only have a few bucks to spend and want something that can be easily toted to picnics or tailgate parties. Ultimately, though, you will find these woefully inadequate for anything beyond the basics. That's why, if you're serious, you need to look at a kettle grill.

Kettle grills have deep, rounded bowls and a removable domed lid. They generally have a lower rack for holding charcoal and an upper grill rack for the food. Cooking temperature is controlled by adjusting vents located on the bottom of the kettle and the top of the lid. These are versatile cooking machines. They are great for direct grilling (open or closed), indirect grilling (barbecuing), and even can be used for smoking.

When shopping for your first kettle grill, there are a number of features to look for. The bowl and lid should be constructed of a heavy-grade metal that is coated with a porcelain finish. Multiple vents in the bowl are essential, along with some type of tray underneath to catch ashes. The lid should fit tightly and be outfitted with both a vent and a heatproof handle. The charcoal and cooking grates should be heavy and durable; look for either stainless steel or a nickel-coated finish. The grill should have sturdy legs, plus wheels that make it easy to move around.

Charcoal grills can get pretty fancy, and a number of add-ons are available that will enhance the unit—plus make it more expensive. Among the options available are built-in thermometers in the lid, elaborate

▲ **Choose a kettle grill constructed of heavy-grade metal and coated with a porcelain finish. The lid should fit tightly and feature a vent and heatproof handle. The grill should have sturdy legs and wheels that make it easy to move around.**

cleaning/ash-catching systems, attached work surfaces and storage racks, and even gas-powered ignition systems! Once you start pricing out these deluxe charcoal grills, you might discover that it's better to consider investing in a gas grill. If you're a beginning griller, probably the best advice is to look for a basic charcoal grill. Look for something durable that will serve you well for a couple years while you hone your skills and give you the confidence to select a higher-end grill that will best suit your long-term needs.

▲ **This removable tray catches ashes that fall from the bottom vents. It is easily cleaned after every grilling session.**

The vent in a kettle grill's lid is there for a lot more than good looks. Opening the vents increases the flow of air through a grill, providing more oxygen, fueling the fire, and increasing the cooking temperature. Closing the vents has the opposite effect, decreasing the cooking temperature or even putting out the fire.

Kettle grills are versatile cooking machines that can be used for direct grilling, indirect grilling, or even smoking.

A handle outside the grill easily and safely controls the vent system in the kettle bottom. The rotating covers do double duty by sweeping away ashes.

Kettle grills employ two grates, a lower one for holding charcoal and an upper one for holding the food. The grates rest on support brackets and are easily lifted out for access and cleaning. Look for a grill that allows you to adjust the height of the cooking grate to change the grilling temperature at its surface.

Choose Your Grill: Gas

Gas grills have become the traditional step up for outdoor cooks who cut their teeth with charcoal. They are usually fueled by a propane tank, though you can safely connect them to a natural gas line if they are set up in a permanent installation. Gas grills typically feature a treasure chest-shape box fitted with a lift-up, hinged lid. Gas burners line the bottom of the box; above the burners sits some type of heating surface, usually ceramic briquettes, lava rock, or metal bars. As food cooks and drips fats and juices on the heating surface, smoke is generated that gives the food its grilled flavor.

Yes, gas grills are more expensive than the charcoal variety, but they offer many advantages. First, there is no more messy charcoal to buy. A typical propane tank fuels 12 to 14 hours of grilling, much more cooking time than the average bag of charcoal. Second, heating up the grill is easy and quick. Forget about starter fluid and a long wait for the coals to gray over; with a gas grill all you do is turn a knob, push a button, and wait 10 to 15 minutes. Finally, you have much greater heat control than with a charcoal grill—no more fussing with vents and adding new briquettes.

As with purchasing a charcoal grill, gas grill shoppers will get what they pay for and need to look for a well-built, durable unit. The grill should consist of solid parts constructed from cast aluminum, stainless steel, or porcelain-coated steel. The racks should feature rust-resistant, easy-to-clean materials such as stainless steel or porcelain enamel coating. The heating mechanism should include push-button ignition and at least three independently operating burners—this will allow better heat control and flexibility for direct or indirect cooking. A built-in thermometer and a gauge to monitor the propane level are must-have features. Carefully consider the heating elements; lava rocks tend to be cheaper and initially work well, but they collect grease and can be prone to flare-ups.

In addition, gas grills are available with a variety of options that might add to the price

▲ **This gas grill has many of the basic features that you should look for, plus some attractive options. It has three primary burners, plus a rotisserie burner and a side burner for keeping food warm.**

but which will also add cooking versatility. Secondary racks sitting in the lid above the main grill rack offer a location to cook items requiring less heat or a place to keep fast-cooking items warm. Make sure they can be removed so you can create room for grilling big things such as whole turkeys. Side burners offer a convenient place to cook stove-top dishes that you'd normally have to run in and out of the kitchen to monitor. Attached racks are a great investment if your deck or patio lacks work space near your grilling zone.

▲ **Features on this model include an attached shelf with flip-up work surface, a storage cabinet underneath the grill, and wheels for mobility.**

■ This gas grill (left) uses metal heating grates installed directly above the burners. Other models use ceramic briquettes or lava rocks as a heating surface. Most gas grills are fueled by propane, available in refillable metal tanks sold at many retail outlets. A short hose, fitted with a device called a regulator, attaches the grill to the fuel tank (above).

Look for a gas grill equipped with at least three burners, allowing flexibility for direct or indirect cooking.

▲ Start-up for many gas grills is a snap: Simply open the grill lid, twist a burner control knob to "high," and press an electronic ignition switch.

▲ The drip pan—which catches grease and juices that drip off cooking food—slides out like a drawer for easy access and cleaning on some models.

Choose Your Grill: Smokers

Smoking is basically a form of grilling where you cook meat using low, indirect heat and smoke generated by chips or chunks of hardwoods placed on the heat source. In addition, a source of moisture—usually a simple water pan—aids the smoking process. Smoked foods can take several hours to cook, but the results are usually worth the time. The unique flavor imparted by different types of woods—hickory, mesquite, and apple are popular choices—can make for a memorable barbecue meal.

Backyard grillers can actually turn their kettle charcoal or gas grill into a smoking machine—and with good results. But if you want to get serious about smoked foods, you should probably consider investing in a specialized cooker built specifically for the task. The most popular type is the vertical water smoker, which looks kind of like a tall, cylindrical kettle grill. These affordable smokers usually stand $2\frac{1}{2}$ or 3 feet tall and have some type of heat source in the base—most feature a simple charcoal grate, but some models have an electrical heating element or even gas burners. Directly above the heat source is the water pan, and above the water pan are (typically) two levels of grill racks for holding the food.

▲ Choosing a vertical water smoker is a lot like choosing a kettle grill—both products share many of the same desirable features. Look for a smoker such as this one, which features porcelain-enameled metal construction, a tight-fitting lid, and heatproof handles.

▲ A charcoal tray in the base is the heat source for this smoker. Start your fire the same way you do with a charcoal grill.

▲ The water pan sits on the next level above the charcoal grate; keep it filled because moisture is essential to the smoking process.

Shopping for a vertical water smoker is a lot like shopping for a kettle grill—some of the desirable construction features are the same for both products. Design elements such as porcelain-enameled metal, tight-fitting lids, and multiple vents are essential for a top-notch smoking experience. In addition, look for a temperature gauge (very important in smoking for monitoring heat levels) and easy access to the lower half of the smoker so you can painlessly add wood, water, and charcoal. When you start costing out models with different fuel types, you will see considerable differences. Not surprisingly, charcoal versions are the cheapest, electric models are somewhat costlier, and gas-fueled varieties are a big investment. Consider how much you plan to use your smoker and spend accordingly.

Maybe you are an experienced smoker and you're looking for an upgrade from your vertical water model—then it's probably time for you to consider a horizontal dry or pit smoker. These can require a significant investment, but this is the style that the barbecue pros use, and they are exactly what you need if you foresee some high-volume smoking in your future. Horizontal smokers employ two separate chambers—a large one for the food and a smaller one for the fuel. Serious smokers often use nothing but wood chunks to fuel their horizontal

smokers, but it's easier and more effective to start the fire with charcoal and to add the wood chunks/chips later. As with other grills/smokers, when shopping for a horizontal smoker look for durable construction—heavy-gauge, rust-resistant metals; welded joints; and

tight-fitting lids. Make sure there are a sturdy frame and wheels to support the smoker and make it easier to move around. An adequate number of vents and a temperature gauge are essential features; racks for storage and prep surfaces are nice add-ons.

▲ This swing-open door provides easy access to the lower half of the smoker so you can painlessly add wood chips, water, and fresh charcoal briquettes.

■ A temperature gauge (above) is a must-have feature for smokers. It allows you to monitor the cooking temperature without lifting the lid. Most vertical water smokers employ two stacked cooking racks (right), which provide plenty of space for a large amount of food.

Choose Your Grill: Fryers

T he cooking device commonly known as a turkey fryer has found a well-deserved home right next to grills and smokers in the world of outdoor cooking. And despite their turkey-oriented roots in the Deep South, fryers are now recognized as a great way to cook a lot more than turkey. They cook food relatively quickly, in the process imparting a delectable crispiness on the outside while maintaining juicy goodness on the inside.

A note about the heating elements: Electric turkey fryers are a relatively new product that you might encounter when you start shopping for a turkey fryer. These cookers appear to have some positive qualities, but they are designed primarily for indoor use. Because this book is about grilling and other types of outdoor cooking, this section will focus on the traditional device used for outside frying—the propane-powered fryer.

Propane fryers employ a large (commonly 30 to 34 quarts) covered pot to hold the cooking oil. A variety of vegetable oils can be used; corn, safflower, peanut, soybean, and canola are common choices. The pot rests in a stand that includes a built-in propane burner for heating the oil. The burner is connected to a standard propane tank, the same kind that you would use to fuel a gas grill. Basic fryer kits

▲ Turkey fryers are simple devices, consisting of a stand fitted with a propane-powered burner that holds and heats a large, oil-filled cooking pot. Buy a fryer with a sturdy stand and cook on a level, stable surface, such as a patio.

▲ The regulator end of the hose screws onto the propane tank. The valve next to the regulator controls the burner.

▲ A 10-quart "fish fry" pot with a lift-out basket is a great accessory for frying small-size foods.

usually include some kind of rack and a hook for lifting a turkey out of the pot.

The booming popularity of this cooking style has spawned a large number of fryers to choose from, spanning a wide range of prices. The first factor to weigh is aluminum versus stainless steel. Less-expensive fryers are generally made from aluminum, which is light, a good heat conductor, and entirely serviceable for frying. If you are serious about frying you will probably want to spend the extra money for stainless steel. It is much more durable and far easier to clean up. Regardless of what it's made of, look for a pot with a vented lid, which is an important safety feature.

Beyond the pot, look for a unit with a sturdy, well-built stand that will resist tipping once it's loaded down with the pot, oil, and food. The burner will be rated by its BTU (British Thermal Unit) output. A higher BTU rating will increase oil-heating speed, but will also rate a higher price. Just as important, look for a unit with a long hose and easy-to-use regulator, ideally one that has been certified by Underwriters Laboratory for safety. Also be sure other amenities can be purchased as part of fryer kits or can be added separately. A frying basket is a great tool for cooking a variety of smaller foods; it will greatly increase your fryer's versatility. A quality thermometer is a must-have for monitoring oil temperature.

▲ A lift-out frying basket that fits inside your cooking pot is a must-have tool if you plan to cook foods smaller than a turkey.

▲ A fryer cooking pot holds about 30 quarts of oil. Aluminum pots are fine, but choose a stainless-steel one if you're serious about frying.

▲ A vented lid prevents steam from building up and is a good cooking pot safety feature. Cover the pot between batches of food, but never have the lid in place while frying.

Fryers are a quick, tasty way to cook more than just turkeys. Foods end up crispy on the outside and juicy on the inside.

Setting Up the Grill Area

Grilling involves cooking with fire, and as wonderful as fire is for cooking, heating, scaring away wild animals, and other jobs, it is also potentially very dangerous. The last thing you want when going out to the deck or patio to cook a simple meal is to end up instead placing a call to your insurance agent or making a trip to the local hospital. Safe grilling is all about setting up your grill area wisely—and a well-planned grill area offers a host of other benefits. Consider: The best chefs maintain well-organized, well-stocked kitchens to help them prepare fantastic meals. Why should things be any different for a grill chef operating in the backyard?

Getting started with grilling first involves choosing the best place to set up your grill, and safety considerations jump to the forefront with site selection. First, remember that grilling is outdoor cooking, which rules out the house, garage, carport, or any enclosed space that might present both a burning hazard and an opportunity for dangerous carbon monoxide gas to build up. Good ventilation is essential. Second, don't put your grill too close to the house, other structures, shrubbery, or trees. Sparks can ignite flammable items nearby, plus the intense heat can kill plants and damage even things that aren't flammable. Third, choose a level, stable spot for the grill so you don't have to worry about it tipping. A concrete patio is probably the best choice, but a flat spot in the grass will work if the legs can be steadied (and the grass isn't dead and dry). The majority of grills probably sit on decks, which are nice, steady platforms, but remember that the wood is still flammable. Consider investing in a sheet of metal or some type of inflammable material to set underneath the grill.

As you scope out possible locations, consider three additional factors:

- Traffic patterns—Grills are hot and potentially hazardous to pets, kids, and other passersby; stay out of their way. Plus, it doesn't make sense to be in a place where pedestrians can get in your way.
- Proximity to the kitchen—Because most grilling prep time is spent in the kitchen, and you will invariably need to run there once or twice while cooking, don't locate your grill in a spot that requires an epic journey just to fetch your cooking mitt or a jar of seasoning.

▲ **Set up the grill in an open area with good ventilation and well away from the house and any vegetation. Keep the grill away from busy walkways and as close to the kitchen as possible.**

- Light sources—Grilling often takes place at sunset or after dark. Position yourself in a place that has a bright, reliable source of artificial light. There is nothing more frustrating than trying to check the doneness of an expensive steak with a weak flashlight.

When you find a safe, convenient, and well-lit spot for your grill, the next challenge will be to create an organized cooking zone fully capable of supporting your efforts to create a culinary masterpiece. As barbecue mania has swept the country, serious outdoor chefs have responded by setting up full-blown outdoor kitchens, complete with refrigerators, sinks, and ample counter space.

Most grillers don't have the resources to commit to this type of installation (and the weather in many parts of the country is often too harsh), but that doesn't mean you can't do a few things to make your cooking experience more enjoyable.

A flat work space is probably the best thing you can add to your grill zone. The various racks that attach to grills are helpful, but they are no replacement for a table or some type of cabinet with a countertop. Make sure whatever you choose is tall enough to work at comfortably—and to keep food out of reach of kids and dogs—and has a sanitary work surface that is easily cleaned off. Speaking of cleanup, a nearby source of water—be

▲ Your grill area can't have enough flat work surfaces, such as this flip-up tray attached to a gas grill.

▲ Set up supplies close to your grill so you don't have to constantly run to the kitchen to retrieve them.

Safety is the most important factor to consider when setting up a grilling area.

it a small sink, a hose, or some type of basin filled with water—is another amenity that should be added to your grilling set-up. Along the same lines, buy a garbage can (ideally the covered type), put a plastic bin liner it, and park it near your cooking area.

The final thing you need to plan for is storage. Sure, you can keep your various tools, fuels, fire starters, seasonings, and so on scattered all over the kitchen and garage, but it sure is handier to keep them nearby. Because this is an outdoor cooking zone, any grill-site storage should be weatherproof and secure.

One option is to build something substantial and secure out of wood, but there are quicker, cheaper options. For example, locking storage cabinets, made out of plastic and available in a variety of sizes, can be purchased at any home center. If on-site storage isn't an option, buy yourself a couple of chest-style plastic storage bins with snap-down lids. Use one for tools and another one for charcoal and wood chips. These have the advantage of being highly portable, so you can keep them in the garage and haul them out at cooking time.

▲ Choose a level, stable site for your grill to minimize the danger of tipping. This paving-stone patio also makes a good work surface because it is inflammable. The wood decks that many grills occupy are a fire hazard and should be fitted with a sheet of metal or other inflammable material directly under the grill.

▷ A freestanding battery-powered light, or one that attaches to the grill, is an essential tool when a grilling session runs after sundown.

Feeding the Fire: Fuel

I f you buy a charcoal grill, then it seems pretty obvious that you are going to fuel your grill with charcoal. Yet you actually have more options than you realize, and even choosing a simple bag of charcoal deserves a little thought.

The most common type of charcoal is composition briquettes, which are made from burned wood scraps, coal dust, petroleum binders, and various types of fillers. Cheaper brands contain a higher percentage of fillers, which can give food an unpleasant taste, take longer to light, burn for a shorter time, and result in a higher volume of ash. Therefore, buy wisely.

The next step up in quality is natural briquettes, which are made from pulverized lumps of wood charcoal bound together with natural starches. These typically light faster, burn hotter and longer, produce less ash, and impart fewer off flavors than composition briquettes. They are also more expensive.

The highest-end charcoal choice—and the costliest—is lump charcoal, also known as charwood. This fuel is made from hardwood trees—oak, hickory, and maple are common varieties—and they light quickly and produce very high temperatures. Charwood is also clean-burning and has no additives—so no odd flavors—and has the advantage of giving food some of the natural wood flavor.

There is actually another alternative for building a fire in your kettle-style charcoal grill—wood, and it's not really that exotic a choice. Simply start a fire in the grill using hardwood chunks roughly the size of a baseball—either make your own or buy commercially prepared varieties—and let them burn until they are hot coals. Cook your meat as you normally would over charcoal and prepare to be impressed with the flavor. Two things to note: First, it takes a little longer to start a fire this way; and second, use only dry hardwoods—common choices are mesquite, hickory, oak, and apple. Avoid soft woods such as pine, which contain pitch that will give food an off taste as it burns, and lumber, because it contains toxic chemicals.

▲ Hardwood chunks, burned until they are hot coals, are a little more work for fueling your charcoal grill, but they give food a great smoky flavor.

▲ Composition briquettes are a convenient, reliable, and inexpensive method for fueling a charcoal grill. Avoid cheaper brands, which contain fillers that can give food an odd taste.

▲ A batch of charcoal provides about one hour of cooking heat. Longer sessions require adding fresh briquettes. Use a chimney starter to light more charcoal and add fresh, hot coals when your grill starts to cool.

▶ After lighting charcoal briquettes and allowing them to burn until they are ashed over, use a long-handled tool to spread them out in the bottom of your grill.

Most gas grillers use liquid propane as their primary fuel. Sold in refillable tanks that are relatively easy to move around and can be replenished or traded in for a full tank at retail outlets everywhere, propane is one of the main reasons that grilling has become so popular. The fuel is clean-burning, cost-effective, and just plain easy to use. If your house uses liquid propane for heat, it's also possible to hook your grill to the line and do away with propane tanks for fuel. Along those lines, another option for fueling your grill is natural gas, if that's what your house uses for heat. Contact your utility company if you are interested in exploring this option, which might make sense if you are a serious griller. On the other hand, a natural gas hookup is a relatively permanent installation; make sure you have an appropriate location and are willing to make a commitment to that spot.

◀ **Propane is stored in portable metal tanks and supplied to the grill through a short hose fitted with a regulator that controls the flow of gas to the grill.**

Grillers have several choices for fueling their cooking fires beyond the standard bag of charcoal or tank of propane.

▲ Once the regulator and fuel hose have been attached to the tank, all it takes is a twist of the valve to start the propane flowing to the grill.

▲ With the grill cover open and the burner knobs turned on, lighting a gas grill is only a matter of pushing an electronic switch on most models.

Hooking Up a Gas Tank

Propane has become the fuel of choice for most grillers, with more than 60 percent choosing gas for their outdoor cooking. The propane is delivered to the grill from a refillable tank that can be taken to a variety of retail outlets, including home centers, hardware stores, and many gas stations, for recharging or exchange for a full tank.

Before you ever hook up any tank to your grill, take a good look at it. Because the tanks are often used for several years, they take a lot of abuse. Avoid using a tank that has large dents or excessive corrosion. Also, take note of the valve on the top of your tank. Since 2002 all propane tanks are required to be fitted with the new OPD—Overfill Prevention Device—valve, which features a safety device that prevents overfilling. OPD valves are easy to spot because of their distinctive, three-lobe handwheels. Though you are unlikely to see them, never use an old tank that is not fitted with an OPD valve.

There are a couple of important safety issues to note before you start hooking up (or disconnecting) a propane tank to your grill. Never smoke while you are working with a propane tank. This offers a serious risk for fire or even an explosion. Always wear heavy

▲ Overfill Prevention Device (OPD) valves have been required on all propane tanks since 2002. OPD valves are easy to spot because of their distinctive three-lobe handwheels. Avoid using a tank still equipped with the old-style valve.

▲ Always wear gloves when working with propane tanks. Escaping gas is extremely cold and can freeze-burn your skin.

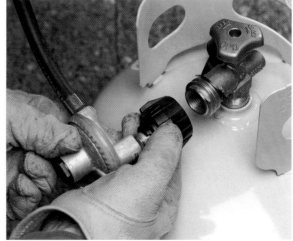

▲ The regulator end of your grill's fuel hose attaches to the propane tank with a simple screw-on fitting.

gloves when working with the tank. Escaping gas is extremely cold and can give you a painful freeze-burn.

The end of the propane hose has a gas-delivery control device called a regulator that in many models includes a built-in pressure gauge that in a glance will tell you how much gas is left in the tank. The regulator end of the hose attaches to the tank with a simple threaded screw-on connector. Before attaching the device check all the threaded surfaces and make sure they are clean and free of debris. Align the connector with the tank valve opening and twist to tighten. Continue turning until the connection is hand-tight. Do not overtighten. You do not need a wrench to create a suitable connection.

Open the valve on the top of the propane tank and check the connection for leaks with a few simple tricks. First, use your ears; many leaks are loud enough to hear. Next, use your nose. Sniff the air just below the connection for a gas odor. Why below? Because the propane is heavier than air and will sink as it escapes. Finally, mix up a 50:50 solution of water and dish detergent in a small spray bottle and coat the surfaces of the connection. Tiny leaks (too small to hear or smell) will present themselves in the form of tiny bubbles. If you detect a leak, carefully clean the threads on both the tank and the regulator and then repeat the installation process. If you can't stop the leak, you should probably trade in the propane tank for a new one. If that doesn't improve the situation, plan on investing in a new hose/regulator. Never light your grill if you are leaking propane (even in minute quantities); the risk of fire and explosion is just too great.

Some new grills feature a hose-regulator with a quick-release connection that allows you to disconnect the propane tank easily between uses. These employ a connection device with a pull-back collar that is screwed into the tank opening and remains in place as long as the tank has propane in it. To attach the regulator, you simply pull back the collar, insert the regulator, and allow the collar to snap back into place and lock the connection tightly. To remove, you simply pull back the collar and remove the regulator.

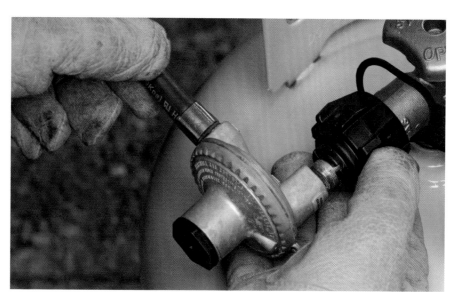

▲ Align the hose connector with the threaded opening on the tank's OPD valve and twist just until it's hand-tight.

Easy-to-use propane tanks are a key reason why 60 percent of grillers choose gas for outdoor cooking.

▲ Check your hose-tank connection for leaks before starting your grill. Spray the area with a 50:50 solution of water and dish soap. Tiny bubbles in the soap spray will indicate a leak.

Lighting a Charcoal Grill

Man has cooked over fire since the dawn of time, but modern man has a much easier time of starting his fire than his prehistoric counterparts. Today's charcoal grillers have to do a little more work than gas-powered outdoor cooks, but they still have several good choices for firing up their grills.

Lighter fluid has emerged as the traditional choice for starting charcoal fires—and why not? It's cheap, quick, and you can tote a can of the stuff anywhere. Squirt some fluid on the coals, allow it to soak in for a minute or two, and light your fire. But, like many "easy" things, lighter fluid has its drawbacks. It's a poisonous, flammable, petroleum-based chemical that you have to take care to store safely. It's also a pollutant—so much so that some areas have banned its use. And for serious outdoor chefs it's probably not the best choice because it can sometimes give food a chemical flavor. If you must use lighter fluid, use it sparingly; too many grillers soak their briquettes to the point of dripping, which is unnecessary. Also, consider investing in a long-stem butane grill lighter, which is easier and safer than fumbling around with matches.

The obvious evolution for charcoal manufacturers was to sell briquettes already impregnated with lighter fluid. These so-called "instant-light" briquettes are really easy to

▲ **Starter fluid is a popular choice for lighting charcoal because it is cheap, easy, and you can use it anywhere. But it's also a pollutant and can give food an odd chemical taste.**

▲ **Create a pile of charcoal briquettes before applying lighter fluid or inserting an electric starter.**

▲ **Electric starters are a quick, efficient way to light charcoal when there is an electrical outlet located nearby.**

use. The one-time-use bags are especially convenient for picnics or camping—throw a bag in the grill, light the ends, and you'll have a fire in little time. Despite their convenience, instant-light briquettes are a poor choice for everyday use. They are expensive, and large bags don't keep that well—if you don't seal them up, the starter fluid can evaporate off the charcoal. And, worst of all, the starter fluid rarely burns all the way off before you start cooking. As a result, food cooked with instant-light briquettes often has a strong chemical flavor.

There are other great charcoal-lighting options beyond starter fluid. Electric starters are inexpensive tools that make quick work of firing up charcoal. They are simple, employing an electric coil that you bury in your briquette pile in the grill. Plug the starter in and wait a few minutes for the coals to start glowing; unplug the starter, set it aside to cool, and let the fire establish itself. Electric starters sound perfect, but they have their drawbacks; first and foremost you need an electrical outlet nearby. Even if you solve that problem, there are safety issues to consider: They are both a serious fire hazard and a serious burn just waiting to happen to kids, pets, and anybody else who accidentally snags the cord. Finally, electric starters have a tendency to burn out fairly quickly, requiring frequent replacement.

The top fire-starting choice for serious grill chefs is the chimney starter, which is a cylindrical steel pipe with a heatproof handle, a grate in the center, and vents underneath. Put crumpled newspaper or a paraffin starter in the base, set the cylinder in your grill, load the cylinder with charcoal or wood chunks, and light. The cylindrical shape encourages quick and even lighting of the coals, which are carefully dumped onto the grill grate when they are white-hot and ready for cooking.

Lighting Charcoal with a Chimney Starter

1

ADD THE PAPER
Crumple a few sheets of newspaper and push them into the bottom of a chimney starter. Alternatively, you could use paraffin starter blocks instead of newspaper.

2

ADD THE CHARCOAL
Place the starter on the bottom rack of your kettle grill. Pour the charcoal briquettes into the top of the chimney starter.

3

LIGHT THE PAPER
Using a long-handled butane lighter or a long match, light the newspaper in the bottom of the chimney starter. Place the starter on the charcoal grate and watch to make sure that the briquettes are lit by the burning newspaper.

4

LET IT BURN
Let the charcoal burn for 20 to 25 minutes until the coals are completely ashed over and they are glowing red-hot.

5

POUR OUT OVER THE COALS
Carefully pour the hot coals from the chimney starter onto the charcoal grate in your grill. Arrange them with a long-handled tool for either direct or indirect grilling.

Heat Control

Gas grills have become popular in large part because they've greatly simplified the process of controlling heat. Once the fire is started in a quality gas grill with multiple burners (ideally at least three), you simply wait for the grill to heat up. Once the grill reaches a certain temperature—based on how you've adjusted the control knobs, it's easily monitored with the built-in thermometer—it should remain at that temperature, at least as long as you have propane in your tank. If you want to cook at a different temperature, you simply adjust the knobs.

Charcoal grills aren't that simple, but it doesn't take a rocket scientist to adjust the cooking temperature on your kettle grill—you just have to understand how the charcoal works. After you light your charcoal and let it burn until the coals are white-hot, your fire will be at its maximum heating point. If you need an extremely hot fire, this is the time to put the coals to work because as they burn they will cool down. If you need a cooler fire, you might want to wait a little while. The amount of charcoal you use and how you arrange it on the grill grate will also affect how hot your fire gets. If you want the hottest possible fire, use enough coals to fully fill the grate so that the burning briquettes are touching. Or, if you want to create a smaller hot zone, use fewer

▲ Holding your hand a few inches above the cooking grate tells you roughly how hot a charcoal fire is. Count how long you can hold your hand there—four seconds indicates a medium (350°F) fire.

▲ A built-in thermometer in the grill lid allows you to monitor temperature without lifting the lid and letting heat escape.

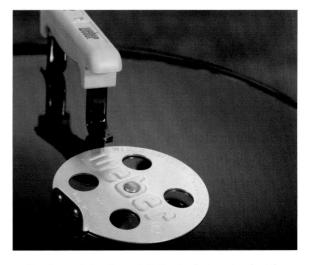

▲ Opening or closing the vents is the simplest way to adjust the cooking temperature in a charcoal grill.

briquettes and push them tightly together; you can also layer them for even more intense heat. For a cooler fire, use fewer briquettes and cook with them spread farther apart.

Once the fire is going and you need to adjust the heat without moving the charcoal around, you have a couple of options. A quick way to increase the heat is to gently tap the coals to knock the accumulated ash off their exterior. A more versatile option for increasing or lowering the temperature is to work with your grill's vents. All fires need oxygen for fuel—provide more oxygen and the fire gets hotter, decrease the oxygen and the burn slows. By opening or closing your vents you will adjust air flow through the grill and thus the oxygen supply. Because air is pulled up through the bottom vents, pay special attention to the lid vent; shutting it completely will probably put the fire out. Instead, make most of your adjustments on the bottom vents only; that's why multiple bottom vents are so useful.

Some charcoal grills offer another feature for controlling cooking temperature: adjustable grill racks. Temperature decreases the farther you move from the coals. Most grills are best positioned about 4 inches above the fire. Use the lowest setting for quick-searing meat and the highest-possible setting for slow cooking.

Some charcoal grills have a thermometer built into the lid, which is great for indirect cooking, but this doesn't tell you the temperature at grill level for direct cooking. You can buy a thermometer specifically made for the grill surface, or you can turn to a built-in tool that offers a reliable method for monitoring heat: your hand. Carefully place your hand, open palm downward, a few inches above the cooking rack and start counting—one-one thousand, two-one thousand, etc.—until the heat forces you to pull your hand away. Two seconds is considered a hot fire (usually 400°F or higher), four seconds is medium (about 350°F), and six seconds or more is a cool temperature (300°F or less).

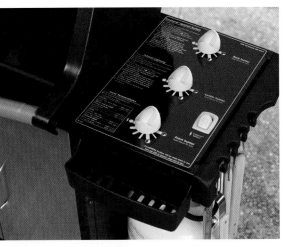

◀ This gas grill is equipped with three burners, each controlled by its own knob. Choosing not to light all three burners is one way to reduce cooking temperature. For example, while indirect grilling you typically light the two side burners but leave the center burner under the food extinguished.

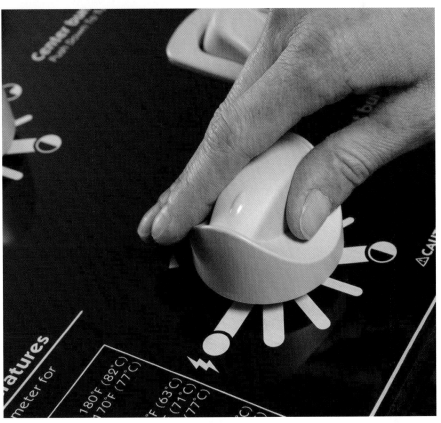

▲ One of the reasons that gas grills are so popular is their simplicity in allowing the cook to adjust the temperature. Just twist one or more of the burner controller knobs and you can change cooking temperature—even in just part of the grill.

When Is It Done?

Determining when your food is done may be the most important, and most underappreciated, topic in grilling, especially when meat is concerned. Too many grill chefs throw a slab of meat on the grill and simply try to guess when its ready, which is a huge mistake. Grill a cut of meat too long and you ruin it; it becomes dry and tough and loses much of its natural flavor. But grill a cut of meat for too short a time and you expose yourself to a variety of health risks. Meat (and some vegetables too) can contain a wide variety of potentially dangerous microorganisms, so you always need to cook your food to an internal temperature that is high enough to kill these microscopic critters. Take note of each recipe's recommended internal temperature and cook meat accordingly. Visit the USDA Food Safety and Inspection Service website (www.fsis.usda. gov) if you need additional information.

By far the best method for monitoring food doneness is to use a food thermometer; several types are available. Oven-/grill-safe meat thermometers have a round dial display and a spike-like metal probe that you insert deep into the meat. These are designed to stay in the food while it cooks and are great for large, long-cooking items such as roasts and whole turkeys. If you first insert these during

▲ The only foolproof way to tell that grilled meat is done and safe to eat is by measuring its internal temperature. Here a quick-read thermometer verifies that the thigh meat in a whole chicken has reached the recommended 180°F.

▲ This chicken breast is no longer pink in the center, a good indication that it is fully cooked.

▲ Grilled fish is done and safe to eat when it turns opaque and flakes easily with a fork.

◀ Different styles of food thermometers have their own benefits and applications. Grill-safe meat thermometers (left) can stay in large items while they cook. Quick-read thermometers are available in both dial (center) and digital (right) versions that once inserted display temperatures in 15 to 20 seconds.

cooking, remember that it will take a couple of minutes to correctly register temperature.

Quick-read thermometers can't stay in foods while they are cooking but offer another advantage—like the name says, you can insert them into the food and know the temperature in 15 to 20 seconds. Quick-read thermometers are available in both dial and digital styles. An interesting twist on the quick-read concept is the thermometer fork, which uses the tines as temperature probes and combines two useful tools in one utensil.

If you don't have a thermometer, you are going to have to be extra diligent to make sure that your food is fully cooked. For some types of food, especially smaller and thinner cuts of meat or fish, it's fairly easy to tell when it's done. For example, fish is fully cooked when

it turns completely opaque and breaks easily into large flakes. For burgers, chicken breasts, pork chops, and steaks, you are generally safe if the meat in the center is no longer pink, though you also can use the "poke test" to gauge doneness on these types of foods. This system compares the tension in the fleshy area at the base of your thumb with the tension in the center of a cooked cut of meat. For rare, the meat tension should be the same as the tension in the fleshy part of your hand when you gently hold your thumb and index finger together. For medium, it's the same as the tension created by holding your thumb and middle finger together. For well-done, you want to match the tension when holding your thumb and pinky together. With some practice you can get pretty good at using this system.

▲ Grilled pork chops are done when juices run clear and the internal temperature reaches 160°F.

A thermometer is an essential tool for cooking meat to a safe internal temperature.

▲ The "poke test": Rare meat has the same tension as the fleshy part of your hand when holding your thumb and index finger together.

▲ Medium-cooked meats have the same tension as when you touch your thumb and middle finger together.

▲ Well-done meats have the same tension as when you touch your thumb and pinky together.

Indirect-Grilling Poultry

For a charcoal grill, arrange medium-hot coals around a drip pan. Test for medium heat. Place unstuffed poultry, breast side up, on grill rack over drip pan. Cover; grill for the time given below or until poultry is no longer pink (180°F for most cuts, 170°F for breast meat), adding more charcoal as necessary. Or if desired, place whole birds on a rack in a roasting pan and omit the drip pan. For a gas grill, preheat grill. Reduce heat to medium. Adjust heat for indirect cooking. Test for doneness using a meat or quick-read thermometer. For whole birds, insert meat thermometer into center of the inside thigh muscle, away from bone. (Poultry sizes vary; use times as a general guide.)

Type of Bird	Weight	Grilling Temperature	Approximate Indirect-Grilling Time	Doneness
Chicken				
Chicken breast half, skinned and boned	4 to 5 ounces	Medium	15 to 18 minutes	170°F
Chicken, broiler-fryer, half	$1\frac{1}{2}$ to $1\frac{3}{4}$ pounds	Medium	1 to $1\frac{1}{4}$ hours	180°F
Chicken, broiler-fryer, quarters	12 to 14 ounces each	Medium	50 to 60 minutes	180°F
Chicken thigh, skinned and boned	4 to 5 ounces	Medium	15 to 18 minutes	180°F
Chicken, whole	$2\frac{1}{2}$ to 3 pounds	Medium	1 to $1\frac{1}{4}$ hours	180°F
	$3\frac{1}{2}$ to 4 pounds	Medium	$1\frac{1}{4}$ to $1\frac{3}{4}$ hours	180°F
	$4\frac{1}{2}$ to 5 pounds	Medium	$1\frac{3}{4}$ to 2 hours	180°F
Meaty chicken pieces (breast halves, thighs, and drumsticks)	$2\frac{1}{2}$ to 3 pounds total	Medium	50 to 60 minutes	180°F (170°F for breast halves)
Game				
Cornish game hen, halved lengthwise	10 to 12 ounces each	Medium	40 to 50 minutes	No longer pink
Cornish game hen, whole	$1\frac{1}{4}$ to $1\frac{1}{2}$ pounds	Medium	50 to 60 minutes	180°F
Pheasant, quartered	$\frac{1}{2}$ to $\frac{3}{4}$ pound each	Medium	50 to 60 minutes	No longer pink
Pheasant, whole	2 to 3 pounds	Medium	1 to $1\frac{1}{2}$ hours	180°F
Quail, semiboneless	3 to 4 ounces	Medium	15 to 20 minutes	180°F
Squab	12 to 16 ounces	Medium	$\frac{3}{4}$ to 1 hour	180°F
Turkey				
Turkey breast, half	2 to $2\frac{1}{2}$ pounds	Medium	$1\frac{1}{4}$ to 2 hours	170°F
Turkey breast tenderloin	8 to 10 ounces ($\frac{3}{4}$ to 1 inch thick)	Medium	25 to 30 minutes	170°F
Turkey breast tenderloin steak	4 to 6 ounces	Medium	15 to 18 minutes	170°F
Turkey breast, whole	4 to 6 pounds	Medium	$1\frac{3}{4}$ to $2\frac{1}{4}$ hours	170°F
	6 to 8 pounds	Medium	$2\frac{1}{2}$ to $3\frac{1}{2}$ hours	170°F
Turkey drumstick	$\frac{1}{2}$ to 1 pound	Medium	$\frac{3}{4}$ to $1\frac{1}{4}$ hours	180°F
Turkey thigh	1 to $1\frac{1}{2}$ pounds	Medium	50 to 60 minutes	180°F
Turkey, whole	6 to 8 pounds	Medium	$1\frac{3}{4}$ to $2\frac{1}{4}$ hours	180°F
	8 to 12 pounds	Medium	$2\frac{1}{2}$ to $3\frac{1}{2}$ hours	180°F
	12 to 16 pounds	Medium	3 to 4 hours	180°F

All cooking times are based on meat removed directly from refrigerator.

Direct-Grilling Poultry

If desired, remove skin from poultry. For a charcoal grill, place poultry on grill rack, bone side up, directly over medium coals. Grill, uncovered, for the time given below or until the proper temperature is reached and meat is no longer pink, turning once halfway through grilling. For a gas grill, preheat grill. Reduce heat to medium. Place poultry on grill rack, bone side down, over heat. Cover and grill. Test for doneness using a meat thermometer (use a quick-read thermometer to test small portions). Thermometer should register 180°F, except in breast meat when thermometer should register 170°F. If desired, during last 5 to 10 minutes of grilling, brush often with a sauce.

Type of Bird	Weight	Grilling Temperature	Approximate Indirect-Grilling Time	Doneness
Chicken				
Chicken breast half, skinned and boned	4 to 5 ounces	Medium	12 to 15 minutes	170°F
Chicken, broiler-fryer, half or quarters	1½- to 1¾-pound half or 12- to 14-ounce quarters	Medium	40 to 50 minutes	180°F
Chicken thigh, skinned and boned	4 to 5 ounces	Medium	12 to 15 minutes	180°F
Meaty chicken pieces (breast halves, thighs, and drumsticks)	2½ to 3 pounds total	Medium	35 to 45 minutes	180°F
Turkey				
Turkey breast tenderloin	8 to 10 ounces (¾ to 1 inch thick)	Medium	16 to 20 minutes	170°F

All cooking times are based on meat removed directly from refrigerator.

Direct-Grilling Meat

For a charcoal grill, place meat on grill rack directly over medium coals. Grill, uncovered, for the time given below or to desired doneness, turning once halfway through grilling. For a gas grill, preheat grill. Reduce heat to medium. Place meat on grill rack over heat. Cover the grill. Test for doneness using a meat thermometer.

Cut	Weight	Grilling Temperature	Approximate Indirect-Grilling Time	Doneness
Beef				
Boneless steak (beef top loin [strip], ribeye, shoulder top blade [flat-iron], tenderloin)	1 inch	Medium	10 to 12 minutes	145°F medium rare
	1 inch	Medium	12 to 15 minutes	160°F medium
	1½ inches	Medium	15 to 19 minutes	145°F medium rare
	1½ inches	Medium	18 to 23 minutes	160°F medium
Boneless top sirloin steak	1 inch	Medium	14 to 18 minutes	145°F medium rare
	1 inch	Medium	18 to 22 minutes	160°F medium
	1½ inches	Medium	20 to 24 minutes	145°F medium rare
	1½ inches	Medium	24 to 28 minutes	160°F medium
Boneless tri-tip steak (bottom sirloin)	¾ inch	Medium	9 to 11 minutes	145°F medium rare
	¾ inch	Medium	11 to 13 minutes	160°F medium
	1 inch	Medium	13 to 15 minutes	145°F medium rare
	1 inch	Medium	15 to 17 minutes	160°F medium
Flank steak	1¼ to 1¾ pounds	Medium	17 to 21 minutes	160°F medium
Steak with bone (porterhouse, T-bone, rib)	1 inch	Medium	10 to 13 minutes	145°F medium rare
	1 inch	Medium	12 to 15 minutes	160°F medium
	1½ inches	Medium	18 to 21 minutes	145°F medium rare
	1½ inches	Medium	22 to 25 minutes	160°F medium
Ground Meat Patties				
Patties (beef, lamb, pork, or veal)	½ inch	Medium	10 to 13 minutes	160°F medium
	¾ inch	Medium	14 to 18 minutes	160°F medium
Lamb				
Chop (loin or rib)	1 inch	Medium	12 to 14 minutes	145°F medium rare
	1 inch	Medium	15 to 17 minutes	160°F medium
Chop (sirloin)	¾ to 1 inch	Medium	14 to 17 minutes	160°F medium
Miscellaneous				
Kabobs (beef or lamb)	1-inch cubes	Medium	8 to 12 minutes	160°F medium
Kabobs (pork or veal)	1-inch cubes	Medium	10 to 14 minutes	160°F medium
Sausages, cooked (frankfurters, smoked bratwurst, etc.)		Medium	3 to 7 minutes	Heated through
Pork				
Chop (boneless top loin)	¾ to 1 inch	Medium	7 to 9 minutes	160°F medium
	1¼ to 1½ inches	Medium	14 to 18 minutes	160°F medium
Chop with bone (loin or rib)	¾ to 1 inch	Medium	11 to 13 minutes	160°F medium
	1¼ to 1½ inches	Medium	16 to 20 minutes	160°F medium
Veal				
Chop (loin or rib)	1 inch	Medium	12 to 15 minutes	160°F medium

All cooking times are based on meat removed directly from refrigerator.

For a charcoal grill, arrange medium-hot coals around a drip pan. Test for medium heat above pan, unless chart says otherwise. Place meat, fat side up, on grill rack over drip pan. Cover and grill for the time given below or to desired temperature, adding more charcoal to maintain heat as necessary. For a gas grill, preheat grill. Reduce heat to medium. Adjust heat for indirect cooking. To test for doneness, insert a quick-read thermometer to test small portions. Temperature should register the "final grilling temperature." Remove meat from grill. For larger cuts, such as roasts, cover with foil and let stand 15 minutes before slicing. The meat's temperature will rise 10°F during the time it stands. Thinner cuts, such as steaks, do not have to stand.

Cut	Thickness/Weight	Approximate Indirect-Grilling Time	Final Grilling Temperature (when to remove from grill)	Final Doneness Temperature (after 15 minutes of standing)
Beef				
Boneless top sirloin steak	1 inch	22 to 26 minutes	145°F medium rare	No standing time
	1 inch	26 to 30 minutes	160°F medium	No standing time
	1½ inches	32 to 36 minutes	145°F medium rare	No standing time
	1½ inches	36 to 40 minutes	160°F medium	No standing time
Boneless tri-tip roast (bottom sirloin)	1½ to 2 pounds	35 to 40 minutes	135°F	145°F medium rare
	1½ to 2 pounds	40 to 45 minutes	150°F	160°F medium
Flank steak	1¼ to 1¾ pounds	23 to 28 minutes	160°F medium	No standing time
Rib roast (chine bone removed) (medium-low heat)	4 to 6 pounds	2 to 2¾ hours	135°F	145°F medium rare
	4 to 6 pounds	2½ to 3¼ hours	150°F	160°F medium
Ribeye roast (medium-low heat)	4 to 6 pounds	1¼ to 1¾ hours	135°F	145°F medium rare
	4 to 6 pounds	1½ to 2¼ hours	150°F	160°F medium
Steak (porterhouse, rib, ribeye, shoulder blade [flat-iron], T-bone, tenderloin, top loin [strip])	1 inch	16 to 20 minutes	145°F medium rare	No standing time
	1 inch	20 to 24 minutes	160°F medium	No standing time
	1½ inches	22 to 25 minutes	145°F medium rare	No standing time
	1½ inches	25 to 28 minutes	160°F medium	No standing time
Tenderloin roast (medium-high heat)	2 to 3 pounds	¾ to 1 hour	135°F	145°F medium rare
	4 to 5 pounds	1 to 1¼ hours	135°F	145°F medium rare
Ground Meat				
Patties (beef, lamb, pork, or veal)	½ inch	15 to 18 minutes	160°F medium	No standing time
	¾ inch	20 to 24 minutes	160°F medium	No standing time
Lamb				
Boneless leg roast (medium-low heat)	3 to 4 pounds	1½ to 2¼ hours	135°F	145°F medium rare
	3 to 4 pounds	1¾ to 2½ hours	150°F	160°F medium
	4 to 6 pounds	1¾ to 2½ hours	135°F	145°F medium rare
	4 to 6 pounds	2 to 2¾ hours	150°F	160°F medium
Boneless sirloin roast (medium-low heat)	1½ to 2 pounds	1 to 1¼ hours	135°F	145°F medium rare
	1½ to 2 pounds	1¼ to 1½ hours	150°F	160°F medium
Chop (loin or rib)	1 inch	16 to 18 minutes	145°F medium rare	No standing time
	1 inch	18 to 20 minutes	160°F medium	No standing time
Leg of lamb (with bone) (medium-low heat)	5 to 7 pounds	1¾ to 2¼ hours	135°F	145°F medium rare
	5 to 7 pounds	2¼ to 2¾ hours	150°F	160°F medium

All cooking times are based on meat removed directly from refrigerator.

continued on page 32

GRILLING BASICS

1

Cut	Thickness/Weight	Approximate Indirect-Grilling Time	Final Grilling Temperature (when to remove from grill)	Final Doneness Temperature (after 15 minutes of standing)
Pork				
Boneless top loin roast (medium-low heat)	2 to 3 pounds (single loin)	1 to 1$\frac{1}{2}$ hours	150°F	160°F medium
	3 to 5 pounds (double loin, tied)	1$\frac{1}{2}$ to 2$\frac{1}{4}$ hours	150°F	160°F medium
Chop (boneless top loin)	$\frac{3}{4}$ to 1 inch	20 to 24 minutes	160°F medium	No standing time
	1$\frac{1}{4}$ to 1$\frac{1}{2}$ inch	30 to 35 minutes	160°F medium	No standing time
Chop (loin or rib)	$\frac{3}{4}$ to 1 inch	22 to 25 minutes	160°F medium	No standing time
	1$\frac{1}{4}$ to 1$\frac{1}{2}$ inch	35 to 40 minutes	160°F medium	No standing time
Country-style ribs		1$\frac{1}{2}$ to 2 hours	Tender	No standing time
Ham, cooked (boneless) (medium-low heat)	3 to 5 pounds	1$\frac{1}{4}$ to 2 hours	140°F	No standing time
	6 to 8 pounds	2 to 2$\frac{3}{4}$ hours	140°F	No standing time
Ham, cooked (slice) (medium-high heat)	1 inch	20 to 24 minutes	140°F	No standing time
Loin back ribs or spareribs		1$\frac{1}{2}$ to 1$\frac{3}{4}$ hours	Tender	No standing time
Loin center rib roast (backbone loosened) (medium-low heat)	3 to 4 pounds	1$\frac{1}{4}$ to 2 hours	150°F	160°F medium
	4 to 6 pounds	2 to 2$\frac{3}{4}$ hours	150°F	160°F medium
Sausages, uncooked (bratwurst, Polish, or Italian sausage links)	about 4 per pound	20 to 30 minutes	160°F medium	No standing time
Smoked shoulder picnic (with bone), cooked (medium-low heat)	4 to 6 pounds	1$\frac{1}{2}$ to 2$\frac{1}{4}$ hours	140°F heated through	No standing time
Tenderloin (medium-high heat)	$\frac{3}{4}$ to 1 pound	30 to 35 minutes	155°F	160°F medium
Veal				
Chop (loin or rib)	1 inch	19 to 23 minutes	160°F medium	No standing time

All cooking times are based on meat removed directly from refrigerator.

Direct-Grilling Fish and Seafood

Thaw fish or seafood, if frozen. Rinse fish or seafood; pat dry. Place fish fillets in a well-greased grill basket. For fish steaks and whole fish, grease the grill rack. Thread scallops or shrimp on skewers, leaving a ¼-inch space between pieces. For a charcoal grill, place fish on the grill rack directly over medium coals. Grill, uncovered, for the time given below or until fish begins to flake when tested with a fork (seafood should look opaque), turning once halfway through grilling. For a gas grill, preheat grill. Reduce heat to medium. Place fish on grill rack over heat. Cover the grill. If desired, brush fish with melted butter or margarine after turning.

Form of Fish	Thickness, Weight, or Size	Grilling Temperature	Approximate Direct-Grilling Time	Doneness
Dressed whole fish	½ to 1½ pounds	Medium	6 to 9 minutes per 8 ounces	Flakes
Fillets, steaks, cubes (for kabobs)	½ to 1 inch thick	Medium	4 to 6 minutes per ½-inch thickness	Flakes
Lobster tails	6 ounces	Medium	10 to 12 minutes	Opaque
	8 ounces	Medium	12 to 15 minutes	Opaque
Sea Scallops (for kabobs)	12 to 15 per pound	Medium	5 to 8 minutes	Opaque
Shrimp (for kabobs)	20 per pound	Medium	5 to 8 minutes	Opaque
	12 to 15 per pound	Medium	7 to 9 minutes	Opaque

All cooking times are based on fish or seafood removed directly from refrigerator.

Indirect-Grilling Fish and Seafood

Thaw fish or seafood, if frozen. Rinse fish or seafood; pat dry. Place fish fillets in a well-greased grill basket. For fish steaks and whole fish, grease grill rack. Thread scallops or shrimp on skewers, leaving a ¼-inch space between pieces. For a charcoal grill, arrange medium-hot coals around drip pan. Test for medium heat above the pan. Place fish on grill rack over drip pan. Cover and grill for the time given below or until fish begins to flake when tested with a fork (seafood should look opaque), turning once halfway through grilling, if desired. For a gas grill, preheat grill. Reduce heat to medium. Adjust heat for indirect cooking. If desired, brush with melted butter or margarine halfway through grilling.

Form of Fish	Thickness, Weight, or Size	Grilling Temperature	Approximate Indirect-Grilling Time	Doneness
Dressed fish	½ to 1½ pounds	Medium	15 to 20 minutes per 8 ounces	Flakes
Fillets, steaks, cubes (for kabobs)	½ to 1 inch thick	Medium	7 t o 9 minutes per ½-inch thickness	Flakes
Sea scallops (for kabobs)	12 to 15 per pound	Medium	11 to 14 minutes	Opaque
Shrimp (for kabobs)	20 per pound	Medium	8 to 10 minutes	Opaque
	12 to 15 per pound	Medium	9 to 11 minutes	Opaque

All cooking times are based on fish or seafood removed directly from refrigerator.

Cleaning and Maintenance

Cleanup after any kind of cooking is never fun, but with grilling it's important. Grills naturally take a lot of abuse—they are located outside, are exposed to the elements, often get banged around, and operate at very high temperatures. Regular cleaning will extend the life of your equipment and help it function properly each and every time you put it to work. In addition, dirty grills (especially the charcoal variety) can actually give your food an odd taste because of the buildup of chemical residue from burning briquettes. And, in extreme situations, dirty grills can be dangerous—an accumulation of grease can lead to unexpected flare-ups.

For charcoal grills, maintenance is pretty easy. It's a good idea to let your fire continue burning at least a few minutes after you pull the food off the grate; this will burn off food residue. Either let the coals burn out (never pour water on them) or close the vents to suffocate the fire. When the grill has cooled somewhat, give it a good scrubbing with a wire grill brush, the first tool you should buy when you get a new grill. Repeat the clean-up process with the brush the next time you fire up your grill, giving it a quick scrub when it first heats up, before you add your food. Remember, the grate does not have to be washed or scrubbed clean.

After the fire is fully out and the grill is cooled, scoop out the ash residue. Never let the ash build up over multiple fires—it can clog the vents, suffocate the fire, and absorb grease that can ignite and flare up. Plus the ash tends to kick up and coat your food with an ugly, gritty white layer. After cleaning out the kettle, turn your attention to the ash catcher below, scraping out the inevitable ash/grease mixture with a putty knife.

Other than cleaning out the ash, your grill kettle and lid don't need additional cleaning after each fire. Instead, plan on a periodic cleaning of the grill (fully cooled, of course) with warm, soapy water. Use a soft cloth or a sponge to wash the entire grill, inside and out. Avoid using any type of abrasive because this can damage the enameled coating.

To some extent, gas grills should follow a similar cleaning regimen. After every use of your grill, burn off any residue on the cooking grate by turning the burners to high for 10 to 15 minutes until the smoke subsides. Let the grate cool somewhat and then scrape it with a grill brush. After the entire grill is fully cooled, clean out the bottom tray and the grease catch pan. Do this after every cooking session, using a putty knife to fully scrape out any residue. If your gas grill uses lava rocks or ceramic briquettes as a heating element, turn them over periodically to burn off minor grease buildup. Replace them if they are heavily saturated with grease. Finally, give all the surfaces of your grill, inside and out, an occasional gentle cleaning with a soft cloth and warm, soapy water.

Whatever your grill type, in addition to cleaning, the other important step to improving its longevity and performance is to protect it from the elements. This is an outdoor cooking tool and for safety reasons should stay outside,

▲ **When you're done cooking with your gas grill and it has cooled down, slide out and check the grease-catching pan.**

▲ **Scrape out your gas grill catch pan with a putty knife after every cooking session to remove grease and debris.**

▲ Your cooking grate needs only occasional cleaning with water. Dry it thoroughly to keep it from rusting.

▲ Use a paper towel to apply a light layer of cooking oil to your cooking grate to keep food from sticking.

but storing it under a covered area when it's not in use is a great idea. In addition, invest in a heavy, weatherproof cover and always keep your grill covered between uses.

Most people choose to keep their grills active year-round (no matter what the climate), but if you are from the old school that shuts down during the winter, you can take a couple of extra steps to prep a grill for winter storage. Give the unit one last, thorough cleaning and dry it completely. All grills can be stored outside (if they are covered) with minimal problems. Leave the propane tank attached to gas grills. You also can move grills indoors. A clean, empty charcoal grill can be safely stored inside with no additional preparation, but you must remove the propane tank before bringing a gas grill indoors. Leave the propane tank outside, sitting in an upright position.

▲ Rub your grate clean with a wire brush both before and just after cooking.

▷ Clean out the ash catcher below the grill kettle after the fire has cooled.

◁ Always store your grill under a cover to protect it from the elements.

Gadget Guide

Grill covers

Part of the fun of grilling is exploring all its possibilities, and to get the most enjoyment out of cooking with the grill you need to outfit yourself with a nice selection of accessories. Sure, some of these things are just plain fun, but some are essential items that every grill chef needs in his or her arsenal.

Must-Have Accessories

Many of these things deserve to be purchased with your new grill. If you don't buy them right away, you'll be buying them in the near future—guaranteed.

Grill cover: Protect your investment from the elements; most grill models have a custom-fit cover available. Choose a cover that is flame resistant, immune to the effects of UV, and resists cracking.

Grill brush: Clean the cooking rack before and after every use. Look for a brush with a long handle and stiff, wire bristles—a built-in scraping blade is really useful.

Spatula, fork, and tongs: The must-have triumvirate of grilling tools is often sold in sets. Look for versions with long, sturdy, heatproof handles; stainless steel construction; and some type of loop or lanyard for hanging on a rack. The tongs will be your most-used piece in the set. Choose a model with long arms that don't flex easily and a spring-loaded hinge—locking versions are great. Use the fork sparingly (it can encourage juices to drain from meat), but models with a built-in food thermometer offer two great tools in one.

Long grill mitts: Buy two. These should be both well insulated and flame retardant. Look for the long versions that run all the way up to your elbow, especially if you will also use them for turkey frying.

Meat thermometers: The essential tool for ensuring safe, perfectly cooked food. Quick-read varieties are the most versatile, but the traditional oven-/grill-safe dial thermometers simplify grilling big things such as roasts and turkeys. Buy one of both kinds, which are not that expensive—your family will thank you.

Fire extinguisher: Always keep one nearby when you cook—a better option than water, which can actually spread a grease fire.

Basting brush: You will use it frequently to oil the rack and spread on sauces—long-handled models with natural bristles are the best.

Disposable foil drip pans: An essential accessory if you plan on doing any indirect grilling; also great for a variety of other uses including soaking wood chips and holding cooked food. Use once for grilling and then toss to make cleanup a snap.

Extra Accessories

Some of these are fun or just make cooking more convenient, but some of these accoutrements will rise to must-have status as you explore the various possibilities of grilling.

Electric starter: A step up from starter fluid. You simply bury the starter in the charcoal, plug it in, and wait a few minutes for the fire to ignite.

Chimney starter. This is the best tool for starting charcoal fires, using just newspaper or paraffin starter chunks. (See pages 22 to 23 for more information on fire starters.)

Grill thermometers: Varieties are available that fit in the lid (good for monitoring temperature while indirect grilling) or on the cooking surface (for checking direct grilling temperatures).

Grill brush

Tongs

Spatula

Fork

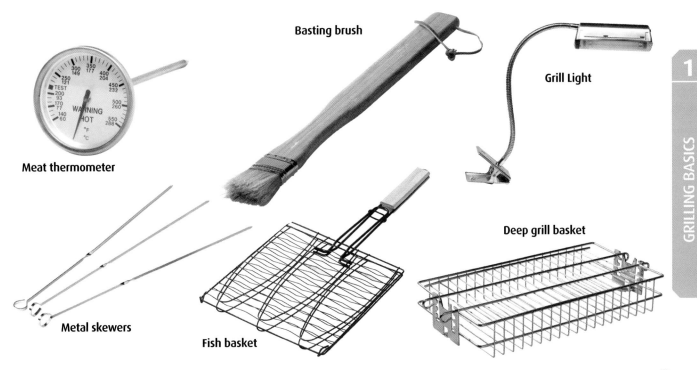

Meat thermometer

Basting brush

Grill Light

Metal skewers

Fish basket

Deep grill basket

Grill lights: Though you are better off setting up in a well-lit area, these clip-on, adjustable lights are a huge, handy step up from a flashlight if you ever find yourself cooking in the dark.

Skewers: There are an endless variety of skewers, which you will find ideal for grilling chunks of meat and vegetables. Wood and bamboo styles are cheap and disposable and must be soaked in water before using. You'll thank yourself for investing in a set of eight to twelve stainless-steel skewers; two-pronged varieties hold food chunks better and keep food from spinning.

Grill baskets: There are many varieties of these (including types specifically designed for fish and vegetables), but the purpose is the same—to securely hold food that is small or fragile or needs frequent turning. Look for a style that uses two hinged cooking grates and has a long handle.

Rib rack: These look like a desktop file holder. They hold ribs vertically, allowing you to greatly increase the barbecuing capacity of your grill and encouraging fat to drip off more easily.

Roast rack: Allows roasting in a disposable aluminum pan; keeps the meat raised above the drippings.

Grill-top pizza pan: Pizza is the latest craze in the grilling; these pans have holes in them so the grill flavor can get to the bottom of the crust.

Grill wok: Turns your grill into a tool for stir-frying vegetables, meat, poultry, and seafood; perforated sides help more of the smoky goodness to envelope your food. These can also double as a rack for grilling fish, vegetables, and other small or fragile foods.

Chicken rack: Yes, this is for the "beer can chicken" you've heard about. It allows you to roast a bird standing on end with a can of your favorite beverage inserted safely inside.

Grilling planks: These pieces of hardwood are soaked in water, placed in a hot grill, and topped with your favorite meat, fish, or poultry. The food ends up with a delicious hardwood flavor like you'd get from smoking.

Rotisserie: This is a motorized, rotating spit or basket that offers the perfect system for slow cooking all types of meats, including whole chickens, roasts, and ribs. Most grills can be transformed into rotisseries with custom kits that contain all the necessary parts.

Grill basket with handle

Rib rack

Rotisserie

Grilling Safety

Yes, fire is a great thing. Many anthropologists think that harnessing fire may be the single greatest achievement for mankind, helping fuel the development of man's big brain and all the wonderful human things that followed: language, culture, and, of course, grilling. Unfortunately, over the years, some humans behaved as if they actually had very small brains. Their actions have resulted in the development of fire extinguishers, fire departments, and a whole host of other things to deal with grilling accidents.

You, fortunately, have the advantage of historical hindsight and can employ the single most important factor in grilling safety: prevention. The best way to ensure a hazard-free outdoor cooking experience is to plan your grilling in advance and set up accordingly. In addition, there are a variety of tools available—many of which have been discussed earlier in the book—that will add to your grilling enjoyment and safety.

The first step in safe grilling is to learn how to use your new grill. Before you ever use your new cooking appliance, read the manufacturer's instructions carefully. If your grill needs to be put together—this is a tough one for many men to follow—read the step-by-step assembly instructions and follow them

▲ Grillers should dress with safety in mind before they start cooking. Always wear close-toed shoes; long, heavyweight pants (such as jeans); and long-sleeve shirts to minimize your risk for burns from splattering grease or flying cinders.

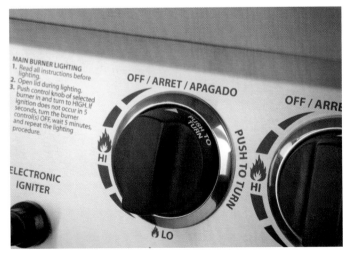

▲ When preparing to light your gas grill, keep the burner knob turned to "off" until after you have opened the lid.

▲ Keep a charged-up fire extinguisher nearby during every grilling session—and make sure you know how to use it.

exactly. If parts are missing, or things don't fit correctly, get help from the manufacturer or retail outlet where you purchased the product. Once your grill is assembled and you know how to operate it, select an appropriate location for using it. Pages 16 to 17 provide more information about setting up your grill, but there are a few things that bear repeating: Choose a level, stable, and well-ventilated spot for your grill; keep it away from trees, shrubs, houses, or anything else combustible (10 feet is a good minimum distance); and keep it out of pedestrian walkways and safely isolated from areas frequented by kids and pets. Once you start your grill, never move it until you are finished cooking and it has fully cooled.

Before you fire up things, think about your clothing and choose a grill-appropriate wardrobe. Keep in mind that serious grillers usually wear jeans and long-sleeve shirts to minimize the chance of burns on their arms and legs. That level of dress may be a lot to ask for in hot weather, but always wear a shirt to protect your midsection from splattering grease. In addition, avoid loose-fitting or flowing clothing (including ties and scarves) that might droop into the fire or snag the grill or tools. Look also at the fabric and avoid anything that might be especially flammable. As far as footwear, never cook in bare feet or open-toed shoes—there is too much risk of injury from dripping grease, dropped tools, and runaway cinders. Finally, people laugh about those "Kiss the Cook" aprons, but there is a good reason to wear them: In addition to protecting your clothes from stains, they can protect you from burns from splattering foods or popping cinders.

There are many good ways to light a charcoal fire, but people still manage to make it unsafe by not using their heads. Lighter fluid is the only liquid that is safe for starting a fire; use it sparingly, let it soak in before lighting, and never add more fluid after the fire has been lit. Consider investing in a chimney starter if you want the safest, most effective method of starting a fire. In addition, avoid using standard kitchen or book matches to light your fire; instead choose long-handled matches or a butane lighter with a long stem—your fingers will thank you in the long run.

Gas grillers should always incorporate a quick safety check into their routine before firing up. Do a quick visual inspection of the propane tank, the hose, and the fittings. Replace any tanks that are excessively dented or rusted, along with any hoses that are cracked or brittle. Spray the fittings with a soapy water solution and look for bubbles, which are a sign of leaks. Plus, don't forget to use your nose—it's a good tool for detecting leaks. Don't light the grill if you smell gas before you open any valves.

Once you are satisfied that your grill is in good working order, open the lid (very important first step for preventing gas buildup), open the valve on the top of the propane tank, turn the knob for the burner designated for lighting, and finally light the grill with a match or the ignition switch.

There are many things that you can do to ensure a safe cooking experience. In addition to dressing correctly, take other precautions to protect yourself from burns. Use only long-handled tools with heat-resistant handles. Buy yourself a pair of long insulated cooking mitts, the kind that reach to the elbow provide the most protection.

Always remember that you are working with fire—it's unpredictable and potentially

▲ **All grill chefs—even guys—should get in the habit of wearing an apron while cooking. Aprons protect your clothes from stains and protect your body from burns caused by popping cinders or splattering grease.**

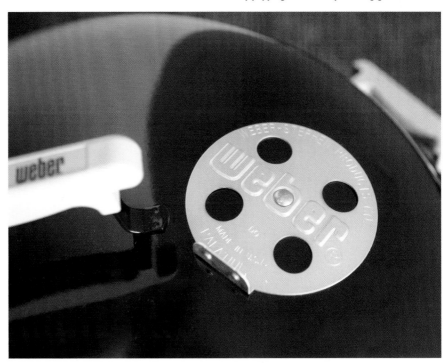

▲ **The lid does a lot more than trap heat for cooking. In the event of a flare-up—usually caused by dripping grease—simply put your grill's lid in place and close the vent to extinguish unwanted and potentially dangerous flames.**

dangerous. Never leave your fire unattended, and monitor it carefully. Your grill lid and vents are your best tools for managing the fire. Leaving the lid on will reduce cooking time and keep the fire under better control. Closing a vent or two will slow down a hot fire. If you are cooking with an open grill and experience a flare-up (caused when grease is ignited), don't panic. Simply close the lid—and the vents if necessary—to extinguish the flame. Never squirt a flare-up with water; that can spread a grease fire. Finally, keep a fire extinguisher close at hand, just in case you have a real emergency.

When you are done cooking with a charcoal fire, cover the grill with its lid, close all the vents, and let the fire completely extinguish itself. Never try to put a fire out with water. When you are finished cooking with a gas grill, turn off the burners and close the gas valve. Once everything has cooled completely, unhook the propane tank to minimize the potential for leaks. Store the tanks outside (not in the garage or in any building where gas can build up) and in an upright position.

Remember that when grilling you are working with fire—it's unpredictable and potentially dangerous.

▲ A pair of long, heavy-duty mitts is an essential purchase for every serious griller. Wear them whenever you are working in the vicinity of your fire to protect yourself from burns and so you can handle grill parts and food with more security and confidence.

▲ Always set up your grill on a level, stable surface to help prevent it from tipping.

▲ Always wear cooking mitts when working with fryers to reduce your risk of burns from the hot oil.

▲ Always store propane tanks outside—never inside your garage—with the valve turned off.

▲ Fryers need to be set up on a stable, level surface that's in a well-ventilated area and far away from structures or any flammable material.

Outdoor cooking demands your constant attention. Never leave your grill or fryer unattended, even for a short time.

▶ Fired-up grills need to be situated in a location that keeps them out of backyard activity areas and walkways. Always keep kids and pets a safe distance from the hot grill. Also remember that once you've lit the fire, never spray on additional lighter fluid or you might end up with a dangerous flare-up.

Direct Grilling

 irect grilling is the classic style of outdoor cooking—start your fire, let your grill get hot, and then slap the meat on the cooking rack. This is a simple and straightforward way to cook, not foolproof, but probably the best place to start for a beginning grill chef. The problem is that too many grillers get too comfortable with the simplicity of direct grilling and don't explore its versatility. Or, even worse, they never quite grasp the nuances of their grill and subject their family to years of the mediocre-tasting entrées.

It's time to move beyond humdrum burgers, brats, and steaks. The first step is to become an expert with heat control. No matter what type of grill you use, learn how to consistently generate a fire temperature that's appropriate for what you are cooking. This is a little more easily done with gas, but it's not that hard with charcoal if you pay attention to the fire and aggressively work the vents and coals to maintain the optimum cooking temperature.

The next step is to learn to cook food—especially meat—to the right internal temperature. This is essential for ensuring safe food, and your grilled meals will be tastier and juicier if you use a food thermometer to monitor their progress and cook to exactly the right doneness.

Chapter 2 Recipes

Finally, you will thank yourself for exploring ways to add great flavors with the help of the fire. For charcoal grillers, this means moving beyond cheap composition briquettes and trying lump charcoal or even hardwood chunks to fuel your fire. Gas grillers can get in the act, too, by using wood chips or chunks to add hardwood flavor while direct grilling.

After honing your fire-management skills, elevate your grilled entrées even further by doing a little more than just tossing meat on the grill. Top grillers employ a mouthwatering arsenal of spices, sauces, rubs, and marinades. A little bit of extra kitchen prep time—often while the grill is heating up—will allow you to transform your burgers, steaks, chops, and chicken from okay to awesome.

Finally, start expanding your definition of grill food. There is no rule that limits what you can cook on a grill over direct heat. Burgers are enhanced by being cooked over an open fire, so why shouldn't shrimp or lobster? Many people aren't crazy about vegetables, but cook veggies on a grill and their attitudes quickly change. And a popular grilling item is pizza, which is easily and oh-so-tastily prepared with basic direct-grilling techniques. The only danger in expanding your skills is that family and friends will start to demand more and more of your grill-cooked masterpieces—but what serious outdoor chefs wouldn't be ecstatic to be "forced" to spend more time next to their grill?

Direct Grilling: Charcoal

Preparing your charcoal grill for direct grilling requires a little advance planning. Consider three key questions:
1. How hot a fire do you need?
2. Will you be simultaneously cooking items that need different cooking temperatures and cooking times?
3. For how long will you need the fire to maintain its cooking temperature?

The simplest meals will require cooking a single food item over a medium fire for an hour or less. Start your fire, wait until it reaches the desired temperature (it might actually have to cool somewhat), and cook your food—but what about more complicated projects?

If you need a very hot fire, plan on using extra briquettes, and after they've ashed over, pack them tightly together. Cook your food immediately;

charcoal fires quickly reach a peak temperature and start cooling. Open the vents to maximize the burn; consider leaving the lid off, but be on the alert for flare-ups.

If you have multiple types of food with different cooking requirements, adjust the structure of your charcoal accordingly—the briquettes don't always have to be evenly spread out. To create a hot spot, bunch some coals together or even double-layer them. To create a cooler cooking zone, spread out fewer coals. If you have quick-cooking items mixed with longer-cooking foods, create a holding area under which you have no coals. Put cooked foods there and replace the lid; the area functions like a warming oven.

The typical charcoal fire will provide enough heat to direct grill for about one hour. If you anticipate needing more cooking time, plan on

adding more charcoal, choosing one of two of methods. First, you can simply add fresh briquettes on top of hot coals. They take about 15 minutes to fully ignite, so add them well before your fire burns itself out. Second, you can light a fresh supply of charcoal in a chimney starter on a concrete patio or other fire-resistant surface and add the briquettes when they are hot and needed. No matter which system you use, adding fresh charcoal is challenging on many grills and is best done by two people—one wearing heatproof mitts lifts the cooking grate while the other quickly adds the new coals. Another option is to look for special cooking grates with a hinged, lift-up panel to make it simple for one cook to add charcoal by her- or himself.

Direct Grilling: Gas

The principles used for effective direct grilling on a gas unit are much the same as you employ on a charcoal grill—except that you have the advantage of a system designed to provide an easily varied flow of fuel and, thus, cooking temperature. Follow the manufacturer's directions for igniting your grill, and that always starts with opening the grill cover to avoid a potentially explosive gas build-up. Once your burners are lit, close the lid and turn your burners to high to help the grill heat up more quickly, even if you eventually will be cooking at a lower temperature.

Regardless of what settings you see on your control knobs, gas grills can be finicky and have unexpected hot spots and cool spots. Serious grillers may want to invest in a thermometer that can be placed at various spots on the cooking grates to measure exactly how hot their grill gets at different spots and under varying knob settings. Such an exercise on some inexpensive grills might reveal that "High" is a fictitious setting. Some economy-priced gas grills struggle to reach a really hot temperature even when all the burners are fueled to the maximum.

Ensuring the best gas-powered direct-grilling experience actually starts when shopping for a new grill. Invest in a unit that has at least three burners for maximum heating ability and the greatest versatility in direct grilling. Three burners ensure the ability to create three regions within the grill for different foods or foods at varying stages of cooking. Just as with a "customized" charcoal setup, you can simultaneously be grilling foods over a hot fire in one area, over a medium or cool fire in another, and be holding cooked foods in yet another "warming" area. And the beauty of the gas system is that you can achieve this multifaceted cooking environment by simply adjusting a few knobs.

Savory Onion Hamburgers

Plain old ground beef gussied up with the right mix of seasonings elevates a grilling favorite from good to great.

2

DIRECT GRILLING

GRILLING DETAILS

PREP: 20 minutes
GRILL: 14 minutes
MAKES: 4 servings

INGREDIENTS

- ½   cup finely chopped onion (1 medium)
- 2   tablespoons steak sauce
- 1   tablespoon Worcestershire sauce
- 1½ teaspoons garlic powder
- ¼   teaspoon black pepper
- 1   pound lean ground beef
- 4   kaiser rolls or hamburger buns, split and toasted (see tip, page 139)
     Cheddar cheese slices, tomato slices, sweet onion slices, dill pickle slices (optional)

SAFETY ALERT

Ground meats present a high risk for getting sick from E. coli and other microorganisms, but taking a few precautions will help you avoid infection. After working with ground meats, thoroughly wash your hands and all utensils, dishes, and work surfaces with an antibacterial cleanser. On the grill, cook all ground meat entrées until they reach a safe internal temperature as measured with a quick-read thermometer. Ground poultry products should be cooked to 170°F, while ground beef, pork, and lamb should be cooked to 160°F.

1 In a medium bowl combine onion, steak sauce, Worcestershire sauce, garlic powder, and pepper. Add ground beef; mix well. Shape mixture into four ¾-inch-thick patties.*

2 For a charcoal grill, grill patties on the rack of an uncovered grill directly over medium coals for 14 to 18 minutes or until meat is done (160°F), turning once halfway through grilling. (For a gas grill, preheat grill. Reduce heat to medium. Place patties on grill rack over heat. Cover; grill as above.)

3 Remove burgers from grill. Serve burgers on rolls. If desired, serve burgers with cheese, tomato, onion, and pickles.

*Note: If you prefer thinner burgers, shape the beef mixture into four ½-inch-thick patties. Grill as above, but grill patties for 10 to 13 minutes or until done (160°F).

Preparing the Grill

1

LIGHT THE CHARCOAL

Light the charcoal using one of the methods described on pages 22 to 23. Allow the charcoal to burn until it glows red-hot and is fully covered with a layer of white ash.

2

SPREAD OUT THE COALS

Using a sturdy, long-handled tool such as a pair of tongs, a garden rake, or a hoe, spread the coals so that they evenly cover the charcoal grate. Put the cooking rack in place, and when it has heated, give it a quick cleaning with a wire grill brush.

3

CHECK THE TEMPERATURE

Using a thermometer or your hand (see pages 24 to 25), check the temperature of the cooking rack. Start cooking when the heat is medium (about 350°F). If the heat is too high, wait for the coals to burn down and cool on their own or adjust the grill vents to reduce air flow.

Preparing the Hamburgers

Top with a slice of cheddar and serve on a fresh kaiser roll.

1

COMBINE THE INGREDIENTS

Combine all the ingredients, except the ground beef, in a medium-size bowl. Add the ground beef and, using a wooden spoon, mix thoroughly so that the seasonings are evenly dispersed throughout the meat.

2

MAKE THE PATTIES

Separate the meat mixture into four even portions. Using your hands, shape each portion into a round, uniformly shaped patty about 1/2 to 3/4 inch thick—thicker patties will be difficult to cook through. Grill immediately or keep refrigerated until cooking time.

Texas Hill Country Ribeyes

Many think ribeyes are the tastiest cut of steak, and this recipe will take them to a whole other level of flavor.

GRILLING DETAILS

PREP: 20 minutes
GRILL: 26 minutes
MAKES: 4 servings

INGREDIENTS

- ⅓ cup snipped fresh sage or 4 teaspoons dried sage, crushed
- 1½ teaspoons coarse salt
- 1½ teaspoons ground cumin
- 1 teaspoon crushed red pepper
- 2 medium red onions
- 4 8-ounce boneless beef ribeye steaks, cut 1 inch thick
- 1 recipe Sweet Pepper Salsa (see recipe, below)

CLOSER LOOK

TOP GRILLING STEAKS
There are several cuts of beefsteak, but here are a few styles that are grilling favorites:
Ribeyes: Flavorful, tender, boneless cuts from the rib section with a higher fat content and price tag.
Tenderloin: Small, thick, lean, and oh-so-tender cuts from the short loin—think filet mignon.
Porterhouse: Part tenderloin, part loin separated by a bone; flavorful and tender and improves with grilling.
T-bone: Similar to porterhouse but with a smaller tenderloin and usually cut thinner.
Sirloin: Large, versatile steaks from "hip" region; less flavorful than other cuts but more economical.

1 For rub, in a small bowl combine sage, salt, cumin, and red pepper; set aside. Peel onions. If desired, cut onions in half lengthwise. Very thinly slice whole or half onions with a sharp knife. Place onions in a grill basket. For a charcoal grill, grill onions in basket directly over medium coals about 15 minutes or until brown and crisp, rearranging and turning once. (For a gas grill, preheat grill. Reduce heat to medium. Place onions in basket directly over heat. Cover; grill as above.) Remove onions and set aside.

2 Meanwhile, trim fat from steaks. Sprinkle rub evenly over both sides of steaks; pat in with your fingers.

3 For a charcoal grill, grill steaks on the rack of an uncovered grill directly over medium coals to desired doneness, turning once halfway through grilling. Allow 11 to 15 minutes for medium-rare doneness (145°F) or 14 to 18 minutes for medium doneness (160°F). (For a gas grill, place steaks on grill rack over medium heat. Cover; grill as above.) Serve with grilled onions and Sweet Pepper Salsa.

Sweet Pepper Salsa: In a medium bowl combine ¾ cup finely chopped red sweet pepper (1 medium); ½ cup finely chopped papaya; ½ cup snipped fresh cilantro; ¼ cup finely chopped jicama; 2 tablespoons lime juice; 1 small fresh habanero chile pepper or 1 medium fresh jalapeño chile pepper, seeded and finely chopped (see tip, page 52); 1 tablespoon honey (if desired); and ¼ teaspoon salt. Cover and refrigerate for up to 24 hours. Makes 1½ cups.

1

LIGHT THE CHARCOAL

Light the charcoal using one of the methods described on pages 22 to 23. Allow the charcoal to burn until it glows red-hot and is fully covered with a layer of white ash.

2

SPREAD OUT THE COALS

Using a sturdy, long-handled tool such as a pair of tongs, a garden rake, or a hoe, spread the coals so that they evenly cover the charcoal grate. Put the cooking rack in place, and when it has heated, give it a quick cleaning with a wire grill brush.

3

CHECK THE TEMPERATURE

Using a thermometer or your hand (see pages 24 to 25), check the temperature of the cooking rack. Start cooking when the heat is medium (about 350°F). If the heat is too high, wait for the coals to burn down and cool on their own or adjust the grill vents to reduce air flow.

Preparing the Steaks

1

PREPARE THE RUB

Using kitchen scissors, snip fresh sage leaves into tiny pieces until you have enough to equal ⅓ cup. Add the remaining rub ingredients and mix. Sprinkle the mixture evenly over both sides of the steaks and rub in gently with the tips of your fingers.

2

GRILL THE ONIONS

Peel two red onions and, if desired, halve lengthwise. Thinly slice the onions with a sharp knife, as shown, and place the slices in a grill basket. Grill the onions over medium heat about 15 minutes, turning once, until they are brown and crispy. Set the onions to the side while you grill your ribeyes and serve them with the steaks.

Sweet Pepper Salsa gives these steaks a spicy Tex-Mex personality.

Stuffed Tenderloin Platter

These big, juicy tenderloins are naturally lean, so grill to medium doneness for the best flavor and tenderness.

GRILLING DETAILS

PREP: 30 minutes
GRILL: 14 minutes
MAKES: 6 servings

INGREDIENTS

- 6 beef tenderloin steaks, cut 1 inch thick
  Salt and black pepper
- 1 12-ounce jar roasted red sweet peppers, drained
- 6 to 12 fresh basil leaves
- ⅓ cup bottled red wine vinaigrette or Italian salad dressing
- 6 small yellow summer squash and/or zucchini, halved lengthwise
- 3 cloves garlic, quartered
- 1 green onion, sliced in chunks
- 1 tablespoon snipped fresh basil or oregano or ½ teaspoon dried basil or oregano, crushed
  Green onions, cut into 1-inch pieces (optional)

TOOL SAVVY

STAYING ON THE CUTTING EDGE

Knives are probably a grill chef's most important tools, and just as important as acquiring a variety of high-quality blades is keeping those blades sharp. A dull knife can make a mess of an expensive cut of meat, and it is more likely to slip and cut you than a sharp blade. Invest in sharpening tools and use them regularly to keep your blades nicely honed. A kitchen steel is great for quickly cleaning up a dull edge, but you'll thank yourself for acquiring a multiple-grit diamond sharpening tool (very inexpensive) or even a motorized sharpener (pricier but quick and easy).

1 Sprinkle steaks lightly with salt and black pepper. Cut a 2-inch-wide pocket in the side of each steak, cutting to but not through the other side. Cut six 2×1-inch pieces roasted red pepper; set remaining peppers aside. Place a red pepper piece and 1 or 2 basil leaves in the pocket of each steak.

2 Brush 3 tablespoons of the vinaigrette on steaks and squash. For a charcoal grill, grill steaks on the rack of an uncovered grill directly over medium coals for 7 minutes. Turn steaks and add squash. Grill for 7 to 9 minutes more for medium doneness (160°F), turning squash once. (For a gas grill, preheat grill. Place steaks on grill rack over heat. Cover; grill steaks and squash as above.)

3 Meanwhile, for the relish, in a food processor combine remaining sweet peppers, garlic, the sliced green onion, and herb. Process until finely chopped. Stir in remaining vinaigrette.

4 Arrange steak and squash on a platter. Serve with relish and, if desired, green onion pieces.

Preparing the Grill

1 LIGHT THE CHARCOAL

Light the charcoal using one of the methods described on pages 22 to 23. Allow the charcoal to burn until it glows red-hot and is fully covered with a layer of white ash.

2 SPREAD OUT THE COALS

Using a sturdy, long-handled tool such as a pair of tongs, a garden rake, or a hoe, spread the coals so that they evenly cover the charcoal grate. Put the cooking rack in place, and when it has heated, give it a quick cleaning with a wire grill brush.

3 CHECK THE TEMPERATURE

Using a thermometer or your hand (see pages 24 to 25), check the temperature of the cooking rack. Start cooking when the heat is medium (about 350°F). If the heat is too high, wait for the coals to burn down and cool on their own or adjust the grill vents to reduce air flow.

Preparing the Tenderloins

1 SEASON THE STEAKS

Cut a "pocket" into the side of each steak and insert a piece of roasted red pepper and one or two fresh basil leaves, as shown. Press the pocket openings closed and generously brush each steak with the vinaigrette or salad dressing. Grill over medium coals.

2 PREPARE THE RELISH

Combine the remaining roasted peppers, garlic, green onions, and herbs in a food processor. Process until the ingredients are finely chopped and well mixed. Combine in a small bowl with the remaining vinaigrette or salad dressing and serve on the side with the grilled tenderloins.

Grill the steaks and squash side by side over a medium-hot fire.

Tex-Mex Fajitas

The steak marinade in this Tex-Mex classic uses jalapeño peppers and golden tequila, also called dorado tequila.

GRILLING DETAILS

PREP: 20 minutes
MARINATE: 2 to 4 hours
SOAK: 30 minutes
GRILL: 17 minutes
STAND: 5 minutes
MAKES: 6 servings

INGREDIENTS

- 1   1¼- to 1½-pound beef flank steak
- ¼   cup olive oil
- ⅓   cup lemon juice
- ¼   cup golden tequila
- ¼   cup sliced green onion (2)
- 4   cloves garlic, minced
- 2   fresh small jalapeño chile peppers, seeded and finely chopped (see safety tip, below)
- 2   tablespoons snipped fresh cilantro
- ½   teaspoon salt
     Wooden skewers
- 1   medium sweet onion
- 2   medium red and/or green sweet peppers
- 1   tablespoon olive oil
     Salt and black pepper
- 2   tablespoons golden tequila
- 2   limes, cut into wedges
- 6   9- to 10-inch flour tortillas
- 1   large tomato, peeled, seeded, and chopped
- 1   large avocado, halved, seeded, peeled, and chopped

SAFETY ALERT

Take special care when working with jalapeño, habanero, and other types of hot chile peppers. These peppers—especially the seeds—contain oils that can irritate your eyes and skin. Always wear rubber or plastic gloves when cutting chile peppers and avoid touching your eyes or mouth. Wash your hands, the knife, and the cutting board with warm, soapy water when you're finished.

1 Trim fat from steak. Score both sides of steak in a diamond pattern by making shallow diagonal cuts at 1-inch intervals.

2 For marinade, in a small bowl combine the ¼ cup olive oil, the lemon juice, the ¼ cup tequila, the green onions, garlic, jalapeño peppers, snipped cilantro, and the ½ teaspoon salt. Place steak in a resealable large plastic bag set in a shallow dish. Pour marinade over steak; seal bag. Marinate in the refrigerator for 2 to 4 hours, turning bag occasionally.

3 Soak several wooden skewers in water for 30 minutes. Cut onion into thick slices. Secure slices by inserting wooden skewers into the sides of onion slices through to the center. Remove stems from sweet peppers. Quarter peppers lengthwise; remove seeds and membranes. Brush onion slices and sweet pepper quarters with the 1 tablespoon olive oil; set aside. Drain steak, discarding marinade. Sprinkle steak with salt and black pepper.

4 For a charcoal grill, grill steak on the rack of an uncovered grill directly over medium coals for 17 to 21 minutes for medium doneness (160°F), turning once halfway through grilling. (For a gas grill, preheat grill. Reduce heat to medium. Place steak on grill rack over heat. Cover; grill as above.) Add onion slices and sweet pepper quarters to grill the last 8 to 10 minutes of cooking time; grill until tender, turning once.

5 Transfer steak to a cutting board; immediately drizzle with the 2 tablespoons tequila. Squeeze 1 or 2 of the lime wedges over steak. Cover steak with foil and let stand for 5 minutes. Wrap tortillas tightly in foil. Heat on grill rack for 10 minutes or until heated through, turning once. Remove skewers from onion slices. Break onion slices into rings; cut sweet pepper quarters into strips.

6 To serve, thinly slice meat diagonally across the grain. Serve on tortillas with onion, sweet pepper, tomato, avocado, and remaining lime wedges. If desired, serve with *salsa*, chopped *avocado*, and *sour cream*.

Preparing the Grill

1

LIGHT THE CHARCOAL

Light the charcoal using one of the methods described on pages 22 to 23. Allow the charcoal to burn until it glows red-hot and is fully covered with a layer of white ash.

2

SPREAD OUT THE COALS

Using a sturdy, long-handled tool such as a pair of tongs, a garden rake, or a hoe, spread the coals so that they evenly cover the charcoal grate. Put the cooking rack in place, and when it has heated, give it a quick cleaning with a wire grill brush.

3

CHECK THE TEMPERATURE

Using a thermometer or your hand (see pages 24 to 25), check the temperature of the cooking rack. Start cooking when the heat is medium (about 350°F). If the heat is too high, wait for the coals to burn down and cool on their own or adjust the grill vents to reduce air flow.

Preparing the Fajitas

The marinade both flavors and tenderizes the flank steak.

1

CHOP THE PEPPERS

With a sharp knife, remove the seeds and membranes from two small jalapeño peppers and chop the peppers into tiny pieces. In a small bowl mix the chopped peppers with the remaining marinade ingredients. Place the steak in a resealable plastic storage bag, top with the marinade, and seal the bag. Marinate in the refrigerator for 2 to 4 hours.

2

PREPARE THE VEGETABLES

Cut a sweet onion into thick slices; thread a wooden skewer through each slice. Quarter two peppers (red, green, or both) lengthwise. Use a basting brush to coat all the vegetables with olive oil, as shown, and set aside until ready to grill.

3

GRILL AND SERVE

Discard the marinade and grill the flank steak over medium coals. Add onions and peppers during the last 8 to 10 minutes. Place the grilled flank steak on a cutting board, drizzle with tequila and lime juice, cover with foil, and let stand for 5 minutes. Slice the meat diagonally (across the grain) into thin strips, as shown, and serve.

Memphis-Style Pork Chops

Barbecue taste varies in different parts of the country. This Southern-style recipe uses chili sauce instead of ketchup and includes molasses and cider vinegar.

2

DIRECT GRILLING

🌀 GRILLING DETAILS

PREP: 15 minutes
GRILL: 12 minutes
MAKES: 4 servings

✓ INGREDIENTS

- ½ cup chili sauce
- 2 tablespoons molasses
- 2 tablespoons cider vinegar
- 1 teaspoon chili powder
- 4 boneless pork loin chops, cut ¾ to 1 inch thick (about 1¼ pounds)
- 1 teaspoon dried basil, crushed
- ½ teaspoon paprika
- ¼ teaspoon salt
- ¼ teaspoon onion powder
- ¼ teaspoon cayenne pepper
- Purchased coleslaw (optional)

🔍 CLOSER LOOK

WHAT'S A RUB?

A rub is a dry mixture of spices that is applied to the surface of meat before grilling and then literally rubbed in. The spices in rubs start flavoring meat immediately, before cooking, and then they really kick into action on the grill once the juices start to flow. Rubs also tend to trap those juices in the meat, and some mixtures that include sugar can protect meat from scorching.

1 In a small saucepan stir together chili sauce, molasses, vinegar, and chili powder. Bring to boiling; reduce heat. Simmer, uncovered, for 3 minutes. Remove from heat.

2 Trim fat from chops. For rub, in a small bowl stir together basil, paprika, salt, onion powder, and cayenne pepper. Sprinkle evenly over both sides of chops; pat in with your fingers.

3 For a charcoal grill, grill chops on the rack of an uncovered grill directly over medium coals for 12 to 15 minutes or until juices run clear (160°F), turning once and brushing with chili sauce mixture during the last 5 minutes of grilling. (For a gas grill, preheat grill. Reduce heat to medium. Place chops on grill rack over heat. Cover; grill as above.) If desired, serve with coleslaw.

Preparing the Grill

1

LIGHT THE CHARCOAL

Light the charcoal using one of the methods described on pages 22 to 23. Allow the charcoal to burn until it glows red-hot and is fully covered with a layer of white ash.

2

SPREAD OUT THE COALS

Using a sturdy, long-handled tool such as a pair of tongs, a garden rake, or a hoe, spread the coals so that they evenly cover the charcoal grate. Put the cooking rack in place, and when it has heated, give it a quick cleaning with a wire grill brush.

3

CHECK THE TEMPERATURE

Using a thermometer or your hand (see pages 24 to 25), check the temperature of the cooking rack. Start cooking when the heat is medium (about 350°F). If the heat is too high, wait for the coals to burn down and cool on their own or adjust the grill vents to reduce air flow.

Preparing the Pork Chops

1

APPLY THE RUB

Prepare the rub by combining the basil, paprika, salt, onion powder, and cayenne pepper in a small bowl. Sprinkle the mixture evenly over both sides of all the chops and rub in gently with the tips of your fingers.

2

GRILL THE CHOPS

Place the chops on the cooking rack of a grill over medium heat (about 350°F). Cook, uncovered, for 12 to 15 minutes, turning once. Check the internal temperature of the chops with a quick-read thermometer, as shown; pull chops from heat when it reaches 160°F.

Use a quick-read thermometer to ensure perfect doneness every time.

Brats with Jalapeño-Green Apple Kraut

These sausages will blitz your taste buds and fire up the crowd at your next tailgate party.

GRILLING DETAILS

PREP: 10 minutes
COOK: 20 minutes
GRILL: 3 minutes
MAKES: 6 servings

INGREDIENTS

- 6   uncooked bratwurst
- 3   cups apple juice or apple cider
- ⅓   cup apple jelly
- 1   8-ounce can sauerkraut, drained
- 1   tart green apple, cored and cut into thin bite-size pieces
- 2   to 3 fresh jalapeño chile peppers, seeded and cut into thin strips (see tip, page 52)
- 6   bratwurst or hot dog buns, split and toasted (see tip, page 139)

CLOSER LOOK

ALL ABOUT BRATWURST

Bratwurst is a German word meaning "fry sausage," and, yes, brats are a sausage, but most grillers consider it a sacrilege to fry them. Traditionally they are made from a mixture of ground pork and veal, but most commercial sausages use beef instead of veal. Wisconsin is the American epicenter of bratwurst cuisine, but they are a popular entrée at picnics, tailgate parties, and backyard cookouts across the country.

1 Use the tines of a fork to pierce the skin of each bratwurst several times. In a Dutch oven combine bratwurst and apple juice. Bring to boiling; reduce heat. Simmer, covered, about 20 minutes or until bratwurst are no longer pink and juices run clear (160°F); drain.

2 Meanwhile, in a small saucepan melt apple jelly over low heat. In a medium bowl combine 2 tablespoons of the melted jelly, the sauerkraut, apple, and chile peppers. Set aside remaining melted jelly to brush on bratwurst.

3 Tear off a 30×18-inch piece of heavy foil; fold in half to make a 15×18-inch rectangle. Mound sauerkraut mixture in center of foil. Bring up two opposite edges of foil and seal with a double fold. Fold remaining edges together to completely enclose sauerkraut mixture, leaving space for steam to build.

4 For a charcoal grill, grill bratwurst and foil packet on the rack of an uncovered grill directly over medium coals for 3 to 7 minutes or until bratwurst are brown, turning bratwurst and foil packet once halfway through grilling and brushing bratwurst with the reserved melted jelly during the last 2 minutes of grilling. (For a gas grill, preheat grill. Reduce heat to medium. Place bratwurst and foil packet on grill rack over heat. Cover; grill as above.)

5 Serve bratwurst in toasted buns; top with sauerkraut mixture.

Preparing the Grill

1 **LIGHT THE CHARCOAL**

Light the charcoal using one of the methods described on pages 22 to 23. Allow the charcoal to burn until it glows red-hot and is fully covered with a layer of white ash.

2 **SPREAD OUT THE COALS**

Using a sturdy, long-handled tool such as a pair of tongs, a garden rake, or a hoe, spread the coals so that they evenly cover the charcoal grate. Put the cooking rack in place, and when it has heated, give it a quick cleaning with a wire grill brush.

3 **CHECK THE TEMPERATURE**

Using a thermometer or your hand (see pages 24 to 25), check the temperature of the cooking rack. Start cooking when the heat is medium (about 350°F). If the heat is too high, wait for the coals to burn down and cool on their own or adjust the grill vents to reduce air flow.

Preparing the Brats

Serve on bratwurst rolls for authentic flavor.

1 **PRECOOK THE BRATWURST**

Using a fork, gently pierce the skin of each brat several times, as shown. Simmer the brats in apple juice, in a Dutch oven or large saucepan, for 20 minutes. Drain and discard the juice and set aside until ready to grill.

2 **MAKE THE KRAUT PACKET**

Tear off a 30×18-inch piece of aluminum foil and fold in half. Place the sauerkraut mixture in the center of the foil and create a packet, carefully sealing the edges, as shown. Leave space for steam to build up inside. Place on the grill with the brats.

Honey-Herb Glazed Chicken

Turn chicken breasts into a gourmet treat, thanks to an oh-so-easy-to-make brush-on sauce.

GRILLING DETAILS

PREP: 20 minutes
GRILL: 12 minutes
MAKES: 4 servings

INGREDIENTS

- 2 tablespoons honey
- 2 tablespoons orange juice
- 2 tablespoons sliced green onion (1)
- 1 tablespoon olive oil
- ½ teaspoon dried thyme, crushed
- ½ teaspoon dried rosemary, crushed
- 2 cloves garlic, minced
- ¼ teaspoon salt
- ⅛ teaspoon black pepper
- 4 skinless, boneless chicken breast halves (1 to 1½ pounds)
  Sliced green onion (optional)

CLOSER LOOK

ONION VARIETIES DIFFER

When a recipe calls for green onions, don't just assume you can substitute any old onion. It's true that green onions are simply immature onions that are harvested before their bulbs get large, but they have a distinctly different flavor from traditional bulb onions and are purposely matched to many recipes. Green onions are versatile because you can use both the bulb and the green tops—the tops often serve as a colorful and flavorful garnish. Green onions are usually sold in bunches held together with a rubber band, which should be removed to increase the time they can be stored in the refrigerator.

1 In a small bowl combine honey, orange juice, the 2 tablespoons green onion, the oil, thyme, rosemary, garlic, salt, and pepper. Set aside.

2 For a charcoal grill, grill chicken on the rack of an uncovered grill directly over medium coals for 12 to 15 minutes or until tender and no longer pink (170°F), turning once and brushing with the honey mixture the last 5 minutes of grilling. (For a gas grill, preheat grill. Reduce heat to medium. Place chicken on the grill rack over heat. Cover; grill as directed at left.)

3 If desired, sprinkle chicken with additional green onion before serving.

Preparing the Grill

1

LIGHT THE CHARCOAL

Light the charcoal using one of the methods described on pages 22 to 23. Allow the charcoal to burn until it glows red-hot and is fully covered with a layer of white ash.

2

SPREAD OUT THE COALS

Using a sturdy, long-handled tool such as a pair of tongs, a garden rake, or a hoe, spread the coals so that they evenly cover the charcoal grate. Put the cooking rack in place, and when it has heated, give it a quick cleaning with a wire grill brush.

3

CHECK THE TEMPERATURE

Using a thermometer or your hand (see pages 24 to 25), check the temperature of the cooking rack. Start cooking when the heat is medium (about 350°F). If the heat is too high, wait for the coals to burn down and cool on their own or adjust the grill vents to reduce air flow.

Preparing the Chicken

1

MINCE THE GARLIC

Peel 2 cloves of garlic and cut into thin slices with a sharp knife. Use a steady up-and-down cutting motion to chop the slices into tiny pieces. Combine the minced garlic in a small bowl with the honey, orange juice, green onion, oil, thyme, rosemary, salt, and pepper. Mix well.

2

GRILL AND BRUSH ON SAUCE

Grill the chicken breasts over medium-hot coals for 12 to 15 minutes, turning once during this time. During the last 5 minutes, brush on the honey-herb sauce. Cook the chicken until it is no longer pink and its internal temperature reaches 170°F.

Serve with orange slices and salad greens for a fresh summertime treat.

Grilled Chicken Fettuccine

The rich, creamy sauce combines with grilled chicken for a memorable new twist on an old pasta favorite.

GRILLING DETAILS

PREP: 20 minutes
GRILL: 12 minutes
MAKES: 6 servings

INGREDIENTS

- 1 cup whipping cream
- 1/3 cup butter or margarine
- 3/4 cup grated Parmesan cheese
- 4 skinless, boneless chicken breast halves
- 12 ounces dried fettuccine
- 1/4 cup purchased pesto
- 1 cup cherry tomatoes, halved
- Freshly ground black pepper
- Toasted pine nuts (optional)
- Shredded fresh basil (optional)

TIME SAVER

BUY BONELESS BREASTS

Sure, you can save a little money by buying whole chicken breasts and boning them yourself, but why waste the time? Frozen boneless, skinless chicken breasts, usually sold in 3- or 4-pound packages, are one of today's best healthy convenience foods. Pull only what you need from the freezer the night before grilling and let the chicken defrost in the refrigerator. When you factor in no more waste from bones and skin—plus your time savings—the boneless breasts are a great deal.

1 In a small saucepan heat whipping cream and butter until butter melts. Gradually add Parmesan cheese, stirring until combined. Cover and keep warm over low heat.

2 For a charcoal grill, grill chicken on the rack of an uncovered grill directly over medium coals for 12 to 15 minutes or until chicken is no longer pink (170°F), turning once halfway through grilling. (For a gas grill, preheat grill. Reduce heat to medium. Place chicken on grill rack over heat. Cover; grill as above.)

3 Meanwhile, cook fettuccine according to package directions. Drain and keep warm.

4 Cut grilled chicken into bite-size pieces. In a medium bowl toss chicken with 1 tablespoon of the pesto. Add the remaining pesto and the cream mixture to the hot cooked fettuccine. Add tomatoes. Toss to coat. Arrange fettuccine on a serving platter; sprinkle with pepper. Top with grilled chicken. If desired, garnish with pine nuts and basil.

Preparing the Grill

1

LIGHT THE CHARCOAL

Light the charcoal using one of the methods described on pages 22 to 23. Allow the charcoal to burn until it glows red-hot and is fully covered with a layer of white ash.

2

SPREAD OUT THE COALS

Using a sturdy, long-handled tool such as a pair of tongs, a garden rake, or a hoe, spread the coals so that they evenly cover the charcoal grate. Put the cooking rack in place, and when it has heated, give it a quick cleaning with a wire grill brush.

3

CHECK THE TEMPERATURE

Using a thermometer or your hand (see pages 24 to 25), check the temperature of the cooking rack. Start cooking when the heat is medium (about 350°F). If the heat is too high, wait for the coals to burn down and cool on their own or adjust the grill vents to reduce air flow.

Preparing the Chicken

Fresh-grated Parmesan cheese will give you the best flavor.

1

PREPARE THE SAUCE

Heat the whipping cream and butter in a small saucepan until the butter melts. Slowly add the Parmesan cheese (use fresh grated for best results), as shown, stirring continuously. Cover and keep warm. Boil the fettuccine according to the directions on the package, drain, and set aside, keeping warm.

2

GRILL THE CHICKEN BREASTS

Grill the chicken breasts, uncovered, over medium heat (about 350°F). Turn once and cook until the chicken is no longer pink and reaches an internal temperature of 170°F. Immediately cut into bite-size pieces and toss with 1 tablespoon pesto.

Basil Halibut Steaks

Cooked on the grill, fish steaks can be every bit as juicy and delicious as beefsteaks—plus they are lower in fat and cholesterol.

GRILLING DETAILS

PREP: 25 minutes
GRILL: 8 minutes
MAKES: 4 servings

INGREDIENTS

- 1½ pounds fresh or frozen halibut steaks, about 1 inch thick
- ½ cup chopped onion (1 medium)
- 1 clove garlic, minced
- 2 tablespoons olive oil
- 2 to 3 cups chopped, seeded, peeled tomatoes (4 to 6)
- ¼ teaspoon salt
- ¼ teaspoon black pepper
- 4 tablespoons snipped fresh basil
- 1 tablespoon butter or margarine, melted
- Salt and black pepper

REAL WORLD

FROZEN IS FRESHER?

Not everyone has access to a fresh-from-the sea fish, and some must be content with buying frozen fish—meaning that they aren't going to be able to really enjoy "fresh" fish, true? No, actually this is "false" in many cases. Today most fish are cleaned and frozen right on the boat, within hours of being caught. It can be stored frozen and maintain its flavor for up to 3 months. "Fresh" (unfrozen) fish, on the other hand, might take up to 10 days before reaching consumers, long enough for the flavor to start deteriorating.

1 Thaw fish, if frozen; rinse and pat dry. Set aside. In a medium skillet cook onion and garlic in hot oil until tender. Stir in tomato, the ¼ teaspoon salt, and the ¼ teaspoon pepper. Bring to boiling; reduce heat. Simmer, uncovered, for 15 minutes. Stir in 2 tablespoons of the basil.

2 Meanwhile, combine melted butter and the remaining basil; brush over one side of the halibut steaks.

3 Lightly grease an unheated grill rack. For a charcoal grill, grill fish, brushed sides up, on the greased grill rack of an uncovered grill directly over medium coals for 5 minutes. Turn fish; grill for 3 to 7 minutes more or until fish flakes easily when tested with fork. (For a gas grill, preheat grill. Reduce heat to medium. Place fish, brushed side up, on greased grill rack over heat. Cover; grill as above.)

4 Season fish to taste with additional salt and pepper. Serve with tomato mixture.

Preparing the Grill

1 LIGHT THE CHARCOAL
Light the charcoal using one of the methods described on pages 22 to 23. Allow the charcoal to burn until it glows red-hot and is fully covered with a layer of white ash.

2 SPREAD OUT THE COALS
Using a sturdy, long-handled tool such as a pair of tongs, a garden rake or a hoe, spread the coals so that they evenly cover the charcoal grate. Put the cooking rack in place, and when it has heated, give it a quick cleaning with a wire grill brush.

3 CHECK THE TEMPERATURE
Using a thermometer or your hand (see pages 24 to 25), check the temperature of the cooking rack. Start cooking when the heat is medium (about 350°F). If the heat is too high, wait for the coals to burn down and cool on their own or adjust the grill vents to reduce air flow.

Preparing Fresh Peeled Tomatoes

For maximum juiciness, take care not to overcook grilled fish.

1 LOOSEN THE SKIN
Cut an × in the bottom of each tomato. Fill a medium pan with enough water to cover a tomato; bring to a boil. Using a large spoon, dip each tomato in boiling water for 5 to 30 seconds until the × separates. Immediately place in a bowl of ice water.

2 REMOVE THE SKIN
Hold a tomato in one hand with the × facing upward. Peel by grasping a skin flap at the × between your thumb and a paring knife blade, as shown, and giving the skin a gentle, steady tug. Repeat until all the peel is removed.

Thai Shrimp Kabobs

This Asian-inspired spicy-sweet dish can be prepared in less than an hour, but let your dinner guests think you worked a lot harder as they compliment your efforts.

GRILLING DETAILS

PREP: 20 minutes
MARINATE: 30 minutes
GRILL: 5 minutes
MAKES: 4 to 6 servings

INGREDIENTS

- 1½ pounds fresh or frozen large shrimp (about 26 to 30), peeled and deveined
- 1 13½- or 14-ounce can unsweetened coconut milk
- 1½ teaspoons finely shredded lime peel
- 3 tablespoons lime juice
- 1½ teaspoons sugar
- 1½ teaspoons green curry paste
- 1½ teaspoons fish sauce
- 1 teaspoon grated fresh ginger
- 2 to 3 cups hot cooked rice
- Lime wedges (optional)

TOOL SAVVY

CHOOSE YOUR SKEWERS

Wood skewers are the traditional choice for grilling Asian fare like the dish on this page. They are functional and inexpensive, but they have some drawbacks: They must be soaked in water for 30 minutes before grilling, and they can only be used one time. Serious grillers usually prefer working with metal skewers, which are durable, reusable, and require no advance planning—just pull them from the drawer, thread on the food, and grill.

1 Thaw shrimp, if frozen. Rinse shrimp; pat dry with paper towels. If using wooden skewers, soak in water for 30 minutes (see tip, left). In a small bowl stir together coconut milk, lime peel, lime juice, sugar, curry paste, fish sauce, and ginger.

2 Place shrimp in a medium bowl. Pour ½ cup of the coconut milk mixture over shrimp. Cover shrimp and refrigerate for 30 minutes. Cover and refrigerate remaining milk mixture.

3 Drain shrimp, discarding marinade. Thread shrimp onto skewers, leaving a ¼-inch space between pieces.

4 Lightly grease an unheated grill rack. For a charcoal grill, grill kabobs on the greased rack of an uncovered grill directly over medium coals for 5 to 8 minutes or until shrimp are opaque, turning kabobs once halfway through grilling. (For a gas grill, preheat grill. Reduce heat to medium. Place kabobs on greased grill rack over heat. Cover; grill as above.)

5 Meanwhile, heat reserved coconut milk mixture over medium heat until boiling. Reduce heat; simmer, uncovered, for 5 minutes (mixture will be thin). Serve with shrimp and rice. If desired, garnish with lime wedges.

Preparing the Grill

1 LIGHT THE CHARCOAL

Light the charcoal using one of the methods described on pages 22 to 23. Allow the charcoal to burn until it glows red-hot and is fully covered with a layer of white ash.

2 SPREAD OUT THE COALS

Using a sturdy, long-handled tool such as a pair of tongs, a garden rake, or a hoe, spread the coals so that they evenly cover the charcoal grate. Put the cooking rack in place, and when it has heated, give it a quick cleaning with a wire grill brush.

3 CHECK THE TEMPERATURE

Using a thermometer or your hand (see pages 24 to 25), check the temperature of the cooking rack. Start cooking when the heat is medium (about 350°F). If the heat is too high, wait for the coals to burn down and cool on their own or adjust the grill vents to reduce air flow.

Preparing the Shrimp

1 PEEL THE SHRIMP

Working from the bottom (leg side) of the shrimp and starting at the head end, grasp the shell between the thumb and forefinger of each hand and gently peel back, as shown. Tear off the shell at the joint with the tail section.

2 DEVEIN THE SHRIMP

Make a sharp slice down the full length of the back of each shrimp, as shown, revealing the dark-colored vein. Pull out the vein with the knife tip and remove completely. Rinse each shrimp clean under cool running water.

Choose brown rice as a healthy, whole grain side dish for this meal.

Grilled Lobster with Rosemary Butter

Grilling takes this upscale seafood favorite to a level of taste that few fancy restaurants can match.

🕐 GRILLING DETAILS

PREP: 15 minutes
GRILL: 12 minutes
MAKES: 4 servings

✓ INGREDIENTS

4	8-ounce frozen lobster tails
2	teaspoons olive oil
½	cup butter
4	teaspoons finely shredded orange peel
2	rosemary sprigs
1	medium orange, cut into wedges (optional)

💡 GOOD IDEA

FLAVORED CLARIFIED BUTTERS
In restaurants, clarified butter is often called "drawn butter." You clarify butter by removing its water and milk solids, leaving nothing but the golden liquid butterfat. You can enhance the rich flavor of clarified butter by adding herbs, as in this recipe. Create your own combinations by experimenting with other flavor additions, such as star anise, fennel seeds, coriander seeds, peppercorns, and snipped fresh dill.

1 Thaw lobster. Rinse lobster; pat dry with paper towels. Place lobster, shell sides down, on a cutting board. To butterfly, with kitchen scissors cut each lobster in half lengthwise, cutting to, but not through, the back shell. Bend backward to crack back shell and expose the meat. Brush lobster meat with olive oil.

2 Lightly grease an unheated grill rack. For a charcoal grill, grill lobster, shell sides down, on the greased rack of an uncovered grill directly over medium coals for 12 to 15 minutes or until lobster meat is opaque and shells are bright red, turning once halfway through grilling. (For a gas grill, preheat grill. Reduce heat to medium. Place lobster, shell sides down, on greased grill rack over heat. Cover; grill as above.)

3 While lobster is grilling, in a small saucepan place butter, orange peel, and rosemary. Cook over very low heat, without stirring, until butter melts; cool slightly. Pour the clear, oily layer through a fine sieve into a serving dish, discarding the milky layer, orange peel, and rosemary. Serve with lobster; store any remaining butter covered in refrigerator up to 1 month. If desired, serve lobster with orange wedges.

Preparing the Grill

1
LIGHT THE CHARCOAL
Light the charcoal using one of the methods described on pages 22 to 23. Allow the charcoal to burn until it glows red-hot and is fully covered with a layer of white ash.

2
SPREAD OUT THE COALS
Using a sturdy, long-handled tool such as a pair of tongs, a garden rake, or a hoe, spread the coals so that they evenly cover the charcoal grate. Put the cooking rack in place, and when it has heated, give it a quick cleaning with a wire grill brush.

3
CHECK THE TEMPERATURE
Using a thermometer or your hand (see pages 24 to 25), check the temperature of the cooking rack. Start cooking when the heat is medium (about 350°F). If the heat is too high, wait for the coals to burn down and cool on their own or adjust the grill vents to reduce air flow.

Preparing the Lobster

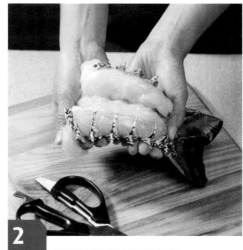

Grill until the meat is opaque and the shell turns bright red.

1
CUT THE LOBSTER TAIL
Using sharp kitchen scissors and holding a lobster tail bottom up in the palm of one hand, cut lengthwise through the tail, as shown. Cut deeply into the meat but not through the top shell.

2
BUTTERFLYING THE LOBSTER
Bend each cut tail backward, as shown, to "butterfly" the lobster and expose the meat for grilling. Using a basting brush, coat the exposed meat with olive oil. Grill lobster tail, shell sides down, over medium coals for 12 to 15 minutes, turning once.

Greek Pizza

Packaged dough makes this dish easy to prepare, and toppings such as lamb and feta cheese give the pizza a distinctive eastern Mediterranean personality.

GRILLING DETAILS

PREP: 15 minutes
GRILL: 12 minutes
MAKES: 4 servings

INGREDIENTS

- 12 ounces ground lamb or beef
- ½ cup chopped green sweet pepper
- 1 8-ounce can tomato sauce
- 1 clove garlic, minced
- ¼ teaspoon allspice
- 1 10-ounce package refrigerated pizza dough
- 2 roma tomatoes, thinly sliced
- ½ cup crumbled feta cheese (2 ounces)
- ¼ cup minced fresh mint
- 1 tablespoon pine nuts, toasted
  Plain low-fat yogurt (optional)

 **TOOL SAVVY**

PIZZA GRILL PANS
You have different options when choosing a pizza pan for grill cooking. A traditional round aluminum or stainless-steel pizza pan will work just fine for grilling. Alternatively, you can choose a perforated pizza pan made specifically for grilling. The holes allow more smoke to penetrate the bottom of the crust, which imparts more grilled flavor. Whichever pan you use, get in the habit of "parbaking" the dough—cooking it on the grill for a few minutes without toppings. This seals the crust and keeps it from getting soggy after the toppings are added.

1 For the sauce, in a large skillet cook ground lamb and sweet pepper over medium heat until meat is no longer pink. Drain well. Stir in tomato sauce, garlic, and allspice.

2 Unroll pizza dough. With your fingers, pat the dough evenly onto a greased 12- to 14-inch pizza pan (you don't need to build up the sides).

3 For a charcoal grill, grill pizza crust in pan on the rack of an uncovered grill directly over medium coals for 6 minutes. (For a gas grill, preheat grill. Reduce heat to medium. Place pizza crust in pan on grill rack over heat. Cover; grill as above.) Carefully remove pizza from grill.

4 Using tongs or a wide spatula, turn crust over; spread crust with sauce. Top with tomatoes. Return pizza to grill. Cover and grill for 6 to 8 minutes more or until pizza is heated through and bottom crust is brown, checking occasionally to make sure the crust doesn't overbrown. Remove pizza from grill.

5 Sprinkle with feta cheese, mint, and pine nuts. If desired, serve with yogurt.

1 LIGHT THE CHARCOAL
Light the charcoal using one of the methods described on pages 22 to 23. Allow the charcoal to burn until it glows red-hot and is fully covered with a layer of white ash.

2 SPREAD OUT THE COALS
Using a sturdy, long-handled tool such as a pair of tongs, a garden rake, or a hoe, spread the coals so that they evenly cover the charcoal grate. Put the cooking rack in place, and when it has heated, give it a quick cleaning with a wire grill brush.

3 CHECK THE TEMPERATURE
Using a thermometer or your hand (see pages 24 to 25), check the temperature of the cooking rack. Start cooking when the heat is medium (about 350°F). If the heat is too high, wait for the coals to burn down and cool on their own or adjust the grill vents to reduce air flow.

Preparing the Crust

On this pizza, the cheese is added after grilling.

1 SPREAD THE DOUGH
Grease a 12- to 14-inch pizza pan with shortening. Using your fingers, gently spread the dough out on the pan, working into a circular shape and filling the pan as much as possible.

2 GRILL THE DOUGH
Place the pan on the grill cooking grate over medium coals. Grill for 5 minutes and remove. Return to the kitchen and flip the crust over in the pan to expose the slightly browned bottom. Cover with toppings and return the pizza to the grill for the remaining cooking time.

Roasted Garlic and Sausage Pizzas

The innovative pizza chef's formula for success: the taste of Italy + open fire = a distinctively American treat.

GRILLING DETAILS

PREP: 25 minutes
REST: 10 minutes
GRILL: 41 minutes
MAKES: 4 to 6 servings

INGREDIENTS

- 2 heads garlic
  Olive oil
- 1 package active dry yeast
- 1 cup warm water (105°F to 115°F)
- 2 tablespoons cornmeal
- 1 teaspoon olive oil
- ½ teaspoon salt
  Dash sugar
- 2½ to 2¾ cups all-purpose flour
  Cornmeal
- 1 pound bulk Italian sausage
- 2 cups sliced fresh mushrooms
- 1 8-ounce can pizza sauce
- 1 medium green sweet pepper, cut into thin bite-size strips (½ cup)
- 2 cups shredded provolone cheese (8 ounces)
- 2 roma tomatoes, sliced

TOOL SAVVY

DO PIZZAS NEED PEELING?

Ever caught the action in a traditional pizza joint? The chefs are often wielding what looks like a giant flat spatula with a long handle. That tool is called a pizza peel and if you make lotsa pie you need one. Aluminum versions are sturdier, but light wood varieties are authentic and more versatile—you can use them as an all-in-one surface for building the pizza, moving it on and off the grill, and even cutting and serving it. A generous layer of cornmeal is the key to helping the pizza slide on and off easily.

1 To roast garlic, cut ½ inch off the top of each garlic head to expose the individual cloves. Leaving garlic heads whole, remove loose, papery outer layers of skin. Place garlic heads, cut sides up, in center of a 10-inch square of heavy foil. Brush garlic heads with olive oil. Bring up 2 opposite edges of foil; seal with a double fold. Fold remaining edges together to completely enclose the garlic, leaving space for steam to build.

2 For a charcoal grill, grill foil packet on the rack of an uncovered grill directly over medium coals about 35 minutes or until garlic heads feel soft, turning packet occasionally. (For a gas grill, preheat grill. Reduce heat to medium. Place foil packet on grill rack over heat. Cover; grill as above.) Remove packet from grill; let cool. Squeeze the roasted garlic cloves from the skins, leaving cloves intact. Discard skins.

3 Meanwhile, for crust, in a large bowl dissolve yeast in warm water. Let stand for 5 minutes. Stir in the 2 tablespoons cornmeal, the 1 teaspoon olive oil, salt, and sugar. Stir in as much of the flour as you can. Turn dough out onto a lightly floured surface. Knead in enough of the remaining flour to make a moderately stiff dough that is smooth and

elastic (about 6 minutes total). Shape dough into two balls. Cover; let rest 10 minutes. Line 2 baking sheets with waxed paper; sprinkle each with additional cornmeal. Roll each dough portion into a 10-inch circle. Transfer each circle to a prepared baking sheet. Cover dough; set aside.

4 In a large skillet cook sausage and mushrooms until sausage is no longer pink; drain well.

5 For a charcoal grill, use a pizza peel or the waxed paper to carefully invert one of the dough circles onto the rack of an uncovered grill directly over medium coals; remove waxed paper (if using). Grill for 1 to 2 minutes or until dough is puffed in some places, starting to become firm, and bottom is light brown. Remove crust from grill; turn crust browned side up. Spread with half each of the sauce, sausage mixture, roasted garlic cloves, sweet pepper, cheese, and tomatoes. Return crust to grill. Cover; grill 2 minutes more or until cheese is melted and bottom crust is crisp. Repeat with remaining dough circle, sauce, sausage mixture, roasted garlic, sweet pepper, cheese, and tomato slices. (For a gas grill, preheat grill. Reduce heat to medium. Place dough circles on grill rack over heat. Cover and grill as above.)

Preparing the Grill

1
LIGHT THE CHARCOAL
Light the charcoal using one of the methods described on pages 22 to 23. Allow the charcoal to burn until it glows red-hot and is fully covered with a layer of white ash.

2
SPREAD OUT THE COALS
Using a sturdy, long-handled tool such as a pair of tongs, a garden rake, or a hoe, spread the coals so that they evenly cover the charcoal grate. Put the cooking rack in place, and when it has heated, give it a quick cleaning with a wire grill brush.

3
CHECK THE TEMPERATURE
Using a thermometer or your hand (see pages 24 to 25), check the temperature of the cooking rack. Start cooking when the heat is medium (about 350°F). If the heat is too high, wait for the coals to burn down and cool on their own or adjust the grill vents to reduce air flow.

Preparing the Dough

Grill this crispy-crusted pizza right on your cooking rack.

1
ROAST THE GARLIC
Cut the top off each garlic head and remove the outer layers of skin, as shown. Brush the garlic with oil and wrap in a foil pouch. Grill over medium heat for 35 minutes. Allow the garlic to cool and then squeeze the cloves from the skins.

2
ASSEMBLE AND GRILL
Grill each crust for 1 to 2 minutes. Turn it cooked side up on a pizza peel generously coated with cornmeal. Add the toppings to the crust and carefully slide a pizza off the peel and onto the cooking grate, as shown. Grill, one pizza at a time, for 2 minutes more.

Grilled Eggplant Parmesan

Leave the skin on the eggplant to help it keep its shape and use slices cut from the center, which are perfect for this tasty side dish.

🌀 GRILLING DETAILS

PREP: 8 minutes
GRILL: 7 minutes
MAKES: 4 side-dish servings

✓ INGREDIENTS

- 4 slices eggplant, cut ¾ inch thick
  Salt and black pepper
- 3 tablespoons olive oil
- 1 clove garlic, minced
- ⅓ cup finely shredded Parmesan cheese
- ⅓ cup finely shredded mozzarella cheese
- 2 medium roma tomatoes, thinly sliced
- 2 tablespoons finely shredded basil (optional)

💲 BUYER'S GUIDE

EGGPLANT DOS AND DON'TS

This odd purple-skinned food is actually a member of the potato family. Thomas Jefferson is given credit for introducing it to American tables. When buying eggplant, stick with smaller ones, which tend to have better taste. To tell if it's ripe, give the skin a gentle poke with your finger. If it gives a little but bounces back, it's perfect. Avoid hard eggplants or ones that have started developing dark blotches on the skin. Use eggplants as quickly as possible after buying them because they don't keep well—you can usually get away with storing them in the refrigerator for only a couple of days.

1 Sprinkle eggplant slices lightly with salt and pepper. Combine olive oil and garlic; brush on both sides of eggplant slices. In a small bowl toss together Parmesan and mozzarella cheeses; set aside.

2 For a charcoal grill, grill eggplant slices on the rack of an uncovered grill directly over medium coals for 5 minutes. Turn eggplant slices and sprinkle with half of the cheese. Top with tomato slices and remaining cheese. Cover and grill for 2 to 3 minutes more or until eggplant is tender and cheese has melted. (For a gas grill, preheat grill. Reduce heat to medium. Place eggplant on grill rack over heat. Cover; grill as above.) If desired, top with shredded basil before serving.

Preparing the Grill

1

LIGHT THE CHARCOAL

Light the charcoal using one of the methods described on pages 22 to 23. Allow the charcoal to burn until it glows red-hot and is fully covered with a layer of white ash.

2

SPREAD OUT THE COALS

Using a sturdy, long-handled tool such as a pair of tongs, a garden rake or a hoe, spread the coals so that they evenly cover the charcoal grate. Put the cooking rack in place, and when it has heated, give it a quick cleaning with a wire grill brush.

3

CHECK THE TEMPERATURE

Using a thermometer or your hand (see pages 24 to 25), check the temperature of the cooking rack. Start cooking when the heat is medium (about 350°F). If the heat is too high, wait for the coals to burn down and cool on their own or adjust the grill vents to reduce air flow.

Preparing the Eggplant

1

GRILL THE EGGPLANT

Grill the eggplant slices for 5 minutes over medium-hot coals. Turn and sprinkle with half of the mixture of Parmesan and mozzarella cheeses. Top each eggplant slice with one or two roma tomato slices, then sprinkle with the remaining cheese.

2

MELT THE CHEESE

Cover the grill and allow the eggplant to cook for an additional 2 to 3 minutes until the eggplant is tender and the cheese is melted. Carefully remove the eggplant by sliding a spatula under individual slices while holding them steady with a grilling fork, as shown. If desired, sprinkle the eggplant with basil and serve.

Choose smaller-size, firm eggplants for the best flavor.

Buttery Grilled Corn on the Cob

Grill-roasted corn is tender, moist, and flavorful—plus you can cook it side by side with your grilled meat. If your corn isn't freshly picked, soak the ears in water for 20 to 30 minutes.

GRILLING DETAILS

PREP: 20 minutes
COOK: 30 minutes
GRILL: 25 minutes
MAKES: 6 side-dish servings

INGREDIENTS

- 6   fresh ears sweet corn with husks
- 1   recipe Crazy Cajun Butter, Pesto Butter, Ginger and Garlic Butter, Chipotle Butter, or Nutty Butter

Crazy Cajun Butter: In a small mixing bowl combine ²/₃ cup softened butter, 1 teaspoon garlic salt, ¼ teaspoon black pepper, ¼ teaspoon cayenne pepper, ⅛ teaspoon ground ginger, ⅛ teaspoon ground cinnamon, and ⅛ teaspoon ground cloves. Beat with an electric mixer on low speed until combined.

Pesto Butter: In a small mixing bowl combine ½ cup softened butter and ¼ cup purchased basil or dried tomato pesto. Beat with an electric mixer on low speed until combined.

Ginger and Garlic Butter: In a small mixing bowl combine ²/₃ cup softened butter; 2 cloves garlic, minced; 1 teaspoon seasoned salt; and ½ teaspoon ground ginger. Beat with an electric mixer on low speed until combined.

Chipotle Butter: Coarsely chop 1 or 2 chipotle chiles in adobo sauce. In a small mixing bowl combine chopped peppers; ²/₃ cup softened butter; 1 clove garlic, minced; and ½ teaspoon salt. Beat with an electric mixer on low speed until combined.

Nutty Butter: In a small mixing bowl combine ½ cup softened butter, ¼ cup very finely chopped peanuts or pecans, 1 tablespoon honey, ½ teaspoon garlic salt, and several dashes bottled hot pepper sauce

1 Carefully peel back corn husks but do not remove. Remove and discard the silk. Gently rinse the corn. Pat dry. Spread about 1 tablespoon flavored butter over each ear of corn. Carefully fold husks back around ears. Tie husk tops with 100-percent-cotton string to secure.

GOOD IDEA

AN ALTERNATIVE TO HUSKS

The leaves surrounding each ear of corn make a great built-in grilling jacket, but sometimes you find yourself with husk-free ears—or you don't want to force guests to deal with messy husks during dinner. In these cases, aluminum foil is a perfectly acceptable alternative. Wrap each ear individually in a tight foil packet and pierce the foil with the tines of a fork in a couple of places to allow steam to escape. Grill the corn as you would the husk-wrapped ears for 20 to 30 minutes over medium heat.

2 For a charcoal grill, grill corn on the rack of a covered grill directly over medium coals for 25 to 30 minutes or until kernels are tender, turning and rearranging ears with long-handled tongs 3 times. (For a gas grill, preheat grill. Reduce heat to medium. Place corn on grill rack over heat. Cover; grill as above.)

3 To serve, remove string from corn. Peel back husks. If desired, return husked ears of corn to grill for a few minutes to make grill marks. If desired, serve with additional flavored butter. Store any remaining flavored butters in tightly covered containers in the refrigerator up to 3 days.

Preparing the Grill

1

LIGHT THE CHARCOAL

Light the charcoal using one of the methods described on pages 22 to 23. Allow the charcoal to burn until it glows red-hot and is fully covered with a layer of white ash.

2

SPREAD OUT THE COALS

Using a sturdy, long-handled tool such as a pair of tongs, a garden rake or a hoe, spread the coals so that they evenly cover the charcoal grate. Put the cooking rack in place, and when it has heated, give it a quick cleaning with a wire grill brush.

3

CHECK THE TEMPERATURE

Using a thermometer or your hand (see pages 24 to 25), check the temperature of the cooking rack. Start cooking when the heat is medium (about 350°F). If the heat is too high, wait for the coals to burn down and cool on their own or adjust the grill vents to reduce air flow.

Preparing the Corn

1

PEEL AND CLEAN CORN

Peel back all the husks from each ear of corn, as shown, but do not remove. Clean off all the silk, wash each ear, and pat dry with paper towels.

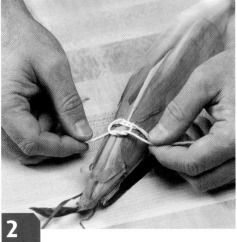

2

ADD BUTTER AND SEAL

Spread about 1 tablespoon of the flavored butter of your choice all over the ear of corn. Carefully fold the husks back into place, fully covering the corn. Secure the husks by tying off with a length of 100-percent-cotton string, as shown; knot to ensure the string is secure. Grill over medium coals.

Serve hot off the grill with one of the great-tasting flavored butters.

Black Pepper Steak Fries

The ultimate grilling side dish—leave the skins on to make the potatoes easier to handle during prep and cooking.

GRILLING DETAILS

PREP: 15 minutes
COOK: 10 minutes
GRILL: 6 minutes
MAKES: 6 servings

INGREDIENTS

1½   pounds russet potatoes (about 4 medium)
2   tablespoons cooking oil
1   teaspoon coarse salt
1   to 1¼ teaspoons coarsely ground black pepper

GOOD IDEA

KEEP THAT SKIN ON!

Many of us learned as kids that potatoes were best eaten without those dirty skins—which, unfortunately, isn't true. Potatoes are healthy food, but many of the nutrients and the most of the fiber are located in or very near to the skin. Grillers should also take note that leaving the skin on potato wedges helps hold them together better as they cook. Before grilling your skin-on potatoes scrub them thoroughly, rinse in cold water, and cut out any sprouts or dark spots.

1 Scrub potatoes thoroughly with a brush; pat dry. Cut the potatoes in half lengthwise; cut each half into 6 wedges

2 In a covered medium saucepan cook potatoes in a small amount of boiling water about 10 minutes or until almost tender. Drain; cool. Place potatoes in a large bowl. In a small bowl combine oil, salt, and pepper; drizzle over potatoes. Toss potatoes gently, being careful not to break wedges.

3 For a charcoal grill, grill potatoes on the rack of an uncovered grill directly over medium coals for 6 to 10 minutes or until brown, turning occasionally. (For a gas grill, preheat grill. Reduce heat to medium. Place potatoes on grill rack over heat. Cover; grill as above.)

Preparing the Grill

1 LIGHT THE CHARCOAL
Light the charcoal using one of the methods described on pages 22 to 23. Allow the charcoal to burn until it glows red-hot and is fully covered with a layer of white ash.

2 SPREAD OUT THE COALS
Using a sturdy, long-handled tool such as a pair of tongs, a garden rake, or a hoe, spread the coals so that they evenly cover the charcoal grate. Put the cooking rack in place, and when it has heated, give it a quick cleaning with a wire grill brush.

3 CHECK THE TEMPERATURE
Using a thermometer or your hand (see pages 24 to 25), check the temperature of the cooking rack. Start cooking when the heat is medium (about 350°F). If the heat is too high, wait for the coals to burn down and cool on their own or adjust the grill vents to reduce air flow.

Preparing the Potatoes

Grill this tasty side dish alongside your meat entrée.

1 PLACING POTATOES ON GRILL RACK
Cut each potato lengthwise in six wedges; leave the skin in place. Boil for 10 minutes, drain, and cool. Coat the potatoes with mixture of cooking oil, coarse salt, and pepper. Using a pair of long-handled tongs, place the potatoes on the grilling rack, as shown.

2 GRILL THE POTATOES
Grill the potatoes over medium heat for 6 to 10 minutes. Using the tongs, turn the wedges periodically so that they cook evenly on both sides and don't burn. Grill the potatoes until they are lightly browned and tender.

Indirect Grilling

While direct grilling is a great way to cook small, thinner pieces of food, it just doesn't cut it for big things such as roasts and whole birds. Such items need a longer, slower, lower-temperature regimen allowing them to fully cook through without getting charred beyond recognition on the outside. Fortunately, your grill, whether it's charcoal- or gas-powered, is a fantastic tool for this type of cooking—in many ways better than your kitchen's oven.

The trick to cooking these big things is actually to use your grill like an oven. You fire it up, then structure your fire in such a way that you can place your entrée on the rack with no hot coals or burners beneath it, only a pan to catch drippings—thus the name indirect grilling. Once you close the lid, your grill stays hot and keeps the food cooking until it reaches the correct internal temperature.

But what's this about the grill being better than an oven? There are a couple of reasons. First, even though most of the cooking is not done directly over the fire, you can still use the open flame to quick-sear cuts of meat before you move them to the indirect heating position. This helps seal in juices and offset the drying effects of cooking. The hot coals are also handy to direct-grill side dishes while your large item continues to cook away in its indirect-heat zone.

Chapter 3 Recipes

The other advantage of indirect grilling is flavor. If you cook a roast or a whole bird in the oven, you are simply using dry heat—effective, but offering no special taste enhancement. The grill represents a whole different world. Grills fueled the normal way, with gas or charcoal, almost always yield tastier slow-cooked foods than an oven. Then, you can add a few hardwood chips or chunks to your fire and suddenly your indirect-grilled entrées turn into smoke-enhanced masterpieces that will wow your friends and family.

Indirect grilling requires attention to a few key details for the best results. First, always use a water-filled pan to catch the drippings (most gas grills have a built-in pan). Otherwise, you'll end up with a greasy,

flammable mess in the bottom of your grill and ash tray. Second, pay close attention to the grill temperature. Buy a thermometer to monitor the temperature (if your grill doesn't have one already built in) and try to keep heat in the zone recommended by the recipe—in most cases 325°F to 350°F. Along these same lines, many foods will require more than 1 hour of indirect grilling time—the typical heating life for a batch of charcoal. That means you will have to be prepared to add new coals to maintain your grill's temperature. If you're using gas, check your propane gauge before you fire up and make sure you have enough gas in the tank for the full cooking time.

Indirect Grilling: Charcoal

You don't have to do anything special to prep your charcoal grill for an indirect-cooking setup, but you will have to purchase one piece of special equipment—disposable aluminum drip pans. Buy a generous supply for yourself and never indirect-grill without using one. The drippings from a roast or turkey can create a huge mess in your charcoal grill, and the grease is flammable and can cause dangerous flare-ups.

Open the grill vents, light your charcoal (a chimney starter is the preferred method), and allow the briquettes to burn until they have ashed over. When they are ready for cooking, take a garden rake, a hoe, or some other type of heavy long-handled tool and separate the coals into two even piles separated by an open spot wide enough to fit your drip pan. Drop the pan into place and build the coals up evenly on either side of it. Partially fill the pan with hot water. This provides a helpful source of moisture, plus keeps the drippings from burning. You can also use other liquids, such as beer or apple juice, to give your food additional flavor.

Place the cooking rack on the grill and allow it to heat up. Place your meat on the grill rack above the drip pan; some recipes recommend a few minutes of cooking directly over the heat to sear all the surfaces before moving meat above the pan. Cover the grill—this is important! Indirect grilling only works if you trap heat like an oven. Resist the temptation to lift the lid to peek at the food or you will let valuable heat escape. Temperature control is critical during indirect cooking, and invariably you will probably want to invest in a thermometer if your grill isn't equipped with one. Use the vents to control the heat level, closing them somewhat to cool the fire or opening them to heat up the grill.

Because many recipes require more than an hour of cooking time, you will be faced with the challenge of adding new charcoal. If you choose to simply replenish fresh briquettes, add them 45 to 50 minutes after the initial coals were fully ignited to get the maximum benefit. A better strategy is to use a chimney starter to light a fresh batch of charcoal (again about 45 minutes into cooking time) and add them when the original coals start to cool below desired cooking temperatures. Whichever method you use, take care in adding the fresh briquettes. Typically, it's easiest to get a partner to lift the grilling rack while you replenish the fire. An alternative, more convenient method is to invest in a cooking rack with a hinged, lift-up section, which makes adding coals a breeze.

Indirect Grilling: Gas

G as grills are outstanding indirect grilling machines. A quality gas grill with multiple independent burners (at least three is ideal) heats quickly and provides easy temperature control with just the twist of a knob. Plus, as long as you have plenty of propane in the tank, the grill will cook as long as you need it without the hassle of adding fresh charcoal. Even with these positive points, gas grills don't cook the food all by themselves, and grill chefs need to pay attention to a few details to make sure their meals turn out tasty every time.

One great thing about gas grills is that most of them are equipped with a built-in grease catch pan—no need to invest in disposable aluminum pans. Unfortunately, too many grillers forget to clean out the grease trap. Check yours before you fire up your grill and make sure it's clean; allowing too much grease to build up can lead to a nasty flare-up.

There are different schools of thought for preheating a gas grill, but the best strategy is generally to light all the burners and turn them on high. Lighting all the burners speeds grill heating; some inexpensive two-burner models might struggle to reach the appropriate cooking temperature without the firepower of both burners. Plus, an all-burner, high-flame preheat will help burn off any residue from previous cooking sessions and minimize the possibility of flare-ups or odd flavors.

Once your grill is lit, close the lid and monitor the temperature. When the heat reaches the desired level (usually 325°F to 350°F), shut down one of the burners to create your indirect heating area. For a three- or four-burner grill you will find that it is usually best to shut down the middle burner(s), creating a cooking zone in the center of the cooking grate. Add your food, close the lid, and let the grill do its job—but don't ignore the food. While you probably won't need to peek at the food very often, you will need to monitor the thermometer and keep the temperature in the proper cooking zone by adjusting burner intensity as necessary. In addition, invest in a quality meat thermometer so that you cook foods to the correct internal temperature for safety and optimum juiciness and flavor.

You can also add hardwood-smoked flavor to your indirect-grilled foods. Many gas grills are equipped with a smoker box—complete with its own heating element—in which you can maintain a supply of hardwood chips. If your grill doesn't have a smoker box, there are ways to add hardwood flavor. A simple way is to drop a large chunk of hardwood (soaked first in water) right on the heating element and let it burn. You'll probably need to replace it a couple of times during long cooking sessions. Or you can fashion a pouch out of a piece of folded aluminum foil, fill it with soaked wood chips, seal it, and poke several holes in the top. Drop the foil pouch on the heating element (holes facing upward) and the chips will burn, smoke, and give you the flavor you desire.

K.C.-Style Beef Ribs

In Kansas City's renowned barbecue joints, pork is more common than beef. But these succulent ribs are proof that K.C. chefs know their way around both kinds of meat.

GRILLING DETAILS

PREP: 25 minutes
MARINATE: 4 to 24 hours
SOAK: 1 hour
GRILL: 1¼ hours
MAKES: 6 to 8 servings

INGREDIENTS

- ½ cup cider vinegar
- 3 tablespoons sugar
- 2 teaspoons dry mustard
- ⅛ teaspoon salt
- 2 cups pineapple juice
- ½ cup Worcestershire sauce
- ⅓ cup chopped onion (1 small)
- 2 tablespoons cooking oil
- 2½ to 3 pounds boneless beef short ribs
- 4 teaspoons paprika
- 1½ teaspoons sugar
- 1 teaspoon garlic powder
- ½ teaspoon black pepper
- ¼ teaspoon salt
- 4 cups hickory or oak wood chips or 10 to 12 wood chunks

CLOSER LOOK

ALL ABOUT BEEF RIBS

There are two main types of beef ribs—short and back—and even variations within these categories.

Short ribs refer to small pieces trimmed from the rib cage. Cuts from the first five ribs are called chuck ribs; they are meatier and less fatty than other cuts and great for grilling.

Boneless short ribs (also called English-style ribs) are meaty pieces cut parallel to the bone.

Back ribs are longer pieces left over after a rib roast is boned. They are not terribly meaty but can be tender and tasty when grilled; make sure you cook enough for everyone to get a generous serving.

1 For marinade, in a medium saucepan bring vinegar to boiling. Remove from heat. Stir in the 3 tablespoons sugar, the dry mustard, and the ⅛ teaspoon salt. Stir until sugar is dissolved. Stir in pineapple juice, Worcestershire sauce, onion, and oil. Cool to room temperature.

2 Trim fat from ribs. Cut ribs into serving-size pieces. Place ribs in a resealable large plastic bag set in a shallow dish. Pour marinade over ribs; seal bag. Marinate in the refrigerator for 4 to 24 hours, turning bag occasionally.

3 Meanwhile, for rub, in a small bowl stir together paprika, the 1½ teaspoons sugar, the garlic powder, pepper, and the ¼ teaspoon salt; set aside. At least 1 hour before grilling, soak wood chips in enough water to cover.

4 Drain ribs, discarding marinade. Pat ribs dry with paper towels. Generously sprinkle rub over both sides of ribs; pat in with your fingers.

5 Drain wood chips. For a charcoal grill, arrange medium-hot coals around a drip pan. Test for medium heat above the drip pan. Sprinkle one-fourth of the wood chips over the coals.

6 Place ribs on grill rack over drip pan. Cover; grill for 1¼ to 1½ hours or until tender. Add more wood chips every 15 minutes and add fresh coals as needed to maintain temperature. (For a gas grill, preheat grill. Reduce heat to medium. Adjust grill for indirect cooking. Add wood chips according to manufacturer's directions. Grill as above, except place ribs, fat sides up, in a roasting pan.)

Preparing the Grill

1 LIGHT THE CHARCOAL

Light the charcoal using one of the methods described on pages 22 to 23. Allow the charcoal to burn until it glows red-hot and is fully covered with a layer of white ash.

2 SEPARATE THE COALS

Using a sturdy, long-handled tool such as a pair of tongs, a garden rake, or a hoe, separate the coals into two equal piles about 10 inches apart. The space between the piles should be wide enough to accommodate a disposable aluminum drip pan.

3 ADD A DRIP PAN

Place an aluminum drip pan in the area between the coals and pour enough hot water into the pan to fill it about ½ inch deep. Replace the grill's cooking grate and allow it to heat up before adding the food.

Preparing the Ribs

Hardwood chips or chunks give the ribs authentic smoked flavor.

1 CUT UP THE RIBS

Hold the rack of ribs vertically and, slicing downward through the meaty sections, cut into individual ribs, as shown. Place the ribs in a resealable plastic bag, cover with the marinade, and marinate in a refrigerator for at least 4 hours.

2 ADD THE WOOD CHIPS

Soak the hardwood chips in water for one hour before starting the fire. When the charcoal is medium hot, sprinkle about one-quarter of the chips directly on the hot coals, as shown. Insert the cooking grate, add the ribs above the drip pan, and cover the grill. Add fresh wood chips to the coals every 15 minutes.

Moroccan Rib Roast

For a more authentic Moroccan feast, prepare this recipe using a 3- to 4-pound leg of lamb grilled for two to three hours.

GRILLING DETAILS

PREP: 15 minutes
GRILL: 1½ hours
STAND: 15 minutes
MAKES: 8 to 10 servings

INGREDIENTS

- 2 tablespoons coriander seeds, crushed
- 2 tablespoons finely shredded lemon peel
- 1 tablespoon olive oil
- 1 teaspoon whole cumin seeds, crushed
- ½ to 1 teaspoon crushed red pepper
- ½ teaspoon coarse salt
- 1 4- to 5-pound beef rib roast*
- 8 cloves garlic, peeled and cut into slivers
  Assorted peeled and cut-up vegetables, such as carrots, turnips, and sweet peppers

REAL WORLD

MODEL T'S AND BRIQUETTES
Humans have been cooking with charcoal for thousands of years, but it has only been recently that the briquette form of the fuel has been in common use. Believe it or not, charcoal briquettes trace their popularity to an unlikely source—Henry Ford, father of the American automobile industry. Starting in 1924, a Ford sawmill manufactured charcoal from waste created by the milling of wood auto parts. Ford sold the charcoal company in 1951, and it was renamed to honor the Michigan city in which it was located—Kingsford.

1 For rub, in a small bowl stir together coriander seeds, lemon peel, olive oil, cumin seeds, crushed red pepper, and salt. Sprinkle rub evenly over meat; pat in with your fingers.

2 Randomly cut ½-inch-wide slits into top and sides of meat. Insert garlic slivers deep into slits. If desired, cover and chill meat for up to 24 hours.

3 Lightly grease an unheated grill rack. For a charcoal grill, arrange medium-hot coals around a drip pan. Test for medium heat above the drip pan. Place meat on the greased grill rack over the drip pan. Cover; grill for 1½ to 2 hours or to desired doneness (155°F for medium). Add assorted cut-up vegetables to grill during the last 45 minutes of grilling, removing and setting them aside as they become tender. (For a gas grill, preheat grill. Reduce heat to medium. Adjust for indirect cooking. Grill as above.)

4 Remove meat from grill. Cover with foil. Let stand for 15 minutes. (The meat's temperature will rise 5°F during standing.) Carve meat and serve with the grilled vegetables.

*Note: You may prepare this recipe using leg of lamb instead of a beef rib roast as part of a more authentic Moroccan feast. For a 3- to 4-pound leg of lamb, grill for 2 to 3 hours or until a meat thermometer registers 155°F for medium doneness.

Preparing the Grill

1

LIGHT THE CHARCOAL

Light the charcoal using one of the methods described on pages 22 to 23. Allow the charcoal to burn until it glows red-hot and is fully covered with a layer of white ash.

2

SEPARATE THE COALS

Using a sturdy, long-handled tool such as a pair of tongs, a garden rake, or a hoe, separate the coals into two equal piles about 10 inches apart. The space between the piles should be wide enough to accommodate a disposable aluminum drip pan.

3

ADD A DRIP PAN

Place an aluminum drip pan in the area between the coals and pour enough hot water into the pan to fill it about ½ inch deep. Replace the grill's cooking grate and allow it to heat up before adding the food.

Preparing the Roast and Vegetables

1

PREPARE THE RUB

Place the coriander and cumin seeds in a plastic sandwich bag and crush with a rolling pin, as shown. Add the crushed seeds to a small bowl and mix with the remaining seasonings. Sprinkle the mixture on both sides of the roast and rub it in with the tips of your fingers.

2

PREPARE THE VEGETABLES

While the roast is grilling, peel and cut up an assortment of vegetables. About 45 minutes before the meat is finished, brush the inside of a grilling basket or wok lightly with oil, place it on the grill, and add the vegetables, as shown. Grill the vegetables alongside the roast, stirring them occasionally and cooking until they are tender.

Use the hot coals to direct-grill the vegetables while the roast slow-cooks.

Tri-Tip Roast with Jambalaya Rice

While the beef grills, prepare the zesty Cajun-style rice flavored with sausage, peppers, and garlic.

3

INDIRECT GRILLING

GRILLING DETAILS

PREP: 25 minutes
GRILL: 34 minutes
STAND: 15 minutes
COOK: 10 minutes
MAKES: 6 servings

INGREDIENTS

- ¼ cup soy sauce
- 2 tablespoons finely chopped onion
- 2 tablespoons granulated sugar
- 2 tablespoons packed brown sugar
- 2 tablespoons lemon juice
- 1 tablespoon vinegar
- ½ teaspoon chili powder
- 1 1½- to 2-pound beef bottom sirloin roast (tri-tip) or boneless beef sirloin steak, cut 1½ to 2 inches thick
- 4 ounces bulk hot Italian sausage
- 1 cup chopped celery (2 stalks)
- ½ cup chopped red sweet pepper
- ½ cup chopped yellow sweet pepper
- ⅓ cup chopped onion (1 small)
- 1 clove garlic, minced
- ¾ cup uncooked rice
- ¼ teaspoon cayenne pepper
- ¼ teaspoon paprika
- 1 10½-ounce can condensed cream of mushroom soup
- 1¼ cups water

CLOSER LOOK

TRI-TIP TIPS

The tri-tip is a triangle-shape beef roast and usually weighs about 2 pounds. It is ideal for grilling or braising. In some regions of the country, you may not find a beef roast labeled "tri-tip" in your supermarket, so look for a sirloin roast or sirloin steak that is cut 1½ to 2 inches thick instead.

1 For brush-on sauce, in a small bowl stir together soy sauce, the 2 tablespoons onion, the granulated sugar, brown sugar, lemon juice, vinegar, and chili powder; set aside.

2 For charcoal grill, arrange medium-hot coals around a drip pan. Test for medium heat above the drip pan. Place meat on grill rack over drip pan. Cover; grill for 34 to 37 minutes for medium rare (145°F) or 36 to 40 minutes for medium (160°F). Brush meat often with the brush-on sauce during the last 10 minutes of grilling. (For gas grill, preheat grill. Reduce heat to medium. Adjust for indirect cooking. Grill as above.)

3 Remove meat from grill. Cover with foil. Let stand for 15 minutes. (The meat's temperature will rise 5°F during standing.) Slice meat.

4 Meanwhile, for jambalaya rice, in a large skillet cook sausage until no longer pink. Drain the grease and transfer sausage to a large saucepan. Add celery, red and yellow sweet peppers, the ⅓ cup onion, and the garlic. Cook and stir for 5 minutes. Add rice, cayenne pepper, and paprika; cook and stir for 2 minutes more. Add soup and water. Bring just to boiling; reduce heat. Simmer, covered, for 15 to 20 minutes or until rice is tender, stirring occasionally. Serve with meat.

Preparing the Grill

1

LIGHT THE CHARCOAL

Light the charcoal using one of the methods described on pages 22 to 23. Allow the charcoal to burn until it glows red-hot and is fully covered with a layer of white ash.

2

SEPARATE THE COALS

Using a sturdy, long-handled tool such as a pair of tongs, a garden rake, or a hoe, separate the coals into two equal piles about 10 inches apart. The space between the piles should be wide enough to accommodate a disposable aluminum drip pan.

3

ADD A DRIP PAN

Place an aluminum drip pan in the area between the coals and pour enough hot water into the pan to fill it about ½ inch deep. Replace the grill's cooking grate and allow it to heat up before adding the food.

Preparing the Roast and Jambalaya Rice

1

GRILL THE ROAST

Grill the roast over a drip pan with the grill cover closed. Check the internal temperature with a meat thermometer to determine doneness: medium rare is 145°F and medium is 160°F. Place the meat on a platter and loosely cover with a piece of aluminum foil, as shown. Let the roast stand for 15 minutes before slicing.

2

PREPARE THE JAMBALAYA RICE

Cook the Italian sausage in a skillet until it is light brown, as shown. Drain the grease. Transfer the sausage to a large saucepan, add celery, sweet pepper, onion, and garlic; cook for 5 minutes. Add rice, cayenne pepper, and paprika; cook for 2 minutes. Stir in soup and water, bring to boiling, reduce heat, and simmer for 15 to 20 minutes.

Slice the roast and serve over a generous bed of the jambalaya rice.

Caribbean Pork with Three-Pepper Salsa

Iowa joins with Jamaica for a memorable grilled entrée. The pop from the peppers livens up the roast, which is sure to be juicy and tender, thanks to several hours swimming in the marinade.

GRILLING DETAILS

PREP: 25 minutes
MARINATE: 6 to 8 hours
GRILL: 1 hour
STAND: 15 minutes
MAKES: 6 to 8 servings

INGREDIENTS

- 1   cup orange juice
- 2   teaspoons finely shredded lime peel
- ¼   cup lime juice
- ¼   cup cooking oil
- ½   cup chopped green onions (4)
- 2   tablespoons soy sauce
- 1   tablespoon grated fresh ginger
- 2   fresh serrano chile peppers, seeded and finely chopped (see tip, page 52)
- 2   cloves garlic, minced
- 1   2- to 2½-pound boneless pork top loin roast (single loin)
- 1   medium green sweet pepper, quartered lengthwise
- 1   medium yellow or orange sweet pepper, quartered lengthwise
- ½   cup cherry tomatoes, quartered
- 2   tablespoons snipped fresh cilantro

SAFETY ALERT

Marinades are a great way to improve the flavor, tenderness, and juiciness of all kinds of food, but pay attention to two issues to avoid food-borne illness. First, always marinate your food in the refrigerator, not on the counter. Second, heat the marinade to a full boil if you plan to use it in a sauce or for basting during grilling. If you aren't going to use the marinade for a sauce or basting, discard it immediately—it can't be reused.

1 For marinade, in a small bowl combine orange juice, lime peel, lime juice, oil, ¼ cup of the green onions, soy sauce, ginger, chile peppers, and garlic. Reserve 2 tablespoons of the marinade for the salsa; cover and refrigerate until needed.

2 Trim fat from meat. Place meat in a resealable large plastic bag set in a shallow dish. Pour remaining marinade over meat; seal bag. Marinate in refrigerator for 6 to 8 hours, turning bag occasionally.

3 Drain pork, discarding the marinade. For a charcoal grill, arrange medium coals around a drip pan. Test for medium-low heat above the pan. Place meat on grill rack over the drip pan. Cover; grill for 1 to 1½ hours or until a meat thermometer registers 155°F. Place sweet peppers, skin sides down, on grill rack directly over the coals. Grill about 10 minutes or until skin is charred. Wrap pepper quarters in foil. Let stand until cool enough to handle. Use a sharp knife to gently and slowly peel off the skin. Discard skin. Chop peppers. (For a gas grill, preheat grill. Reduce heat to medium low. Adjust for indirect cooking. Grill as above, except place meat on a rack in a roasting pan.)

4 For salsa, in a medium bowl combine the reserved marinade, chopped grilled sweet peppers, the remaining ¼ cup green onions, cherry tomatoes, and cilantro.

5 Remove the meat from the grill. Cover with foil. Let stand for 15 minutes. The meat's temperature will rise 5°F during standing. Slice the meat and serve with salsa.

Preparing the Grill

1

LIGHT THE CHARCOAL

Light the charcoal using one of the methods described on pages 22 to 23. Allow the charcoal to burn until it glows red-hot and is fully covered with a layer of white ash.

2

SEPARATE THE COALS

Using a sturdy, long-handled tool such as a pair of tongs, a garden rake, or a hoe, separate the coals into two equal piles about 10 inches apart. The space between the piles should be wide enough to accommodate a disposable aluminum drip pan.

3

ADD A DRIP PAN

Place an aluminum drip pan in the area between the coals and pour enough hot water into the pan to fill it about ½ inch deep. Replace the grill's cooking grate and allow it to heat up before adding the food.

Preparing the Salsa

1

GRILL THE SWEET PEPPERS

Place the quartered sweet peppers, skin sides down, directly over the hot coals on one side of the cooking grate. Grill the peppers about 10 minutes or until the skin is charred, as shown. Wrap the peppers loosely in a piece of aluminum foil and set aside to cool.

2

PEEL THE GRILLED PEPPERS

When the sweet peppers have cooled enough to handle, gently peel off the charred skin by grasping it between your thumb and a paring knife, as shown. Chop the skinned peppers and mix them in a small bowl with the other salsa ingredients. Serve with the sliced pork.

Use your heat source to direct-grill sweet peppers for the salsa.

Pork Stuffed with Orange and Thyme

These peppery tenderloins are tempered with an orange- and mustard-flavored sauce.

GRILLING DETAILS

PREP: 40 minutes
CHILL: 1 to 8 hours
GRILL: 30 minutes
STAND: 15 minutes
MAKES: 6 to 8 servings

INGREDIENTS

 2   12- to 16-ounce pork tenderloins
 ¼   cup finely chopped onion
 3   tablespoons finely shredded
        orange peel
 2   tablespoons snipped fresh thyme
 2   tablespoons olive oil
 4   teaspoons coarsely cracked black
        pepper
 1   teaspoon coarse salt
 1   recipe Orange-Thyme Sauce (see
        recipe, below)

TOOL SAVVY

STRINGING IT UP

Recipes often instruct you to tie up pork, beef, or lamb roasts—why? Sometimes the meat is tied to hold stuffing in place, such as the entrée on this page. Other times tying is used to keep a trimmed, boneless cut in a uniform shape that will cook evenly and offer a more attractive presentation on serving. Any time a grilling recipe specifies tying (whole poultry is another item that must often be tied), it is essential that you use only string designed for the job—generally identified as kitchen string or butcher's string. Kitchen string is 100 percent cotton or linen, organic fibers that will not burn during cooking and offer an easy-to-handle texture and bulkiness. Many types of non-kitchen utility string are manufactured from synthetic fibers that not only are difficult to handle, they may melt or burn at grilling temperatures and ruin your meat.

1 Trim fat from pork. Split each tenderloin lengthwise, cutting from one side almost to, but not through, the other side. Spread meat open. In a small bowl combine onion, orange peel, and thyme; divide between the tenderloins, spreading onto the cut sides of each tenderloin. Fold each tenderloin back together. Tie with 100-percent-cotton string at 1-inch intervals. Brush tenderloins with olive oil. In a small bowl combine pepper and salt. Sprinkle evenly over each tenderloin; pat in with your fingers. Cover and chill tenderloins for 1 to 8 hours.

2 For a charcoal grill, arrange hot coals around a drip pan. Test for medium-high heat above the drip pan. Place meat on grill rack over the drip pan. Cover; grill for 30 to 35 minutes or until a meat thermometer registers 155°F. (For a gas grill, preheat grill. Reduce heat to medium-high. Adjust for indirect cooking. Grill as above, except place meat on a rack in a roasting pan.)

3 Remove meat from grill. Cover with foil. Let stand for 15 minutes. (The meat's temperature will rise 5°F during standing.) Slice pork; serve with the Orange-Thyme Sauce.

Orange-Thyme Sauce: In a small saucepan combine ½ cup orange juice, 2 tablespoons coarse-grain brown mustard, 2 tablespoons olive oil, and 1 tablespoon snipped fresh thyme. Cook and stir over medium heat until heated through. Makes about ¾ cup.

Preparing the Grill

1

LIGHT THE CHARCOAL

Light the charcoal using one of the methods described on pages 22 to 23. Allow the charcoal to burn until it glows red-hot and is fully covered with a layer of white ash.

2

SEPARATE THE COALS

Using a sturdy, long-handled tool such as a pair of tongs, a garden rake, or a hoe, separate the coals into two equal piles about 10 inches apart. The space between the piles should be wide enough to accommodate a disposable aluminum drip pan.

3

ADD A DRIP PAN

Place an aluminum drip pan in the area between the coals and pour enough hot water into the pan to fill it about ½ inch deep. Replace the grill's cooking grate and allow it to heat up before adding the food.

Preparing the Stuffed Tenderloins

Grill to an internal temperature of 155°F and rest for 15 minutes before carving.

1

BUTTERFLY THE TENDERLOINS

Cut a deep slit lengthwise through each tenderloin, being careful not to cut all the way through the meat. Spread the sides of the cut tenderloins apart and fill the cavity of each with half the onion, orange peel, and thyme mixture.

2

TIE THE TENDERLOINS

Cut two long pieces of kitchen string and tie off one end of each tenderloin. Close and secure both pieces of meat by looping and knotting the string at 1-inch intervals, as shown. Coat both tenderloins with oil, season with salt and pepper, and refrigerate until you're ready to grill.

Corn Bread-Stuffed Chops

The corn bread-sausage-cranberry stuffing is a tasty surprise to hide inside a juicy, thick-cut loin chop.

GRILLING DETAILS

PREP: 25 minutes
SOAK: 1 hour
GRILL: 35 minutes
MAKES: 4 servings

INGREDIENTS

3	cups apple or cherry wood chips
1/4	teaspoon black pepper
1/8	teaspoon celery seeds
1/8	teaspoon onion salt or garlic salt
	Dash ground cloves
	Dash cayenne pepper (optional)
4	ounces bulk pork sausage or bulk turkey sausage
1/4	cup chopped onion
1/2	cup corn bread stuffing mix
1/4	cup dried cranberries
1/2	of a 4-ounce can diced green chile peppers, drained
2	tablespoons snipped fresh parsley
1	to 2 tablespoons apple juice, chicken broth, or water
4	pork loin rib chops, cut 1½ inches thick (about 3 pounds)

GOOD IDEA

THE ALL-AMERICAN CRANBERRY
Cranberries were introduced to the Pilgrims by Native Americans, who had long enjoyed the tart fruit as a staple food. Today, there is considerable evidence that cranberries have a well-deserved place in our diets. In addition to containing worthwhile amounts of fiber and vitamin C, cranberries are rich in phytochemicals that serve as antioxidants and might help prevent cancer and heart disease. Plus, research has confirmed an old folk remedy employing cranberries—eating them (or drinking cranberry juice) can help treat and prevent urinary tract infections.

1 At least 1 hour before cooking, soak wood chips in enough water to cover.

2 For the rub, in a small bowl stir together black pepper, celery seeds, onion salt, cloves, and, if desired, cayenne pepper.

3 For stuffing, in a small saucepan cook sausage and onion until sausage is no longer pink and onion is tender. Drain off fat. Stir in stuffing mix, cranberries, chile peppers, and parsley. Add just enough of the apple juice to moisten.

4 Trim fat from pork chops. Cut a pocket in each chop by cutting a slit in the fatty side and working the knife inside to cut almost to bone (keep original slit small). Spoon stuffing into the pockets in chops. If necessary, secure with wooden toothpicks. Sprinkle the rub evenly over both sides of the pork chops; pat in with your fingers.

5 Drain the wood chips. For a charcoal grill, arrange medium-hot coals around a drip pan. Test for medium heat above the drip pan. Sprinkle half of the drained chips over the coals. Place chops on the grill rack over the drip pan. Cover; grill for 35 to 40 minutes or until the juices run clear (160°F), turning chops once halfway through grilling. Add more wood chips every 15 minutes. (For a gas grill, preheat grill. Reduce heat to medium. Adjust for indirect cooking. Add wood chips according to manufacturer's directions. Grill as above.) Remove the toothpicks before serving, if using.

Preparing the Grill

1 LIGHT THE CHARCOAL

Light the charcoal using one of the methods described on pages 22 to 23. Allow the charcoal to burn until it glows red-hot and is fully covered with a layer of white ash.

2 SEPARATE THE COALS

Using a sturdy, long-handled tool such as a pair of tongs, a garden rake, or a hoe, separate the coals into two equal piles about 10 inches apart. The space between the piles should be wide enough to accommodate a disposable aluminum drip pan.

3 ADD A DRIP PAN

Place an aluminum drip pan in the area between the coals and pour enough hot water into the pan to fill it about 1/2 inch deep. Replace the grill's cooking grate and allow it to heat up before adding the food.

3

INDIRECT GRILLING

Preparing the Stuffed Chops

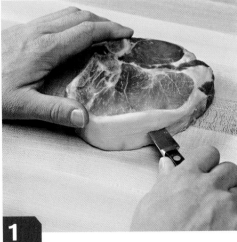

1 CUT A POCKET

Insert the tip of a sharp, pointed knife into the center of the fatty side of a chop, as shown. Keeping the original slit small, gently cut a pocket that reaches almost to the bone and the edges of the chop.

2 STUFF THE CHOPS

Using a teaspoon, fill the pocket in each chop with stuffing, as shown. Close the pocket opening with a wooden toothpick. Sprinkle both sides of each chop with the seasoning and rub in. Grill with indirect heat for 35 to 40 minutes.

Apple or cherry wood chips give a hint of hardwood-smoked flavor.

Peachy Pork Spareribs

Peach nectar is the secret ingredient in the homemade sauce that creates ribs so good you'll probably dream of moving to Georgia.

3

INDIRECT GRILLING

GRILLING DETAILS

PREP: 15 minutes
CHILL: overnight
GRILL: 1½ hours
MAKES: 6 to 8 servings

INGREDIENTS

- ½ cup packed brown sugar
- 2 tablespoons salt
- 1 tablespoon dry mustard
- 2 teaspoons five-spice powder
- 1 teaspoon black pepper
- 1 teaspoon garlic powder
- 6 pounds meaty pork spareribs
- 1 recipe Peachy Barbecue Sauce (see recipe, below)

BUYER'S GUIDE

PORK RIB PRIMER
Here are some pork rib styles popular with grillers:

Spareribs: The rib section from the side or belly region. Fatty, but that's what makes them tasty. St. Louis and Kansas City styles are more trimmed versions.

Back ribs: From the center cut of the loin. Meatier than spareribs, most racks contain 12 or 13 ribs.

Country-style ribs: Meaty ribs from the shoulder end of the loin, but can be difficult to eat because of the fat and bone structure.

1 For rub, in a bowl stir together brown sugar, salt, mustard, five-spice powder, pepper, and garlic powder. Sprinkle rub evenly over ribs; pat in with your fingers. Place ribs on a tray; cover and refrigerate overnight.

2 For a charcoal grill, arrange medium-hot coals around a drip pan. Test for medium heat above the drip pan. Place ribs, bone sides down, on grill rack over the drip pan. Cover; grill for 1½ to 1¾ hours, brushing with about 2 cups of the Peachy Barbecue Sauce during the last 15 minutes of grilling. Add fresh coals as needed to maintain temperature. (For a gas grill, preheat grill. Reduce heat to medium. Adjust for indirect cooking. Grill as above.) Pass remaining sauce with ribs.

Peachy Barbecue Sauce: In a large saucepan stir together 3 cups peach nectar, one 15-ounce can tomato sauce, 1 cup finely chopped onion, ⅓ cup reduced-sodium soy sauce, ¼ cup rice vinegar, and 2 to 3 teaspoons bottled hot pepper sauce. Bring to boiling; reduce heat. Simmer, uncovered, about 50 minutes or until thickened, stirring occasionally. Makes about 3 cups.

Preparing the Grill

1
LIGHT THE CHARCOAL
Light the charcoal using one of the methods described on pages 22 to 23. Allow the charcoal to burn until it glows red-hot and is fully covered with a layer of white ash.

2
SEPARATE THE COALS
Using a sturdy, long-handled tool such as a pair of tongs, a garden rake, or a hoe, separate the coals into two equal piles about 10 inches apart. The space between the piles should be wide enough to accommodate a disposable aluminum drip pan.

3
ADD A DRIP PAN
Place an aluminum drip pan in the area between the coals and pour enough hot water into the pan to fill it about ½ inch deep. Replace the grill's cooking grate and allow it to heat up before adding the food.

Preparing the Ribs and Sauce

1
GRILL THE SPARERIBS
Lay the rub-seasoned rack of spareribs, bone side down, on the grill above the drip pan. Grill, covered, for 1½ to 1¾ hours. Add fresh charcoal to maintain a temperature around 350°F.

2
COOK THE SAUCE
Combine the sauce ingredients in a large pan and heat to boiling. Turn down the heat and simmer, uncovered, for 50 minutes, stirring periodically. Brush the sauce on the ribs during the last 15 minutes of grilling.

Apply your rub and let the seasonings work overnight for maximum flavor.

Lamb with Spinach Pesto

For another flavor dimension, stir sour cream into some of the pesto to make a tangy sauce to serve with the slices of lamb.

🔄 GRILLING DETAILS

PREP: 40 minutes
GRILL: 1³/₄ hours
STAND: 15 minutes
MAKES: 12 servings

✓ INGREDIENTS

- 1¹/₂ cups firmly packed fresh spinach leaves
- ¹/₂ cup grated Romano cheese
- ¹/₄ cup firmly packed fresh basil leaves
- ¹/₄ cup pine nuts
- 4 cloves garlic, quartered
- 4 teaspoons finely shredded lemon peel
- 2 tablespoons lemon juice
- 2 tablespoons olive oil
- ¹/₄ teaspoon salt
- ¹/₈ teaspoon lemon-pepper seasoning
- 1 3¹/₂- to 4-pound boneless leg of lamb, rolled and tied
- 1 teaspoon salt
- ¹/₂ teaspoon lemon-pepper seasoning
- ¹/₂ cup dairy sour cream

🌐 REAL WORLD

LEARNING ABOUT LAMB

While Americans don't eat as much as other countries, lamb is the favored meat in many parts of the world—which should tell us something. Lamb, meat from a sheep less than one year old, has a distinctive but mild flavor and is a lean, nutritious meat: It is a good source of protein, B vitamins, zinc, and iron. A variety of cuts are great for grilling, including legs, roasts, and chops. Meat from older sheep is usually called mutton and is less popular than lamb. It is often stronger in flavor, tends to be tougher, and is probably not the best choice for grilling.

1 For pesto, in a blender or food processor combine spinach, cheese, basil, nuts, garlic, lemon peel, lemon juice, oil, ¹/₄ teaspoon salt, and the ¹/₈ teaspoon lemon-pepper seasoning. Cover and blend or process until a paste forms, stopping and scraping sides as necessary. Set aside.

2 Untie roast and trim fat. If necessary, butterfly meat. (To butterfly, lay roast flat, boned side up. From the center, cut to within ¹/₂ inch of the other side. Place knife in the V of the first cut. Cut horizontally to the cut boned surface and away from the first cut to within ¹/₂ inch of the end of the meat. Repeat on the opposite side of the V. Spread open.) Spread ¹/₃ cup of pesto over cut surface of meat. Roll up; tie securely with 100-percent-cotton string. Sprinkle the 1 teaspoon salt and ¹/₂ teaspoon lemon-pepper seasoning evenly over outside of meat; pat in with your fingers.

3 For a charcoal grill, arrange medium coals around a drip pan. Test for medium-low heat above pan. Place lamb on grill rack over drip pan. Cover; grill until meat thermometer registers desired doneness. Allow 1³/₄ to 2¹/₄ hours for medium-rare doneness (140°F) and 2 to 2¹/₂ hours for medium doneness (155°F). (For a gas grill, preheat grill. Reduce heat to medium-low. Adjust for indirect cooking. Grill as above.)

4 Remove meat from grill. Cover with foil. Let stand for 15 minutes before carving. (The meat's temperature will rise 5°F during standing.) To serve, remove strings and thinly slice meat. Combine remaining pesto and the sour cream; pass with meat.

Preparing the Grill

1
LIGHT THE CHARCOAL
Light the charcoal using one of the methods described on pages 22 to 23. Allow the charcoal to burn until it glows red-hot and is fully covered with a layer of white ash.

2
SEPARATE THE COALS
Using a sturdy, long-handled tool such as a pair of tongs, a garden rake, or a hoe, separate the coals into two equal piles about 10 inches apart. The space between the piles should be wide enough to accommodate a disposable aluminum drip pan.

3
ADD A DRIP PAN
Place an aluminum drip pan in the area between the coals and pour enough hot water into the pan to fill it about ½ inch deep. Replace the grill's cooking grate and allow it to heat up before adding the food.

Butterflying the Leg of Lamb

Discover what the rest of the world knows about grilled lamb.

1
UNTIE AND CUT LAMB
Untie the lamb and lay it flat. Slice downward into the center of the roast, cutting to within ½ inch of the bottom. Turn the knife horizontally and cut outward from the slice, as shown, cutting to within ½ inch of the outside edge.

2
CUT AND SPREAD LAMB
Rotate the lamb 180 degrees and repeat the horizontal cut on the other half of the roast. Open up the roast and spread the pesto over the cut surface of the meat. Roll up the lamb and tie with kitchen string to secure (see page 91).

Dijon-Crusted Lamb Rib Roast

Spicy Dijon mustard, garlic, and thyme grill up into a wonderful crust with a twofold purpose—to provide flavor and to seal the juices in the lamb.

GRILLING DETAILS

PREP: 10 minutes
GRILL: 50 minutes
STAND: 15 minutes
MAKES: 4 servings

INGREDIENTS

1	2¹/₂-pound lamb rib roast (8 ribs)
3	tablespoons Dijon-style mustard
1	tablespoon olive oil
¹/₂	teaspoon dried thyme, crushed
¹/₄	teaspoon salt
¹/₄	teaspoon black pepper
2	cloves garlic, minced
¹/₄	cup dairy sour cream

CLOSER LOOK

MUCH ADO ABOUT MUSTARD

Mustard is one of the most popular and versatile condiments around, and there are thousands of different brands from all over the world. All types originate from tiny mustard seeds and differ, thanks to the ingredients and seasonings used in the preparation. Here is a quick review of some popular styles:

Yellow: Traditional American-style mustard, with a bright yellow color and smooth texture.

Dijon: Brown mustard named after the French city in which it originated; made with unfermented grape juice, plus seasonings that give it a spicy bite.

English: Smooth-textured, bright yellow, and very hot (spicy) mustard that should be used sparingly.

Stone-ground: Coarse-textured brown mustard with a pleasantly spicy flavor.

1 Trim fat from meat. In a small bowl stir together mustard, oil, thyme, salt, pepper, and garlic. Place 2 tablespoons of the mustard mixture in a separate small bowl; cover and set aside. Spread meat with remaining mustard mixture. Insert a meat thermometer into meat, not touching the bone.

2 For a charcoal grill, arrange medium-hot coals around a drip pan. Test for medium heat above the drip pan. Place meat, bone side down, on the grill rack over the drip pan. Cover; grill until the meat thermometer registers 140°F for medium-rare doneness (50 to 60 minutes) or 155°F for medium doneness (1 to 1¹/₂ hours), adding fresh coals as needed to maintain temperature. (For a gas grill, preheat grill. Reduce heat to medium. Adjust for indirect cooking. Grill as above.)

3 Remove meat from grill. Cover with foil. Let stand for 15 minutes. The meat's temperature will rise 5°F during standing. Meanwhile, for sauce, stir sour cream into the reserved mustard mixture in the small bowl. To serve, cut meat into four 2-rib portions. Pass sauce with meat.

Preparing the Grill

1
LIGHT THE CHARCOAL
Light the charcoal using one of the methods described on pages 22 to 23. Allow the charcoal to burn until it glows red-hot and is fully covered with a layer of white ash.

2
SEPARATE THE COALS
Using a sturdy, long-handled tool such as a pair of tongs, a garden rake, or a hoe, separate the coals into two equal piles about 10 inches apart. The space between the piles should be wide enough to accommodate a disposable aluminum drip pan.

3
ADD A DRIP PAN
Place an aluminum drip pan in the area between the coals and pour enough hot water into the pan to fill it about ½ inch deep. Replace the grill's cooking grate and allow it to heat up before adding the food.

Preparing the Lamb

1
PREP FOR GRILLING
Lay the roast, rib side down, in a shallow dish. Using a basting brush, generously apply the mustard mixture to the top of the roast, as shown. Insert a meat thermometer into the lamb. Grill until the temperature is 140°F for medium rare or 155°F for medium.

2
CARVE THE ROAST
Remove the roast from the grill, cover it with aluminum foil, and let it stand for 15 minutes. Holding the roast with tongs, slice it into four portions of two ribs each. Serve with the sauce.

Serve with vegetable chunks grilled alongside the lamb over direct heat.

Lemon and Garlic Grilled Chicken

Forget bread stuffing—the lemon and garlic inside this bird, along with a tasty brush-on sauce and slow cooking on the grill, will let you say good-bye to boring chicken.

GRILLING DETAILS

PREP: 30 minutes

GRILL: 1 hour

STAND: 10 minutes

MAKES: 6 servings

INGREDIENTS

- 2 lemons
- 3 tablespoons butter, melted
- 1 tablespoon snipped fresh rosemary or 1 teaspoon dried rosemary, crushed
- ¼ teaspoon salt
- ⅛ teaspoon black pepper
- 1 2½- to 3-pound whole broiler-fryer chicken
- 4 cloves garlic, halved
- ½ cup chicken broth
- 1 tablespoon butter

BUYER'S GUIDE

CHICKEN TERMINOLOGY

When shopping for whole chickens or chicken parts, you might encounter several confusing classifications. What does each mean?

Broiler-Fryer: Young and tender chickens weighing an average of 3½ pounds that are perfect for just about any type of cooking method, including grilling.

Roaster: Larger chickens (up to 5 pounds) with more meat per pound than a broiler-fryer, though somewhat less tender and juicy. A good choice for roasting whole.

Capon: Castrated roosters raised specifically for tender and juicy meat. Weigh up to 10 pounds and have a high white to dark meat ratio.

Stewing Hen: Large, mature females that are tasty but not very tender. Need moist-heat cooking, so are less desirable for grilling.

1 Cut one of the lemons into thin wedges; set aside. Finely shred 1 teaspoon lemon peel from the remaining lemon; set peel aside. Squeeze juice from the lemon; measure juice. If necessary, add enough water to equal 3 tablespoons. Set aside 1 tablespoon of the juice.

2 Stir together lemon peel, remaining 2 tablespoons lemon juice, the 3 tablespoons melted butter, the rosemary, salt, and pepper.

3 Rinse inside of chicken; pat dry with paper towels. Place lemon wedges and garlic in the cavity. Twist wing tips under the back. Brush chicken with lemon-butter mixture.

4 For a charcoal grill, arrange medium-hot coals around a drip pan. Test for medium heat above the drip pan. Place chicken, breast side up, on grill rack above drip pan. Cover; grill for 1 to 1¼ hours or until chicken is no longer pink and drumsticks move easily in their sockets (180°F). (For a gas grill, preheat grill. Reduce heat to medium. Adjust for indirect cooking. Grill as above, except place chicken on a rack in a roasting pan.) Remove chicken from grill. Cover with foil and let stand for 10 minutes before carving.

5 Meanwhile, for sauce, in a small saucepan combine reserved lemon juice and chicken broth. Bring to boiling; reduce heat. Boil gently, uncovered, for 5 minutes. Stir in the 1 tablespoon butter. Serve with chicken.

Preparing the Grill

1 LIGHT THE CHARCOAL

Light the charcoal using one of the methods described on pages 22 to 23. Allow the charcoal to burn until it glows red-hot and is fully covered with a layer of white ash.

2 SEPARATE THE COALS

Using a sturdy, long-handled tool such as a pair of tongs, a garden rake, or a hoe, separate the coals into two equal piles about 10 inches apart. The space between the piles should be wide enough to accommodate a disposable aluminum drip pan.

3 ADD A DRIP PAN

Place an aluminum drip pan in the area between the coals and pour enough hot water into the pan to fill it about 1/2 inch deep. Replace the grill's cooking grate and allow it to heat up before adding the food.

Preparing the Chicken

1 MAKE THE BRUSH-ON

Using a kitchen grater, finely shred 1 teaspoon of peel from a whole lemon, as shown. Cut the lemon in half and squeeze out 3 tablespoons of juice. Mix the peel and 2 tablespoons of the juice with the melted butter, rosemary, salt, and pepper.

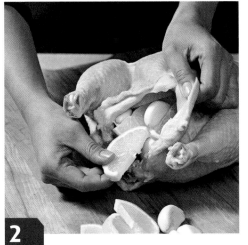

2 STUFF THE CHICKEN

Fill the cavity of the chicken with thin lemon slices and whole garlic cloves. Close the skin flap over the cavity and twist the wing tips under the back. Brush the chicken with the lemon mixture and grill.

The key to this chicken's great flavor is fresh, whole lemons.

Grilled Spiced Turkey

Grilling over indirect heat might be the easiest and most efficient way to prepare a turkey, and the meat will turn out both flavorful and moist.

⟁ GRILLING DETAILS

PREP: 20 minutes
GRILL: 3 hours
STAND: 15 minutes
MAKES: 12 servings

✓ INGREDIENTS

- 1   12- to 14-pound whole turkey, thawed if frozen
- 1   tablespoon olive oil
- 1   tablespoon paprika
- 1   tablespoon coriander seeds
- 1½ teaspoons mustard seeds
- 1½ teaspoons sugar
- 1½ teaspoons salt
- ½   teaspoon dried marjoram

📖 WORK SMARTER

TURKEY TEMPERATURE SMARTS

Cooking to the right level of doneness is the biggest challenge in turkey grilling. Because it takes so long it's tempting to pull the bird too early, which could be a dangerous mistake. So, in the name of safety, many turkeys stay on the grill too long and end up about as moist as the Mojave Desert. The simple solution for a perfectly cooked bird is a quality quick-read thermometer (even if your bird has one of those pop-up doneness indicators). Insert the thermometer tip into the inner thigh meat, taking care not to touch any bone, and give it 20 seconds to take the reading. Your turkey is done when the temperature is 180°F.

1 Remove neck and giblets from body and neck cavities of turkey. Rinse inside of turkey and pat dry with paper towels; brush skin with oil. In a small bowl combine paprika, coriander seeds, mustard seeds, sugar, salt, and marjoram. Sprinkle spice mixture evenly over all sides of turkey; pat in with your fingers.

2 For a charcoal grill, arrange medium-hot coals around a drip pan. Test for medium heat above the drip pan. Place turkey, breast side up, on grill rack over drip pan. Cover; grill for 3 to 4 hours or until turkey is no longer pink and drumsticks move easily in their sockets (180°F in inside thigh muscle), adding fresh coals as needed to maintain temperature. (For a gas grill, preheat grill. Reduce heat to medium. Adjust for indirect cooking. Grill as above.)

3 Remove turkey from grill. Cover with foil; let stand for 15 minutes before carving.

Preparing the Grill

1 LIGHT THE CHARCOAL

Light the charcoal using one of the methods described on pages 22 to 23. Allow the charcoal to burn until it glows red-hot and is fully covered with a layer of white ash.

2 SEPARATE THE COALS

Using a sturdy, long-handled tool such as a pair of tongs, a garden rake, or a hoe, separate the coals into two equal piles about 10 inches apart. The space between the piles should be wide enough to accommodate a disposable aluminum drip pan.

3 ADD A DRIP PAN

Place an aluminum drip pan in the area between the coals and pour enough hot water into the pan to fill it about ½ inch deep. Replace the grill's cooking grate and allow it to heat up before adding the food.

Preparing the Turkey

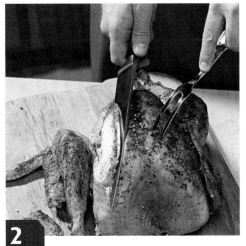

Make sure you have plenty of charcoal or a full tank of gas before you start cooking.

1 GRILL THE TURKEY

Cook the turkey in a covered grill over a drip pan for 3 to 4 hours. Charcoal grillers will need to add water to the drip pan, plus a regular supply of new briquettes to keep the cooking heat between 325°F and 340°F.

2 CARVE THE TURKEY

Remove the turkey from the grill when its internal temperature reaches 180°F. Transfer it to a cutting board, cover it loosely with foil, and let it stand 20 minutes. Carve the bird with a sharp knife, starting with thin slices from the breast, as shown.

Sticky-Sloppy Barbecue Chicken

Country meets city in this finger-lickin' barbecue recipe. Dry sherry supplies the uptown flavor.

GRILLING DETAILS

PREP: 15 minutes
MARINATE: 2 to 4 hours
COOK: 30 minutes
GRILL: 50 minutes
MAKES: 6 servings

INGREDIENTS

3	to 4 pounds meaty chicken pieces (breast halves, thighs, and drumsticks
1½	cups dry sherry
1	cup finely chopped onion (1 large)
¼	cup lemon juice
1	tablespoon bottled minced garlic (6 cloves)
2	bay leaves
1	15-ounce can tomato puree
¼	cup honey
3	tablespoons molasses
1	teaspoon salt
½	teaspoon dried thyme, crushed
¼	to ½ teaspoon cayenne pepper
¼	teaspoon black pepper
2	tablespoons white vinegar

GOOD IDEA

A BETTER MARINADE

Marinades with maximum flavoring and tenderizing action should contain a mixture of acids (such as wine, vinegar, or salsa) or natural enzymes (such as those found in ginger or pineapple), oil (which protects food from the grill heat), and aromatic seasonings, including herbs and spices. A marinade can enhance flavor in a relatively short time—15 minutes to 2 hours—but tough cuts of meat need to be marinated for 4 to 24 hours for maximum tenderness. On the other hand, too much marinating can make some meat mushy; most recipes do not leave food in marinade longer than 24 hours.

1 Place chicken in a resealable large plastic bag set in a shallow dish. For marinade, in a medium bowl stir together sherry, onion, lemon juice, garlic, and bay leaves. Pour marinade over chicken. Seal bag; turn to coat chicken. Marinate in the refrigerator for 2 to 4 hours, turning bag occasionally.

2 Drain chicken, reserving marinade. Cover and refrigerate chicken until ready to grill. For sauce, in a large saucepan combine the reserved marinade, the tomato puree, honey, molasses, salt, thyme, cayenne pepper, and black pepper. Bring to boiling; reduce heat. Simmer, uncovered, about 30 minutes or until reduced to 2 cups. Remove from heat. Discard bay leaves. Stir in white vinegar.

3 For a charcoal grill, arrange medium-hot coals around a drip pan. Test for medium heat above the pan. Place chicken pieces, bone sides down, on grill rack over drip pan. Cover and grill for 50 to 60 minutes or until tender and no longer pink (170°F for breast halves; 180°F for thighs and drumsticks), brushing with some of the sauce during the last 15 minutes of grilling. (For a gas grill, preheat grill. Reduce heat to medium. Adjust for indirect cooking. Grill as above.)

4 To serve, reheat remaining sauce until bubbly; pass with chicken.

Preparing the Grill

1
LIGHT THE CHARCOAL

Light the charcoal using one of the methods described on pages 22 to 23. Allow the charcoal to burn until it glows red-hot and is fully covered with a layer of white ash.

2
SEPARATE THE COALS

Using a sturdy, long-handled tool such as a pair of tongs, a garden rake, or a hoe, separate the coals into two equal piles about 10 inches apart. The space between the piles should be wide enough to accommodate a disposable aluminum drip pan.

3
ADD A DRIP PAN

Place an aluminum drip pan in the area between the coals and pour enough hot water into the pan to fill it about ½ inch deep. Replace the grill's cooking grate and allow it to heat up before adding the food.

Preparing the Chicken

1
MARINATE THE CHICKEN

Place the chicken pieces in a resealable plastic bag, cover with the marinade, seal the bag, and marinate in a refrigerator for 2 to 4 hours. Remove the chicken, allowing the excess marinade to drip off, as shown. Save the marinade for making the barbecue sauce.

2
GRILL THE CHICKEN

Place the chicken over the extinguished center burner (or the drip pan on a charcoal grill), close the lid, and grill for 50 to 60 minutes. Baste with the sauce during the last 15 minutes. Cook until all the meat is tender and no longer pink and it reaches the right internal temperature as measured by a quick-read thermometer.

Marinate the chicken for at least 2 hours before grilling for maximum flavor.

Cranberry-Margarita Turkey Legs

Drumsticks doused in tequila and slathered in a spicy-sweet chipotle-cranberry sauce—this dish has "party" written all over it.

3

INDIRECT GRILLING

GRILLING DETAILS

PREP: 20 minutes
MARINATE: 2 to 24 hours
GRILL: 45 minutes
MAKES: 6 servings

INGREDIENTS

- 6 turkey drumsticks (about 3 pounds)
- 1/4 cup cranberry juice
- 1/4 cup tequila
- 1 tablespoon finely shredded lime peel
- 1/4 cup lime juice
- 2 cloves garlic, minced
- 1 teaspoon salt
- 1/4 teaspoon cayenne pepper (optional)
- 1 16-ounce can whole cranberry sauce
- 2 or 3 canned chipotle peppers in adobo sauce, mashed

CLOSER LOOK

CHECKING OUT CHIPOTLES

Chipotle (pronounce chi-PO-tuh-lay) peppers have reached fad status of late, but they are not really a new food. Chipotles are simply ripe red jalapeños that have been smoked to preserve them and to provide additional flavor. Chipotles are available dried or even powdered, but usually it is most common to find them canned in chile-vinegar adobo sauce. Heat-wise, chipotles rate a "medium," but their smoky flavor makes them a robust addition to any dish.

1 Place turkey in a resealable large plastic bag set in a shallow dish. For marinade, in a small bowl stir together cranberry juice, 2 tablespoons of the tequila, 1 1/2 teaspoons of the lime peel, 2 tablespoons of the lime juice, the garlic, salt, and, if desired, cayenne pepper. Pour over turkey; seal bag. Marinate in the refrigerator for 2 to 24 hours, turning bag occasionally. Drain turkey, discarding marinade.

2 For sauce, in a small saucepan combine remaining tequila, remaining lime peel, remaining lime juice, the cranberry sauce, and chipotle peppers. Bring to boiling; reduce heat. Simmer, uncovered, for 5 minutes. Reserve 1 1/4 cups of the sauce.

3 For a charcoal grill, arrange medium-hot coals around a drip pan. Test for medium heat above the drip pan. Place drumsticks on grill rack over drip pan. Cover; grill for 45 to 60 minutes or until tender and no longer pink (180°F), turning and brushing occasionally with the remaining sauce during the last 10 minutes of grilling. (For a gas grill, preheat grill. Reduce heat to medium. Adjust for indirect cooking. Grill as above.) To serve, reheat and pass the reserved sauce with turkey.

Preparing the Grill

1 LIGHT THE CHARCOAL
Light the charcoal using one of the methods described on pages 22 to 23. Allow the charcoal to burn until it glows red-hot and is fully covered with a layer of white ash.

2 SEPARATE THE COALS
Using a sturdy, long-handled tool such as a pair of tongs, a garden rake, or a hoe, separate the coals into two equal piles about 10 inches apart. The space between the piles should be wide enough to accommodate a disposable aluminum drip pan.

3 ADD A DRIP PAN
Place an aluminum drip pan in the area between the coals and pour enough hot water into the pan to fill it about ½ inch deep. Replace the grill's cooking grate and allow it to heat up before adding the food.

Preparing the Turkey and Sauce

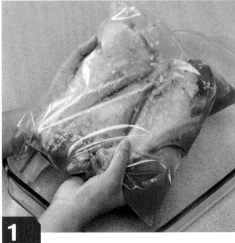

1 MARINATE THE TURKEY
Place the turkey legs in a resealable large plastic bag. Add the marinade, seal the bag, and turn it over several times to coat the turkey. Marinate in the refrigerator for 2 to 24 hours, turning the bag occasionally.

2 PREPARE THE SAUCE
Using a spoon, mash the chipotle peppers in a small bowl. Add the peppers to a saucepan and mix with the tequila, lime peel, lime juice, and cranberry sauce. Heat the mixture to boiling and simmer for 5 minutes. Brush the sauce on the turkey legs while they grill.

Serve with a salad to cool down the spicy goodness of the chipotle peppers.

Rotisserie

 otisserie is an Old French word that, roughly translated, means "roast"—but that only tells half the story. A rotisserie is a grilling setup that allows you to barbecue foods on a slowly rotating spit. In effect, the foods become self-basting because instead of just dripping off, the juices tend to stay on the meat. Foods cooked this way turn out tender, juicy, and tasty.

If you enjoy gyros from your favorite Greek restaurant, there is a good chance that you've eaten lamb cooked on a rotisserie and you understand how good food cooked this way tastes. But you don't need an industrial, restaurant-quality contraption to enjoy rotisserie cooking at home: You can buy a kit to turn your grill—either charcoal or gas—into a fully functioning rotisserie cooker. In fact, rotisserie cooking is just an offshoot from indirect grilling; the only difference is that the meat constantly turns.

When you start shopping for a rotisserie attachment, check into the company that manufactured your grill. There is a good chance that there is a rotisserie kit designed specifically for your model. If not, don't worry; there are also "universal" kits that are meant to work with any kind of grill (though it might take some trial and error to make the attachment function properly on your grill).

Chapter 4 Recipes

The most important element in every rotisserie attachment is the electric motor that rotates the spit. Look for a heavy-duty motor that turns smoothly and quietly and, if possible, buy a model with an on/off switch.

The other parts of the kit are pretty standard: mounting brackets, spit rod, and forks to hold the meat and keep it from spinning. "Premium" attachment kits usually include other useful items, including a spit handle that makes it easy to manually rotate the meat and a counterbalance that can be used to smooth out the spit rotation for large items such as turkeys that are nearly impossible to center on the spit.

If rotisserie grilling is good for big things such as roasts and chickens, shouldn't it also work for smaller things? Yes, it does, and fortunately smart people have already designed a product that makes it easy. The rotisserie basket is a simple accessory that attaches to the spit and rotates along with it. The basket can be used to cook vegetables, chicken pieces, fish, or other small-size foods. There are actually two types: the tumble basket, in which the pieces move around while they cook, and the flat basket, which holds food steady. The flat basket is better for delicate foods such as fish, which otherwise might break apart as they cook.

Rotisserie: Charcoal

4

ROTISSERIE

T he thing to remember about rotisserie cooking on a charcoal grill is that it is simply a form of indirect grilling. Most kettle-style cookers support the rotisserie spit and motor with a metal ring that rests on top of the grill. Once the rotisserie attachment is in place and you've tested the motor to make sure the spit is rotating properly, you start your fire just like you would for any other indirect-grilled entrée. When the coals are hot and ashed over, separate them into two piles, insert an aluminum drip pan, and spread the coals out evenly on either side of the pan. Now you're ready to cook.

Placing the meat on the spit takes some attention to detail. Place the spit rod as close to the center of the food item as possible—sometimes this is really difficult, but it's important. Balance is essential to allow the spit to rotate steadily and evenly. It's possible to get some large things so off-center that the motor can't even turn the item. If you struggle to get your rotisserie rotating effortlessly because of the weight distribution, buy yourself a counterbalance. This little tool is simply a weight that clips on the spit rod and helps balance out an off-center food item.

Once the food is centered on the rod, lock it in place with the holding forks, which simply slide over the ends of the rod and then are pushed tight into the food and secured by turning the setscrew. Before starting the motor, test-turn the spit manually a couple of times to make sure everything rotates freely and check to make sure the grill lid clears the rotating food. Check to see that the drip pan is filled with water and positioned to catch all drippings. When everything is a go, turn on the motor, put the lid in place, and cook.

Because rotisserie is a long, slow cooking process, you will need to add fresh charcoal briquettes to maintain the fire temperature. Since there is no cooking grate in place, this is simple to do. A batch of coals will give you an hour of good heat. Either start feeding fresh briquettes to the hot coals after about 45 minutes of cooking or light a full fresh batch in a chimney starter after each hour of cooking and add briquettes to the grill.

Rotisserie: Gas

Gas grills and rotisserie seem to go hand in hand. Most manufacturers of quality gas grills offer attachment kits that can quickly and easily convert a grill for rotisserie cooking. The simplicity of using gas fuel during long cooking sessions and the precise temperature control gas grills offer are two reasons that should encourage every gas grill owner to give rotisserie a try. Sure, it takes a while to grill things this way, but rotisserie in a gas grill is a relatively hands-off process. Backyard barbecue hosts will find they have plenty of time to converse with guests even while grilling a roast or a couple of chickens on their gas rotisserie.

Probably the most important thing for a gas griller to remember before a rotisserie session is to check the propane level in the fuel tank. Some of these entrées take 2 or more hours to cook, and you'll kick yourself if the last of the gas burns out halfway through a cookout with hungry guests waiting for their dinner. Once you've assured yourself that you have plenty of fuel and the rotisserie attachment is in place and functioning, proceed just like a direct-grilling session. Light all the burners, close the lid, and let the grill heat up.

Meanwhile, turn your attention to centering and securing the food on the spit rod, an essential step no matter what type of grill you are using. Once the grill is heated, turn off the burner under where the food will cook and put the spit rod in place. Test turn the food by hand (this is where a rotisserie with a built-in handle on the spit rod is so convenient) and check clearance with the grill lid. If the food is badly unbalanced, re-center it on the spit rod or attach a counterbalance weight. Never force your motor to struggle with an off-balance load—that's a great way to burn it out. Once the spit rod rotates easily, turn on the motor, close the lid, and let the grill do its job.

Keep an eye on the temperature and adjust your burner levels accordingly. Other than a periodic check to make sure the spit is turning, and maybe occasional basting, keep the lid closed as much as possible to preserve the cooking heat.

Bayou Rotisserie Chicken

The birds are brined in this recipe, a style of saltwater marinating that produces succulently moist and tender chicken, even after slow cooking.

4

ROTISSERIE

GRILLING DETAILS

PREP: 30 minutes
MARINATE: 6 to 8 hours
GRILL: 1 hour
STAND: 10 minutes
MAKES: 8 to 10 servings

INGREDIENTS

- 2 3- to 3½-pound whole broiler-fryer chickens
- 8 cups water
- ½ cup kosher salt
- ½ cup bourbon
- ½ cup honey
- 2 tablespoons finely shredded lemon peel
- ½ cup lemon juice
- ½ cup bottled hot pepper sauce
- 6 cloves garlic, minced
- 1 recipe Cajun Spice Rub (see recipe, below)

Cajun Spice Rub: In a small bowl combine ½ teaspoon ground allspice, ¼ teaspoon cayenne pepper, and ¼ teaspoon black pepper.

WORK SMARTER

DEFROSTING FROZEN CHICKEN

Chicken is great food, but it carries some risk from bacterial illness if you don't handle it properly. Most people buy frozen whole birds, and there are right and wrong ways to thaw them out. Never thaw chicken on the countertop. Instead, place your frozen chicken in the refrigerator and allow it a full 24 hours to thaw. There is also a safe quick-thaw system. Place your chicken in a sink full of cold water—which should be drained and replaced every half hour—and allow 30 minutes of defrosting time for every pound of bird.

1 Remove the neck and giblets from chickens. Place chickens in a resealable 2-gallon plastic bag set in a large bowl. For brine, in a large bowl combine water, salt, bourbon, honey, lemon peel, lemon juice, bottled hot pepper sauce, and garlic. Stir until salt and honey are dissolved. Pour brine over chickens; seal bag. Marinate in the refrigerator for 6 to 8 hours.

2 Remove chickens from brine; discard brine. Pat chickens dry with paper towels. Sprinkle Cajun Spice Rub evenly onto chickens; pat in with your fingers.

3 To secure chickens on a spit rod, place one holding fork on rod with tines toward the point. Insert rod through one of the chickens, neck end first, pressing tines of holding fork firmly into the breast meat. To tie wings, slip a 24-inch piece of 100-percent-cotton string under back of chicken; bring ends of string to front, securing each wing tip. Tie in center of breast, leaving equal string ends. To tie legs, slip a 24-inch piece of string under tail. Loop string around tail, then loop around crossed legs. Tie very tightly to hold bird securely on spit, again leaving string ends. Pull together the strings attached to wings and legs; tie tightly. Trim off excess string. Place second holding fork on rod with the tines toward the chicken; press tines of holding fork firmly into thigh meat. Adjust forks and tighten screws. Repeat with remaining chicken. Test balance, making adjustments as necessary.

4 For a charcoal grill, arrange medium-hot coals around a drip pan. Test for medium heat above the drip pan. Attach spit, turn on the motor, and lower the grill hood. Let the chickens rotate over drip pan for 1 to 1¼ hours or until chicken is no longer pink and drumsticks move easily in their sockets (180°F in thigh muscle). Add fresh coals as needed to maintain temperature. (For a gas grill, preheat grill, reduce heat to medium. Adjust for indirect cooking. Attach spit. Grill as above.)

5 Remove chickens from spit. Cover with foil; let stand for 10 minutes before carving.

Preparing the Grill

1

LIGHT THE CHARCOAL
Light the charcoal using one of the methods described on pages 22 to 23. Allow the charcoal to burn until it glows red-hot and is fully covered with a layer of white ash.

2

ADD ROTISSERIE ATTACHMENT
Wearing mitts to protect your hands and arms from burns, place the rotisserie attachment on the top of the grill kettle.

3

INSERT DRIP PANS
Using a sturdy, long-handled tool such as a pair of tongs, a garden rake, or a hoe, pile the coals on one side of the grill. Position a pair of small aluminum drip pans, as shown, underneath and parallel to where the rotisserie spit will run. Pour enough hot water into the drip pans to fill them each about 1/2 inch deep.

Preparing the Chicken

1

PLACE CHICKEN ON SPIT
Secure a holding fork near one end of the spit rod. Insert the rod through the neck end of a chicken and snug up to the holding fork, inserting the tines into the breast. Make sure the bird is centered on the spit rod as much as possible.

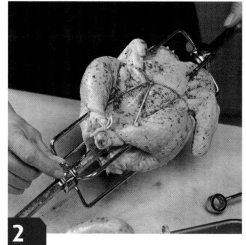

2

SECURE THE CHICKEN
Using a 24-inch length of kitchen string, tie the wing tips tightly to the breast. Use a second piece of string to tie the legs to the tail. Tie the loose ends of the two strings together, knot, and trim. Push a second holding fork into place and tighten the setscrew. Repeat with the second chicken.

Double the goodness by grilling two birds on one spit at the same time.

Marinated Rotisserie Rump Roast

You can't rush this roast—it needs 2 days of marinating and 2 hours of cooking, but the mouthwatering results are worth the wait.

GRILLING DETAILS

PREP: 15 minutes
MARINATE: 2 to 3 days
GRILL: 2 hours
STAND: 15 minutes
MAKES: 8 to 10 servings

INGREDIENTS

- 1 3-pound boneless beef rump roast (rolled and tied)
- 2½ cups water
- 2½ cups vinegar
- 2 medium onions, sliced
- 1 medium lemon, sliced
- 3 bay leaves
- 12 whole cloves
- 6 whole black peppercorns
- 1 teaspoon salt

BUYER'S GUIDE

MAKING THE GRADE

When you are shopping for cuts of beef, you might encounter three different grades: USDA Prime, USDA Choice, and USDA Select. Beef grade is determined primarily by the amount of marbling (fat) and the age of the animal. The higher the grade, (usually) the more tender, juicy, and flavorful the meat. Prime is the highest grade and is most often seen on restaurant menus. Choice and Select are more commonly seen in your local supermarket.

1 Place roast in a resealable large plastic bag set in a large bowl. For marinade, in a large bowl combine the water, vinegar, onions, lemon, bay leaves, cloves, peppercorns, and salt; pour over roast. Seal bag. Marinate in the refrigerator for 2 to 3 days, turning bag occasionally.

2 Drain roast, reserving the marinade. In a saucepan heat the reserved marinade to boiling; set aside. To secure roast on a spit rod, place one holding fork on rod with tines toward point. Insert rod through the narrow end of the roast, pressing tines of holding fork firmly into meat. Place second holding fork on rod with tines toward roast; press tines of holding fork firmly into meat. Adjust forks and tighten screws. Test balance, making adjustments as necessary.

3 For a charcoal grill, arrange medium coals around a drip pan. Test for medium-low heat above the drip pan. Attach spit, turn on the motor, and lower grill hood. Let the roast rotate over drip pan for 2 to 2½ hours or until medium doneness (155°F), brushing occasionally with the reserved marinade during the first 1½ hours of grilling. Add fresh coals as needed to maintain temperature. (For a gas grill, preheat grill. Reduce heat to medium. Adjust for indirect cooking. Attach spit. Grill as above.)

4 Remove roast from spit. Cover with foil. Let stand for 15 minutes. The meat's temperature will rise 5°F during standing. Discard any remaining marinade.

Preparing the Grill

1

LIGHT THE CHARCOAL

Light the charcoal using one of the methods described on pages 22 to 23. Allow the charcoal to burn until it glows red-hot and is fully covered with a layer of white ash.

2

ADD ROTISSERIE ATTACHMENT

Wearing mitts to protect your hands and arms from burns, place the rotisserie attachment on the top of the grill kettle.

3

INSERT DRIP PANS

Using a sturdy, long-handled tool such as a pair of tongs, a garden rake, or a hoe, pile the coals on one side of the grill. Position a pair of small aluminum drip pans, as shown, underneath and parallel to where the rotisserie spit will run. Pour enough hot water into the drip pans to fill them each about ¹/₂ inch deep.

4

ROTISSERIE

Preparing the Roast

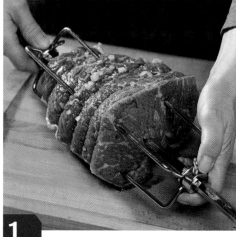

Boil the marinade and use it as a basting brush-on for even more flavor.

1

PLACE ROAST ON SPIT

Secure one holding fork near the center of the spit rod. Insert the spit rod through the center of the marinated roast and push onto the holding fork until the tines are fully embedded. Add the second holding fork and tighten its setscrew.

2

BALANCE THE SPIT ROD

Place the spit rod on the rotisserie rack and test the balance. If the roast is off-center, attach a counterbalance so that the weight is opposite the roast's heaviest side. Test how the rod spins, adjusting the counterbalance weight in or out, as shown, until the roast spins easily and evenly.

Rotisserie Gyro Sandwiches

Getting the authentic taste of your favorite gyro restaurant in your own backyard is a lot easier than you think.

GRILLING DETAILS

PREP: 20 minutes
CHILL: 4 to 24 hours
GRILL: 45 minutes
STAND: 15 minutes
MAKES: 8 servings

INGREDIENTS

- 2 pounds ground lamb
- 1 tablespoon dried minced onion
- 2 teaspoons garlic powder
- 2 teaspoons Greek seasoning, crushed
- 1 teaspoon salt
- ½ teaspoon black pepper
- 1 6-ounce carton plain low-fat yogurt
- ½ cup chopped, seeded cucumber
- 1 tablespoon snipped fresh mint
- 2 cloves garlic, minced
- 8 pita bread rounds, warmed
- 2 medium tomatoes, thinly sliced
- ½ cup crumbled feta cheese (2 ounces)

TOOL SAVVY

THE MAGIC OF FOOD PROCESSORS
Food processors are one of cooking's greatest inventions—which you will understand the first time you use one. These do-it-all appliances mix, chop, grind, puree, shred, whip, juice, etc., just about any kind of food quickly and easily with the push of a button. Some people mistakenly think they are just glorified blenders, but they just don't understand the differences—can a blender knead bread dough? Don't try to save money by skimping on size. Look for a model with a large bowl and a heavy-duty motor. A good variety of cutting/mixing discs is nice, though these can be purchased separately.

1 In a food processor combine lamb, minced onion, garlic powder, Greek seasoning, salt, and pepper. Cover and process until mixture is very smooth, scraping sides as necessary.

2 Shape the meat mixture into a 6- to 7-inch-long cylinder-shape loaf; set aside. On a work surface place two 24-inch-long sheets of plastic wrap, overlapping the sheets slightly on one long side. Place lamb loaf lengthwise in the center of the plastic. Starting from a long side, wrap the plastic around the loaf, squeezing out any air. Twist ends of the plastic tightly to compress the loaf. Place the loaf in a shallow baking pan or on a tray. Refrigerate for 4 to 24 hours until loaf is firm, turning occasionally to maintain the cylinder shape.

3 To secure the loaf on a spit rod, place one holding fork on the rod with the tines toward the point. Insert the rod through the end of the loaf, pressing tines of holding fork firmly into meat. Place second holding fork on rod, tines toward the loaf; press tines of holding fork firmly into the meat. Adjust forks and tighten screws. Test balance, making adjustments as necessary.

4 For a charcoal grill, arrange medium-hot coals around a drip pan. Test for medium heat above the drip pan. Attach spit, turn on the motor, and lower the grill hood. Let the loaf rotate over the drip pan for 45 minutes or until a quick-read thermometer inserted into the center of the meat reads 170°F. (For a gas grill, preheat grill, reduce heat to medium. Adjust for indirect cooking. Attach spit. Grill as above.)

5 Remove loaf from spit. Cover with foil; let stand about 15 minutes or until a quick-read thermometer inserted into the center of the meat reads 180°F.

6 Meanwhile, for yogurt sauce, in a small bowl stir together yogurt, cucumber, mint, and garlic. Thinly slice meat. On each of the warmed pitas place some of the meat, 2 tablespoons of the yogurt sauce, some of the tomato slices, and 1 tablespoon crumbled feta cheese. Fold pita in half; serve immediately.

Preparing the Grill

1

LIGHT THE CHARCOAL

Light the charcoal using one of the methods described on pages 22 to 23. Allow the charcoal to burn until it glows red-hot and is fully covered with a layer of white ash.

2

ADD ROTISSERIE ATTACHMENT

Wearing mitts to protect your hands and arms from burns, place the rotisserie attachment on the top of the grill kettle.

3

INSERT DRIP PANS

Using a sturdy, long-handled tool such as a pair of tongs, a garden rake, or a hoe, pile the coals on one side of the grill. Position a pair of small aluminum drip pans, as shown, underneath and parallel to where the rotisserie spit will run. Pour enough hot water into the drip pans to fill them each about $1/2$ inch deep.

Preparing the Lamb Loaf

1

FORM THE LOAF

Combine the ground lamb and seasonings in a food processor and mix until smooth. Remove the meat and shape it into a uniform, oblong loaf shape, as shown. Place the loaf on a large piece of plastic wrap.

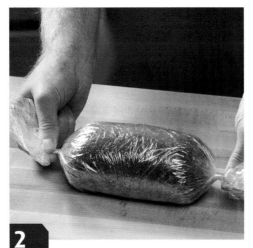

2

WRAP THE LOAF

Roll the loaf in the plastic and twist the ends tightly, securing with tape. Place the loaf on a tray and chill in the refrigerator for at least 2 hours—overnight is better. Rotate the loaf periodically to maintain its shape. When the loaf is firm, remove the plastic, secure it on the spit rod, and grill.

Serve on warm pitas with cucumber dressing for authentic gyro taste.

Southwestern Rotisserie Pork Roast

This dish uses both a sour-sweet brush-on sauce and a spicy rub for double the flavor. Considering how good the roasted pork tastes, it is surprisingly simple to prepare.

GRILLING DETAILS

PREP: 20 minutes
GRILL: 1½ hours
STAND: 15 minutes
MAKES: 6 to 8 servings

INGREDIENTS

- 3 tablespoons honey
- 1 teaspoon finely shredded lime peel
- 1 tablespoon lime juice
- 2 tablespoons chili powder
- 1 tablespoon salt
- 1 tablespoon onion powder
- 1 tablespoon garlic powder
- 2 teaspoons ground cumin
- 2 teaspoons black pepper
- 1 teaspoon paprika
- ¼ teaspoon cayenne pepper
- 1 2½- to 3-pound boneless pork top loin roast (single loin)

WORK SMARTER

WHY REST A ROAST?

Most recipes for large cuts of pork, beef, or lamb will tell you to pull the roast when it reaches a certain temperature, cover it with foil, and let it sit for awhile. This is called "resting" and there are good reasons for doing it. The meat will actually continue to cook during this time, with its internal temperature rising 5 to 10 degrees—that's why recipes sometimes specify a final grilling temperature a little lower than the "safe" temperature. While a roast rests, its juices become better distributed and its fibers relax, ensuring tender, juicy slices from any part of the cut.

1 In a small bowl combine honey, lime peel, and lime juice; set aside. In another small bowl combine chili powder, salt, onion powder, garlic powder, cumin, black pepper, paprika, and cayenne pepper; set aside.

2 Trim fat from meat. Brush meat with the honey mixture. Sprinkle chili powder mixture evenly onto roast; pat in with your fingers.

3 To secure the roast on a spit rod, place one holding fork on the rod with tines toward the point. Insert the rod through the narrow end of the roast, pressing the tines of the holding fork firmly into meat. Place second holding fork on rod with tines toward roast; press tines of holding fork firmly into meat. Adjust forks and tighten screws. Test balance, making adjustments as necessary.

4 For a charcoal grill, arrange medium coals around a drip pan. Test for medium-low heat above the pan. Attach spit; turn on the motor and lower the grill hood. Let the roast rotate over the drip pan about 1½ hours or until a quick-read thermometer inserted into the center of the roast reads 155°F. Add fresh coals as needed to maintain temperature. (For a gas grill, preheat grill, reduce heat to medium. Adjust for indirect cooking. Attach spit. Grill as above.)

5 Remove roast from spit. Cover with foil. Let stand for 15 minutes. The meat's temperature will rise 5°F during standing.

Preparing the Grill

1 LIGHT THE CHARCOAL
Light the charcoal using one of the methods described on pages 22 to 23. Allow the charcoal to burn until it glows red-hot and is fully covered with a layer of white ash.

2 ADD ROTISSERIE ATTACHMENT
Wearing mitts to protect your hands and arms from burns, place the rotisserie attachment on the top of the grill kettle. .

3 INSERT DRIP PANS
Using a sturdy, long-handled tool such as a pair of tongs, a garden rake, or a hoe, pile the coals on one side of the grill. Position a pair of small aluminum drip pans, as shown, underneath and parallel to where the rotisserie spit will run. Pour enough hot water into the drip pans to fill them each about 1/2 inch deep.

Preparing the Roast

1 TRIM THE ROAST
Use a sharp knife to trim the excess fat from the outside of the pork. Brush the roast with the honey mixture, apply the rub, and secure the meat on the spit rod. Grill the roast over medium-low heat (about 300°F) for 1½ to 2 hours.

2 REMOVE THE ROAST
Working with cooking mitts, lift the spit rod from the grill and place the roast on a cutting board. Remove one holding fork and carefully slide the roast off the rod and onto the cutting board with the help of a grill fork. Cover the roast with foil, let it stand for 15 minutes, and carve it.

Cook the roast to an internal temperature of 155°F and let rest for 15 minutes before carving.

Smoking

While cooking foods over an open flame has been around since man tamed fire and figured out that food tastes better when it's hot, cooking with smoke has probably been around nearly as long. Who knows—maybe it all started with a leg of antelope hung near a smoky fire for several hours. Our prehistoric proto-griller tested the smoky antelope and realized that not only was it cooked, but it tasted pretty darn good. Over time, people realized that smoking also worked to tenderize and preserve meats—very important when an antelope or a deer, or in later days, a family's lone hog—might have to provide meals for days or weeks. Today we smoke foods because we like

the flavor, and we don't need to build a smokehouse when craving meat, poultry, or fish with that great hardwood-smoke taste. Smoking is really a form of indirect heat grilling. You can smoke foods in your charcoal or gas grill—or you can buy a smoker built specifically for the job. Whatever cooking tool you use, there are a few things to keep in mind to ensure a tasty smoked dish every time:

Time and Temperature: These two things work together. Smoking is a low-temperature, slow-cooking process and it takes time. If you get impatient and try to fire things up to move the cooking process along, you won't get the full benefit of the smoke—you'll simply be indirect grilling.

Chapter 5 Recipes

Keep the cooking temperature in the specified range and give the food the full time it needs to smoke.

Wood: This is the key ingredient to smoking. Your fuel—whether gas or charcoal or electricity—provides the heat, but burning hardwood chips or chunks provides the smoke and the flavor. Refer to pages 124 to 125 for choosing the right kind of hardwood for different entrées.

Water: Wait a second—water puts fire out, right? Not when it comes to smoking, where water is an essential ingredient in two different ways. First, the wood chips and chunks that you add to your fire need to be soaked in water or they'll burn too quickly and not generate enough smoke. Second, your smoker needs a steady supply of moisture (usually provided by a pan of water) to keep the surface of the meat from sealing and to allow the smoke to penetrate.

Your imagination may be the only limit to the kinds of meats that can be cooked—and end up tasting great—in a smoker. Pork ribs and chops are smoker classics, but smoked beef roasts and steak, poultry, and fish of all types can be fantastic. And how about improving plain old meat loaf? Turn to pages 134 to 135 to see just how versatile your smoker can be.

Smoking: Charcoal

It's simple to set up your charcoal grill for smoking because it's a form of indirect grilling—but you are going to have to do things differently if you want your food to have authentic slow-cooked, hardwood-smoked flavor.

The big thing to keep in mind is temperature—smoke cooking is accomplished in a much cooler environment, anywhere from 200°F to 250°F, with about 220°F to 225°F usually considered ideal. Fire up your grill as if you are going to indirect grill, but take steps to reduce the temperature. First, use fewer charcoal briquettes to start with and maintain fewer hot coals as your food cooks. Next let the coals burn down more than usual before you start cooking. Finally, control the burn rate by carefully adjusting the vents. It's unlikely that you will be cooking with all the vents all the way open.

All this discussion about temperature probably makes it clear that you need a good thermometer—actually you need two. Buy one that monitors temperature on the cooking surface and buy a quality quick-read meat thermometer. Even though you are using low heat, you still have to cook meat to a safe internal temperature.

Water is another essential ingredient for smoking in a charcoal grill. Your aluminum drip pan is going to double as your water pan. Add more water than you normally would for indirect grilling—fill it to a depth of an inch or two—and replenish the supply regularly.

Finally, the smoke—as with a charcoal-fired vertical water smoker, add your hardwood chips or chunks right on top of the hot coals. There are a couple of things to consider: First, always soak your hardwood pieces in water for an hour before you add them to the fire. Second, charcoal-grill smokers will probably find it easier to work with smaller chip-size pieces rather than big chunks. The chips will burn easily on the smaller, cooler charcoal fire and can be replenished as needed.

Smoking: Gas

Gas grills, which are fantastic indirect grilling machines, can also be pretty serviceable smoking machines, especially if they have a smoker box—but more on that shortly. Gas grills have the advantage of fairly precise temperature control. Once you get your grill to the correct cooking temperature, all it takes is some minor adjustments to the gas control knobs to keep the cooking heat in the right zone. Plus, most have a built-in thermometer, so you can constantly check the temperature without lifting the lid and letting both heat and smoke escape.

Many new grills are fitted with a smoker box, which is a really slick device for generating smoke. The smoker box is a long, thin drawer that slides out of the grill; you fill it with soaked hardwood chips. Most smoker boxes have their own burner, so you can heat them independently from the rest of the grill—great for generating smoke without getting the overall grill too hot.

If you don't have a smoker box, generating smoke on a gas grill offers some challenges, and you have two options. The first is to fill a pouch folded out of aluminum foil with soaked wood chips. Seal the pouch, poke several holes in the top, and drop it directly on the heating element. Alternatively, you can place chunks of soaked hardwood directly on the burner. Both options have disadvantages. The burner might have to be turned way up to make the chips or chunks smoke, raising the grill temperature too high—meaning you will have to let it cool before adding the food. In addition, you will have to add a new pouch or wood chunks for longer cooking times, and that will probably require almost starting over—removing the food and cooking grate, adding the hardwood, heating the grill, and cooling it back to cooking temperature.

As with smoke cooking on any type of grill or smoker, a water supply is essential for smoking in a gas grill. Put a water-filled disposable aluminum drip pan off to the side of your cooking grate and keep it replenished as needed.

Choosing the Wood

Smoking meats is a relatively simple process, but choosing the right wood for the job takes some thought. Every type of wood gives off a different "flavor" of smoke, and sometimes the smoke flavor just doesn't complement the meat. Because it takes a long time to cook food in a smoker, you don't want to spend several hours smoking something that's only fit to serve the dog—and, heck, he might even turn his nose up at it.

Before you even start considering matchmaking wood to meat, remember what you can't use for generating smoke. Never use soft woods, such as pine, cottonwood, or poplar, because the pitch and other compounds they contain can give food a terrible flavor. Never use lumber or any kind of composite wood products, which usually have

been treated with chemicals that can be toxic. Never use wood chips that you can't identify or trace the history of—you never know when you will end up with a mixture that includes something toxic or foul-tasting.

Hardwood chips and chunks are really the only thing to consider for smoking. There are a variety of wood types available, and they all have their own distinctive characteristics. Wood chips and chunks are available prepackaged at many retail outlets that sell grilling supplies, including Internet outlets. Here is a quick primer on the various hardwood types and their appropriate meat matches.

Alder
Alders are native to western North America and gained fame in cooking circles as the perfect wood

for smoking salmon. Alder smoke gives foods a delicate, slightly sweet flavor, which makes it a good choice for fish and poultry, but not for smoking beef.

Match with: Fish (especially salmon), poultry, and pork.

Apple
Apple smoke produces a mild, sweet flavor—not surprisingly, some people describe it as "fruity." The flavor is a little on the light side for beef, but pork and other light-flavor meats taste great under the influence of apple smoke.

Match with: Pork (especially ham), poultry, veal, and fish.

Cherry

Also a fruit tree, cherry provides a smoked flavor that is similar to apple—delicate and slightly sweet. The smoke tends to turn meat a deep mahogany color. Some recommend blending with alder, hickory, oak, or pecan for the best results.
Match with: Pork, poultry, and fish.

Hickory

Hickory is probably the most famous smoking wood and is especially popular in the South and Midwest. It gives meat a strong, hearty flavor and is a great match for strong-flavored fare such as wild game. Use sparingly because too much hickory smoke can give food a bitter flavor.
Match with: Beef, pork (especially ribs), and wild game.

Maple

This tree that dominates the hardwood forests of the northeastern U.S. gives foods a mellow, slightly sweet flavor. It has traditionally been used to smoke hams, but it's great for a variety of delicate-flavored foods.
Match with: Pork (especially ham), poultry, vegetables, and fish.

Mesquite

Texas ranchers and farmers hate this tenacious, thorny tree, but grill chefs love mesquite because it burns hot and gives food a distinctive sweet flavor. Smoking is another matter because the flavor can get very strong—even harsh. Use only well-aged mesquite and apply the chips very sparingly. Try mixing a little in with apple or pecan to perk up flavor.
Match with: Beef, chicken, and vegetables.

Oak

Oak is the most popular smoking choice in Europe and is probably the most versatile hardwood. It imparts a strong—but not overpowering—smoked flavor and is a good match for beef, lamb, and other strong-flavored meats. Some authorities claim the red oak is the best oak choice for smoking.
Match with: Beef, lamb, pork, and poultry.

Pecan

Some people describe pecan as a milder version of hickory, though with its own rich character. It is very popular in the southwestern U.S. where the tree is most abundant. It gives meat a slightly fruity flavor and is a great choice for large cuts that need to be smoked for a lengthy period of time.
Match with: Pork (especially roasts and chops), poultry, fish, and beef brisket.

◀ Large, chunk-size pieces of hardwood, such as this mesquite, are best for an entirely wood-fueled fire or gas grills with no smoker box.

◀ Small, chip-size pieces of hardwood, such as this hickory, are best used with charcoal-fueled fires and gas grills with a smoker box.

5

SMOKING

Smokin' Strip Steak Churrasco

Churrasco is a Latin American barbecue and chimichurri is a zesty Argentinian sauce made with parsley and mint; use only fresh herbs for authentic flavor.

GRILLING DETAILS

PREP: 30 minutes
SOAK: 1 hour
MARINATE: 1 hour
GRILL: 16 minutes
MAKES: 4 servings

INGREDIENTS

- 3 cups mesquite or hickory wood chips
- 4 boneless beef top loin steaks, cut 1 inch thick (2¼ pounds total)
  Salt and black pepper
- 1½ cups lightly packed fresh parsley leaves
- 3 tablespoons snipped fresh mint
- 3 tablespoons red wine vinegar
- 1 tablespoon bottled minced garlic
- 1 tablespoon Dijon-style mustard
- 1 teaspoon crushed red pepper
- ½ teaspoon salt
- ⅓ cup olive oil
  Lime wedges (optional)

WORK SMARTER

KEEPING FRESH HERBS FRESH

Sometimes (deep in the winter, for example) it's tough to find fresh herbs and they can be a little pricier than we'd like. Better flavor makes this extra expense worthwhile, but you need to take steps to preserve your investment. Store fresh herbs in the refrigerator, ideally in a perforated bag. Some moisture is good, but too much promotes decay. Shake off any excess water before you put the herbs in a bag and add a crumpled paper towel to absorb excess water.

1 At least 1 hour before smoke cooking, soak wood chips in enough water to cover.

2 Trim fat from steaks. Season steaks with salt and black pepper. Place steaks in a resealable large plastic bag. To make the chimichurri sauce, in a food processor or blender combine parsley, mint, vinegar, garlic, mustard, crushed red pepper, and the ½ teaspoon salt. With food processor or blender running on low speed, very slowly add oil until all the ingredients are finely chopped and combined. Cover and refrigerate half of the sauce until ready to serve.

3 Pour the remaining chimichurri sauce over the steaks. Seal bag, turning bag several times until the steaks are well coated. Refrigerate for 1 hour. Drain steaks, discarding the sauce in bag.

4 Drain wood chips. For a charcoal grill, arrange medium-hot coals around a drip pan. Test for medium heat above the drip pan. Sprinkle wood chips over the coals. Place steaks on grill rack over drip pan. Cover; grill until desired doneness. Allow 16 to 20 minutes for medium rare (145°F) or 20 to 24 minutes for medium (160°F). (For a gas grill, preheat grill. Reduce heat to medium. Adjust for indirect cooking. Add wood chips according to manufacturer's directions. Grill as above.) Serve steaks with the reserved chimichurri sauce and, if desired, lime wedges.

Smoker Directions: Prepare steak and chimichurri sauce as directed. Substitute 6 mesquite or hickory wood chunks for the wood chips. In a smoker arrange preheated coals, drained wood chunks, and water pan according to the manufacturer's directions. Pour water into water pan. Place steaks on grill rack over water pan. Cover and smoke until desired doneness. Allow 40 to 50 minutes for medium rare (145°F) or 50 to 60 minutes for medium (160°F). Serve as above.

Preparing the Grill

1
LIGHT THE CHARCOAL
Light the charcoal using one of the methods described on pages 22 to 23. Allow the charcoal to burn until it glows red-hot and is fully covered with a layer of white ash.

2
ADD THE DRIP PAN
Place a disposable aluminum drip pan in the middle of the charcoal grate. Arrange the hot coals in two equal piles on both sides of the drip pan. (If you light the charcoal with starter fluid or an electric starter, separate the charcoal into two piles with a long-handled tool such as a hoe and place the pan between the piles.)

3
ADD THE WOOD CHIPS
Soak the wood chips in water for at least 1 hour before using. Drain off the water and sprinkle the wet wood chips directly on the hot coals. Add enough hot water to the drip pan to fill it 1 or 2 inches deep and then insert the cooking rack in the grill.

Preparing the Steaks

1
MAKE THE SAUCE
Add all the chimichurri sauce ingredients except for the olive oil to a food processor and cover with the lid. Process the mixture on low speed and, without stopping, slowly add the oil. Continue processing the mixture until it's well blended.

2
MARINATE THE STEAK
Set aside half of the chimichurri sauce in the refrigerator. Place the steaks in a resealable plastic bag and cover with the remaining sauce. Seal the bag and turn it to coat the meat. Marinate the steaks in the refrigerator for 1 hour. Remove the steaks and grill or smoke.

Use half the sauce for marinade and half for serving on the steak.

Beer-Sauced Beef Brisket

In addition to the sauce, this brisket is flavor-enhanced with a spicy rub. Don't forget the cloves—even a dash can make a difference.

GRILLING DETAILS

PREP: 10 minutes
SOAK: 1 hour
GRILL: 2 to 2½ hours
MAKES: 15 servings

INGREDIENTS

4	cups mesquite or hickory wood chips
2	tablespoons sugar
1	tablespoon seasoned salt or garlic salt
1	tablespoon paprika
1½	teaspoons chili powder
1½	teaspoons black pepper
⅛	teaspoon cayenne pepper
⅛	teaspoon celery seeds
	Dash ground cloves
½	cup beer
1	tablespoon cider vinegar
1	tablespoon olive oil
1	tablespoon Worcestershire sauce
1	tablespoon bottled barbecue sauce
½	teaspoon seasoned salt or garlic salt
¼	teaspoon celery seeds
1	3- to 4-pound fresh beef brisket
1	recipe Cajun Beer Sauce (see recipe, page 213) or Smoky Barbecue Sauce (page 218)

CLOSER LOOK

ALL ABOUT BRISKET

"Brisket" sounds a little mysterious, but it is simply a cut of beef from the underside of the animal—sometimes it's referred to as the "breast meat." Brisket is very flavorful and usually boneless, but it is tough. Generally it is used in dishes that must be cooked for a long time, which helps tenderize the meat. Brisket is a perfect candidate for indirect grilling or smoking—match it up with a strong-flavored hardwood such as hickory or pecan for the best results.

1 At least 1 hour before smoke cooking, soak wood chips in enough water to cover.

2 For rub, in a small bowl combine sugar, the 1 tablespoon seasoned salt, the paprika, chili powder, black pepper, cayenne pepper, the ⅛ teaspoon celery seeds, and the cloves. Set aside.

3 For mop sauce, in another small bowl combine beer, vinegar, oil, Worcestershire sauce, barbecue sauce, the ½ teaspoon seasoned salt, and the ¼ teaspoon celery seeds. Set aside.

4 Trim fat from brisket. Sprinkle rub evenly over brisket; pat in with your fingers.

5 Drain wood chips. For a charcoal grill, arrange medium-hot coals around a drip pan. Test for medium heat above the drip pan. Sprinkle half of the drained wood chips over coals. Place brisket on grill rack over the drip pan. Cover; grill for 2 to 2½ hours or until brisket is tender; brush once or twice with mop sauce during the last hour of grilling. Discard any remaining mop sauce. Add additional coals, wood chips, and water as needed to maintain temperature, smoke, and moisture. (For a gas grill, preheat grill. Reduce heat to medium. Adjust for indirect cooking. Add wood chips according to manufacturer's directions. Grill as above.)

6 To serve, thinly slice meat across the grain. Serve with Cajun Beer Sauce or Smoky Barbecue Sauce.

Smoker Directions: Prepare brisket as directed at left. Substitute 8 to 10 mesquite or hickory wood chunks for the wood chips. In a smoker arrange preheated coals, drained wood chunks, and water pan according to manufacturer's directions. Pour water into pan. Place brisket on the grill rack over water pan. Cover and smoke for 5 to 6 hours or until brisket is tender; brush once or twice with mop sauce during the last hour of smoke cooking. Discard any remaining mop sauce. Add additional coals and water as needed to maintain temperature and moisture. Serve as above.

Preparing the Grill

1 LIGHT THE CHARCOAL

Light the charcoal using one of the methods described on pages 22 to 23. Allow the charcoal to burn until it glows red-hot and is fully covered with a layer of white ash.

2 ADD THE DRIP PAN

Place a disposable aluminum drip pan in the middle of the charcoal grate. Arrange the hot coals in two equal piles on both sides of the drip pan. (If you light the charcoal with starter fluid or an electric starter, separate the charcoal into two piles with a long-handled tool such as a hoe and place the pan between the piles.)

3 ADD THE WOOD CHIPS

Soak the wood chips in water for at least 1 hour before using. Drain off the water and sprinkle the wet wood chips directly on the hot coals. Add enough hot water to the drip pan to fill it 1 or 2 inches deep and then insert the cooking rack in the grill.

Preparing the Brisket

1 APPLY THE RUB

Combine the rub ingredients in a small bowl. Trim the fat from the brisket and sprinkle the rub mixture over both sides of the meat. Gently work the seasonings into the brisket with the tips of your fingers. Place in the smoker, cover, and grill or smoke as directed.

2 CARVE AND SERVE

Brush the brisket with the mop sauce during the last hour of cooking. Remove from the grill or smoker and carve into thin slices by cutting across the grain with a sharp knife, as shown.

Serve on toasted kaiser rolls generously covered in sauce.

Ginger-Orange Beef Ribs

Soy sauce and fresh ginger give these meaty ribs Pacific Rim flair. An Asian chef might smoke them in a kamado, the traditional egg-shape ceramic oven used for smoking.

GRILLING DETAILS

PREP: 10 minutes
SOAK: 1 hour
GRILL: 1¼ hours
MAKES: 4 servings

INGREDIENTS

- 3 to 4 cups hickory or oak wood chips
- 2 teaspoons paprika
- ½ to 1 teaspoon salt
- ½ teaspoon black pepper
- 3 to 4 pounds beef back ribs (about 8 ribs)
- ½ cup bottled barbecue sauce
- ¼ cup frozen orange juice concentrate, thawed
- 2 tablespoons soy sauce
- 1 tablespoon grated fresh ginger

REAL WORLD

VERSATILE GINGER

Americans like their ginger ale and their gingerbread but don't incorporate ginger into their cuisine as eagerly as other cultures, especially those from Asia. Ginger probably originated in ancient China, and while we often think of it in its dried, powdery form, it's the fresh root that most of the world enjoys. In Southeast Asia, ginger is sliced and eaten raw; in India it's often fried. Japanese chefs tend to use it in small amounts as a flavoring, while it's used much more liberally in traditional Chinese stir-fries. However you use ginger, forego the powder for the fresh root, which is commonly available in most supermarkets.

1 At least 1 hour before grilling, soak wood chips in enough water to cover.

2 For rub, in a small bowl combine paprika, salt, and pepper. Trim fat from ribs. Sprinkle rub evenly over ribs; pat in with your fingers.

3 For sauce, in a small bowl stir together barbecue sauce, orange juice concentrate, soy sauce, and ginger.

4 Drain wood chips. For a charcoal grill, arrange medium-hot coals around a drip pan. Test for medium heat above the drip pan. Sprinkle one-fourth of the chips over the coals. Place ribs, bone sides down, on the grill rack over drip pan. (Or place ribs in a rib rack; place on grill rack.) Cover; grill for 1¼ to 1½ hours or until tender, brushing once with sauce during the last 15 minutes of grilling. Add more wood chips every 20 minutes and more coals as needed. (For a gas grill, preheat grill. Reduce heat to medium. Adjust for indirect cooking. Add wood chips according to manufacturer's directions. Grill as at left.)

Smoker Directions: Prepare as directed at left. Substitute 4 to 6 hickory or oak wood chunks for the wood chips. In a smoker arrange preheated coals, drained wood chunks, and the water pan according to the manufacturer's directions. Pour water into pan. Place ribs, bone sides down, on the grill rack over the water pan. (Or place ribs in a rib rack; place on grill rack.) Cover and smoke for 2½ to 3 hours or until ribs are tender, brushing once with sauce during the last 15 minutes of cooking. Add additional coals and water as needed to maintain temperature and moisture. Pass any remaining sauce with ribs.

Preparing the Grill

1 LIGHT THE CHARCOAL

Light the charcoal using one of the methods described on pages 22 to 23. Allow the charcoal to burn until it glows red-hot and is fully covered with a layer of white ash.

2 ADD THE DRIP PAN

Place a disposable aluminum drip pan in the middle of the charcoal grate. Arrange the hot coals in two equal piles on both sides of the drip pan. (If you light the charcoal with starter fluid or an electric starter, separate the charcoal into two piles with a long-handled tool such as a hoe and place the pan between the piles.)

3 ADD THE WOOD CHIPS

Soak the wood chips in water for at least 1 hour before using. Drain off the water and sprinkle the wet wood chips directly on the hot coals. Add enough hot water to the drip pan to fill it 1 or 2 inches deep and then insert the cooking rack in the grill.

Preparing the Sauce and Ribs

1 PREPARE THE SAUCE

Finely shred fresh ginger using a kitchen grater until you have 1 tablespoon. Mix the ginger with the barbecue sauce, orange juice concentrate, and soy sauce and set aside in the refrigerator.

2 SMOKE THE RIBS

Place the beef back ribs on the smoker rack. Cover and grill or smoke as directed. Brush the ribs generously with the barbecue sauce mixture during the last 15 minutes of cooking. Serve the remaining sauce with the ribs.

Garnish with orange wedges and squeeze the juice on the ribs for extra flavor.

Sirloin with Horseradish Sauce

English cooks produced a winning dish with this classic chophouse combination of smoky sliced beef and silky horseradish sauce.

GRILLING DETAILS

PREP: 15 minutes
SOAK: 1 hour
CHILL: 1 to 4 hours
GRILL: 32 minutes
MAKES: 6 servings

INGREDIENTS

4	cloves garlic, minced
¾	teaspoon ground cumin
½	teaspoon coarse black pepper
¼	teaspoon salt
1	2- to 2½-pound beef sirloin steak, cut 1½ inches thick
3	to 4 cups oak or hickory wood chips
⅓	cup dairy sour cream
2	tablespoons Dijon-style mustard
1	tablespoon snipped fresh chives
2	teaspoons prepared horseradish
¼	cup whipping cream, whipped

OLD VS. NEW

THE STEAK OF KINGS?

Legend has it that the sirloin steak received its name from English King Henry VIII, who so loved this cut of beef that he "knighted" it with the nickname "Sir Loin." In reality, the name probably derived from an Old French word "surlonge," which translates to "above loin." Today, sirloin is a good candidate to be the steak of grill-kings—it's both tasty and more affordable than other cuts of steak, making it a very popular choice for backyard cookouts.

1 For rub, in a small bowl combine garlic, cumin, pepper, and salt. Trim fat from steak. Place steak in a shallow dish. Sprinkle rub evenly over one side of steak; rub in with your fingers. Cover and refrigerate for 1 to 4 hours.

2 At least 1 hour before smoke cooking, soak wood chips in enough water to cover. Drain before using.

3 Drain wood chips. For a charcoal grill, arrange medium-hot coals around a drip pan. Test for medium heat above the drip pan. Sprinkle half of the drained wood chips over coals. Place steak, seasoned side up, on the grill rack over drip pan. Cover; grill until the steak is the desired doneness. Allow 32 to 36 minutes for medium rare (145°F) or 36 to 40 minutes for medium (160°F). Add additional coals and water as needed to maintain temperature and moisture. (For a gas grill, preheat grill. Reduce heat to medium. Adjust for indirect cooking. Add wood chips according to manufacturer's directions. Grill as above.)

4 Meanwhile, for sauce, in a small bowl stir together sour cream, mustard, chives, and horseradish. Fold in whipped cream.

5 To serve, thinly slice steak across the grain. Pass the sauce with steak.

Smoker Directions: Prepare steak as at left. Substitute 6 to 8 oak or hickory wood chunks for the wood chips. In a smoker arrange preheated coals, drained wood chunks, and water pan according to the manufacturer's directions. Pour water into pan. Place steak, seasoned side up, on the grill rack over water pan. Cover and smoke until steak is desired doneness. Allow about 2 hours for medium-rare doneness (145°F) or about 2½ hours for medium doneness (160°F). Add additional coals and water as needed to maintain temperature and moisture. Prepare sauce and serve as above.

Preparing the Grill

1

LIGHT THE CHARCOAL

Light the charcoal using one of the methods described on pages 22 to 23. Allow the charcoal to burn until it glows red-hot and is fully covered with a layer of white ash.

2

ADD THE DRIP PAN

Place a disposable aluminum drip pan in the middle of the charcoal grate. Arrange the hot coals in two equal piles on both sides of the drip pan. (If you light the charcoal with starter fluid or an electric starter, separate the charcoal into two piles with a long-handled tool such as a hoe and place the pan between the piles.)

3

ADD THE WOOD CHIPS

Soak the wood chips in water for at least 1 hour before using. Drain off the water and sprinkle the wet wood chips directly on the hot coals. Add enough hot water to the drip pan to fill it 1 or 2 inches deep and then insert the cooking rack in the grill.

Preparing the Steak and Sauce

1

SMOKE THE SIRLOIN

Apply the rub to the top side only of the steak and refrigerate it for 1 to 4 hours. Place the steak, seasoned side up, on the smoker rack and cook for 2 to 2½ hours. Add fresh charcoal, wood chunks, and water as needed.

2

PREPARE THE SAUCE

Using an electric mixer, beat the whipping cream in a bowl on high until soft peaks form. Combine the other sauce ingredients in another bowl and then fold in the whipped cream with a spatula, as shown. Serve the sauce over thin slices of the steak.

Serve with roasted potatoes and parsnips for an authentic English-style meal.

Smoked Meat Loaf

This ground beef favorite gets a pleasant buzz, thanks to hardwood smoke, chipotle pepper, and just a taste of red wine and bourbon.

GRILLING DETAILS

PREP: 30 minutes
SOAK: 1 hour
GRILL: 65 minutes
STAND: 15 minutes
MAKES: 6 servings

INGREDIENTS

- 3 to 4 cups hickory or mesquite wood chips
- 6 slices smoked bacon, cut up
- ½ cup chopped onion (1 medium)
- 1¼ cups soft bread crumbs
- ¼ cup milk
- 1 egg, slightly beaten
- 1 cup shredded Monterey Jack cheese (4 ounces)
- ¼ cup dry red wine
- 2 tablespoons Worcestershire sauce
- ½ teaspoon garlic salt
- ½ teaspoon ground chipotle chile pepper
- ½ teaspoon black pepper
- 1½ pounds ground beef
- ⅓ cup bottled barbecue sauce
- 1 tablespoon bourbon

BUYER'S GUIDE

WATCH THE FAT IN GROUND BEEF

Ground beef is tasty and an economical source of protein and other nutrients, but shop carefully if you are trying to limit fat in your diet. Regular ground beef—labeled as 73 percent lean—contains 17 grams of fat (6.5 grams of the least healthy saturated variety) per 3-ounce serving. Leaner varieties are more expensive but contain less fat and more protein per serving:

80 percent lean—15 grams fat/5.8 saturated
85 percent lean—13 grams fat/5.1 saturated
90 percent lean—11 grams fat/4.3 saturated
You should also consider using ground turkey, which has similar flavor and only 11 grams of total fat and 2.9 grams of saturated fat per serving.

1 At least 1 hour before smoke cooking, soak wood chips in enough water to cover.

2 In a large skillet cook bacon until crisp. Remove bacon, leaving 1 tablespoon drippings in the skillet. Drain bacon on paper towels and set aside. Cook onion in the drippings until tender.

3 Combine bread crumbs, milk, and egg. Add the cooked bacon, the onion, cheese, wine, Worcestershire sauce, garlic salt, chipotle chile pepper, and black pepper. Add ground beef; mix well. Divide the beef mixture in half, then pat into two 8×4×3-inch disposable foil loaf pans.

4 Drain wood chips. For a charcoal grill, arrange medium-hot coals around a drip pan. Test for medium heat above the pan. Sprinkle half of the wood chips over the coals. Place the foil pans on grill rack over drip pan. Cover and grill for 60 to 70 minutes or until done (160°F). (For a gas grill, preheat grill. Reduce heat to medium. Adjust for indirect cooking. Add wood chips according to manufacturer's directions. Grill as at left.)

5 Meanwhile, combine barbecue sauce and bourbon. Carefully drain fat from loaf pans. Spread sauce mixture over loaves. Grill for 5 minutes more. Remove pans from grill. Cover loosely with foil and let stand for 15 minutes before slicing.

Smoker Directions: Prepare meat loaf as directed. Substitute 6 to 8 hickory or mesquite wood chunks for the wood chips. In a smoker arrange preheated coals, drained wood chunks, and water pan according to the manufacturer's directions. Pour water into pan. Place the foil pans on grill rack over water pan. Cover and smoke for 1¼ to 1½ hours or until done (160°F). Meanwhile, combine barbecue sauce and bourbon. Carefully drain fat from loaf pans. Spread sauce mixture over loaves. Smoke for 15 minutes more. Remove pans from smoker. Cover loosely with foil and let stand for 15 minutes before slicing.

1

LIGHT THE CHARCOAL

Light the charcoal using one of the methods described on pages 22 to 23. Allow the charcoal to burn until it glows red-hot and is fully covered with a layer of white ash.

2

ADD THE DRIP PAN

Place a disposable aluminum drip pan in the middle of the charcoal grate. Arrange the hot coals in two equal piles on both sides of the drip pan. (If you light the charcoal with starter fluid or an electric starter, separate the charcoal into two piles with a long-handled tool such as a hoe and place the pan between the piles.)

3

ADD THE WOOD CHIPS

Soak the wood chips in water for at least 1 hour before using. Drain off the water and sprinkle the wet wood chips directly on the hot coals. Add enough hot water to the drip pan to fill it 1 or 2 inches deep and then insert the cooking rack in the grill.

5

SMOKING

Preparing the Meat Loaf

1

PRESS INTO PANS

Combine the meat loaf ingredients in a large bowl and mix well; divide the mixture in half. Place each half of the mixture into a disposable aluminum loaf pan and press gently to fill out the pan.

2

SMOKE AND DRAIN

Grill or smoke the two loaves as directed. Holding the meat loaf with a spatula, carefully drain the fat from each pan. Top each loaf with the barbecue sauce mixture and cook until the sauce is hot and starts to glaze meat loaves.

Cook the meat loaf until a quick-read thermometer registers 160°F.

Memphis-Style Smoked Pork

The bourbon- and hot pepper-spiked marinade and serving sauce kicks things up a notch for your taste buds.

GRILLING DETAILS

PREP: 45 minutes
SOAK: 1 hour
MARINATE: 24 hours
GRILL: 4 hours
STAND: 15 minutes
MAKES: 12 servings

INGREDIENTS

- 1   8-ounce can tomato sauce
- 1   cup finely chopped onion (1 large)
- ¾   cup bourbon or beef broth
- ⅔   cup cider vinegar
- ¼   cup packed brown sugar
- ¼   cup Worcestershire sauce
- ¼   teaspoon salt
- ¼   teaspoon black pepper
-     Dash bottled hot pepper sauce
- 1   4½- to 5-pound boneless pork shoulder roast
- 3   to 4 cups hickory wood chips

TOOL SAVVY

BASTING A MASTERPIECE

If you get serious about grilling, you are going to get serious about barbecue sauces, and that means you need the right tool to apply them. Some people try to get by with a wimpy short-handled kitchen basting brush or even a paintbrush, but they are ultimately disappointed. Buy yourself a barbecue basting brush with two important features:
1. A generous head of natural bristles (avoid nylon, which melts at high temperatures).
2. A long handle to protect you from the heat. Regardless of how long your handle is, always baste with oven mitts on to protect your hands and arms from burns.

1 For sauce, in a medium saucepan combine tomato sauce, onion, bourbon, ⅓ cup of the vinegar, the brown sugar, Worcestershire sauce, salt, black pepper, and hot pepper sauce. Bring to boiling; reduce heat. Simmer, covered, for 15 minutes. Remove from heat and cool completely. Reserve 1 cup of sauce; cover reserved sauce and chill.

2 Trim fat from meat. Place meat in a resealable large plastic bag set in a shallow dish. For marinade, mix the remaining sauce and ⅓ cup vinegar. Pour over meat; seal bag. Marinate in the refrigerator for 24 hours, turning bag occasionally.

3 At least 1 hour before smoke cooking, soak wood chips in enough water to cover. Drain meat, reserving marinade. Transfer marinade to a medium saucepan. Bring to boiling; set aside.

4 Drain wood chips. For a charcoal grill, arrange medium-hot coals around a drip pan. Test for medium heat above the drip pan. Sprinkle one-fourth of the drained wood chips over coals. Place meat on grill rack over drip pan. Cover; grill 4 hours or until meat is very tender and internal temperature is 160°F when tested with a quick-read thermometer,

basting occasionally with the marinade during the first 3 hours of grilling. Add coals, wood chips, and water as needed to maintain temperature, smoke, and moisture. (For a gas grill, preheat grill. Reduce heat to medium. Adjust for indirect cooking. Add wood chips according to manufacturer's directions. Grill as at left, except place meat on a rack in a roasting pan.)

5 Remove meat from grill. Cover meat with foil; let stand for 15 minutes before slicing. Meanwhile, in a small saucepan cook the reserved 1 cup sauce over medium heat until heated through. Slice meat. Serve sauce with meat.

Smoker Directions: Prepare sauce and meat as directed. Substitute 6 to 8 hickory wood chunks for the wood chips. In a smoker arrange preheated coals, drained wood chunks, and water pan according to the manufacturer's directions. Pour water into pan. Place meat on grill rack over water pan. Cover and smoke for 4½ to 5½ hours or until meat is tender and temperature is 160°F when tested with a quick-read thermometer, basting meat occasionally with the marinade during the first 3 hours of smoking. Remove meat from smoker; serve as above.

Preparing the Grill

1 LIGHT THE CHARCOAL

Light the charcoal using one of the methods described on pages 22 to 23. Allow the charcoal to burn until it glows red-hot and is fully covered with a layer of white ash.

2 ADD THE DRIP PAN

Place a disposable aluminum drip pan in the middle of the charcoal grate. Arrange the hot coals in two equal piles on both sides of the drip pan. (If you light the charcoal with starter fluid or an electric starter, separate the charcoal into two piles with a long-handled tool such as a hoe and place the pan between the piles.)

3 ADD THE WOOD CHIPS

Soak the wood chips in water for at least 1 hour before using. Drain off the water and sprinkle the wet wood chips directly on the hot coals. Add enough hot water to the drip pan to fill it 1 or 2 inches deep and then insert the cooking rack in the grill.

Preparing the Pork Roast

1 PLACE ROAST IN SMOKER

Marinate the roast for 24 hours in the refrigerator. Drain the marinade from the pork, place the liquid in a saucepan, and heat to boiling. Place the roast on the smoker or grill rack, as shown, and smoke or grill as directed.

2 BASTE WITH MARINADE

During the first 3 hours of cooking, baste the roast periodically with the boiled marinade. Continue cooking the roast until the internal temperature reaches 160°F, replenishing the charcoal, wood chips or chunks, and water as needed.

Use part of the sauce for marinating and basting and the rest for serving.

Carolina Pulled Pork BBQ

"Pulled" pork simply means that when the meat's done smoking, it's pulled apart into shreds and mixed with sauce before serving.

GRILLING DETAILS

PREP: 15 minutes
SOAK: 1 hour
GRILL: 4 hours
STAND: 15 minutes
MAKES: 12 servings

INGREDIENTS

- 8 to 10 cups hickory wood chips
- 1 4½- to 5-pound boneless pork shoulder roast
- 1½ teaspoons salt
- 1½ teaspoons black pepper
- 2 cups cider vinegar
- 3 tablespoons packed brown sugar (optional)
- 1 tablespoon salt
- 1 tablespoon crushed red pepper
- 12 hamburger buns, split and toasted (see tip, page 139)
- Purchased coleslaw
- Bottled hot pepper sauce (optional)

REAL WORLD

WHAT "BARBECUE" MEANS IN THE CAROLINAS

Ask most people about barbecue and they describe grilled or smoked meat covered in a thick, sweet, tomato-based sauce. Try to serve that kind of barbecue in the Carolinas and you're bound to have some disappointed people on your hands. In North Carolina and South Carolina, "barbecue" or "BBQ" refers to slow-cooking a big pork shoulder or whole hog and serving it with a thin, vinegar-based sauce. The tender, juicy, and oh-so-tasty pork cooked this way is quickly finding fans all across America.

1 At least 1 hour before smoke cooking, soak wood chips in enough water to cover.

2 Trim fat from meat. Sprinkle the 1½ teaspoons salt and the black pepper evenly over meat; pat in with your fingers. For sauce, in a bowl combine vinegar, brown sugar (if desired), the 1 tablespoon salt, and the crushed red pepper. Set aside.

3 Drain wood chips. For a charcoal grill, arrange medium-hot coals around a drip pan. Test for medium heat above the drip pan. Sprinkle one-fourth of the drained wood chips over coals. Place meat on grill rack over the drip pan. Cover; grill about 4 hours or until meat is very tender and internal temperature is 160°F when tested with a quick-read thermometer. Add additional coals, wood chips, and water as needed to maintain temperature, smoke, and moisture. (For a gas grill, preheat grill. Reduce heat to medium. Adjust for indirect cooking. Add wood chips according to manufacturer's directions. Grill as above, except place meat on a rack in a roasting pan.)

4 Remove meat from grill. Cover meat with foil; let stand for 15 minutes. Using 2 forks, gently shred the meat into long, thin strands. Add enough of the sauce to moisten the meat.

5 Serve shredded meat on toasted buns. Top meat with coleslaw. Pass the remaining sauce and, if desired, hot pepper sauce.

Smoker Directions: Prepare meat as directed. In a smoker arrange preheated coals, drained wood chunks, and water pan according to the manufacturer's directions. Pour water into pan. Place meat on the grill rack over water pan. Cover and smoke for 4 to 5 hours or until meat is very tender. Add additional coals and water as needed to maintain temperature and moisture. Remove meat from smoker; continue as directed above.

Preparing the Grill

1 LIGHT THE CHARCOAL

Light the charcoal using one of the methods described on pages 22 to 23. Allow the charcoal to burn until it glows red-hot and is fully covered with a layer of white ash.

2 ADD THE DRIP PAN

Place a disposable aluminum drip pan in the middle of the charcoal grate. Arrange the hot coals in two equal piles on both sides of the drip pan. (If you light the charcoal with starter fluid or an electric starter, separate the charcoal into two piles with a long-handled tool such as a hoe and place the pan between the piles.)

3 ADD THE WOOD CHIPS

Soak the wood chips in water for at least 1 hour before using. Drain off the water and sprinkle the wet wood chips directly on the hot coals. Add enough hot water to the drip pan to fill it 1 or 2 inches deep and then insert the cooking rack in the grill.

Preparing the Pork

1 PULL THE PORK

Grill or smoke the shoulder roast about 4 hours, until the meat is very tender. Pull the meat from the smoker, cover it with foil, and let it stand for 15 minutes. Using two forks, shred the meat into long, thin strands, as shown. Moisten with some of the sauce.

2 TOAST THE BUNS

If you are smoking in a grill, keep the fire burning. Place the buns, cut side down, on the cooking rack directly over the heat. Grill until lightly browned. Top each bun with the pulled pork.

For Carolina authenticity, top your sandwich with extra sauce and coleslaw.

Sugar-and-Spice Pork Ribs

Hickory gives pork a truly distinctive flavor. Some people prefer other hardwoods, but many pit masters would never dream of using anything but hickory with smoked pig.

GRILLING DETAILS

PREP: 20 minutes
CHILL: 8 to 24 hours
SOAK: 1 hour
GRILL: 1¼ hours
MAKES: 6 servings

INGREDIENTS

- ⅓ cup sugar
- 2 tablespoons paprika
- 1 tablespoon seasoned salt
- 1 tablespoon hickory-flavor salt
- 2 teaspoons garlic powder
- 2 teaspoons black pepper
- 4 pounds pork loin back ribs
- 4 cups hickory wood chips
- 1 cup bottled barbecue sauce

WORK SMARTER

CHIPS OR CHUNKS?

Does it really matter whether you generate smoke with large, chunk-size pieces of hardwood or tiny, chip-size pieces? Yes, it does, depending on what type of grill you are using. If you are working with either a charcoal-fired smoker or grill, or a gas grill with a smoker box, you will find it easier to work with smaller chips. They burn more readily in these devices and can be easily replenished. When smoking on a gas grill without a smoker box, or when fueling a vertical water smoker exclusively with wood, you'll want to use large chunks of hardwood, which will be easier to handle, last longer, and give you better results.

1 For rub, in a small bowl combine sugar, paprika, seasoned salt, hickory-flavor salt, garlic powder, and pepper. Remove ¼ cup of the rub. (Store remaining rub in a tightly covered container for another use.)

2 Pull membrane off the back of the ribs; trim fat from ribs. Sprinkle the ¼ cup rub evenly over both sides of ribs; pat in with your fingers. Wrap ribs tightly in plastic wrap; refrigerate for 8 to 24 hours.

3 At least 1 hour before grilling, soak wood chips in enough water to cover.

4 Drain wood chips. For a charcoal grill, arrange medium-hot coals around a drip pan. Test for medium heat above the drip pan. Sprinkle half of the wood chips over the hot coals. Place ribs, bone sides down, on grill rack over drip pan. Cover; grill for 1¼ to 1½ hours or until ribs are tender; brush

once with barbecue sauce during the last 15 minutes of grilling. Add additional coals and wood chips as needed to maintain temperature and smoke. (For a gas grill, preheat grill. Reduce heat to medium. Adjust for indirect cooking. Add wood chips according to manufacturer's directions. Grill as at left.)

5 In a small saucepan heat remaining barbecue sauce until bubbly; pass with ribs.

Smoker Directions: Prepare as at left. Substitute 6 to 8 hickory wood chunks for the wood chips. In a smoker arrange preheated coals, drained wood chunks, and water pan according to manufacturer's directions. Pour water into pan. Place ribs, bone sides down, on grill rack over water pan. Cover and smoke for 3 to 4 hours or until ribs are tender; brush once with barbecue sauce during the last 15 minutes of smoke cooking. Add additional coals and water as needed to maintain temperature and moisture.

Preparing the Grill

1

LIGHT THE CHARCOAL

Light the charcoal using one of the methods described on pages 22 to 23. Allow the charcoal to burn until it glows red-hot and is fully covered with a layer of white ash.

2

ADD THE DRIP PAN

Place a disposable aluminum drip pan in the middle of the charcoal grate. Arrange the hot coals in two equal piles on both sides of the drip pan. (If you light the charcoal with starter fluid or an electric starter, separate the charcoal into two piles with a long-handled tool such as a hoe and place the pan between the piles.)

3

ADD THE WOOD CHIPS

Soak the wood chips in water for at least 1 hour before using. Drain off the water and sprinkle the wet wood chips directly on the hot coals. Add enough hot water to the drip pan to fill it 1 or 2 inches deep and then insert the cooking rack in the grill.

5

SMOKING

Preparing the Ribs

1

TRIM THE RIBS

Pull the membrane off the back of the ribs, using a sharp knife to free the membrane from the meat. Use the knife to trim all the excess fat from the ribs.

2

APPLY THE RUB

Sprinkle the rub mixture evenly over both sides of the ribs. Rub the spices into the surface of the meat with your fingertips. Wrap the ribs tightly in a large piece of plastic wrap, as shown. Refrigerate the ribs for 8 to 24 hours before smoking.

Baste and serve with your favorite bottled barbecue sauce.

Smokin' Jerk Chicken

Smoke from allspice tree wood is a mainstay in authentic Jamaican jerk. Fruit woods provide similar smoked flavor, especially coupled with traditional jerk seasonings.

GRILLING DETAILS

PREP: 15 minutes
SOAK: 1 hour
MARINATE: 1 to 4 hours
GRILL: 50 minutes
MAKES: 6 servings

INGREDIENTS

3	pounds meaty chicken pieces (breasts, thighs, and drumsticks)
½	cup tomato juice
⅓	cup finely chopped onion (1 small)
2	tablespoons water
2	tablespoons lime juice
1	tablespoon cooking oil
1	tablespoon Pickapeppa sauce (optional)
4	cloves garlic, minced
½	teaspoon salt
3	to 6 cups fruit wood chips
1	to 2 tablespoons Jamaican jerk seasoning
	Lime wedges

CLOSER LOOK

WHOM ARE YOU CALLING A JERK?

"Jerk" refers both to a style of cooking and a dry seasoning blend for meat (usually chicken or pork) that originated on the Caribbean island of Jamaica. It's not actually one specific mix (each chef might have his or her own recipe), but it generally contains a mixture of most or all of the following ingredients: peppers (black, red, and/or chile), thyme, cinnamon, ginger, allspice, cloves, garlic, salt, and onions. You can buy jerk seasoning in the spice section of most grocery stores.

1 If desired, remove skin from chicken. Place chicken in a resealable large plastic bag set in a deep dish. For marinade, in a small bowl combine tomato juice, onion, water, lime juice, oil, Pickapeppa sauce (if desired), garlic, and salt. Pour over chicken; seal bag. Marinate in the refrigerator for 1 to 4 hours, turning bag occasionally.

2 At least 1 hour before smoke cooking, soak wood chunks in enough water to cover.

3 Drain chicken, discarding marinade. Sprinkle jerk seasoning evenly over chicken; pat in with your fingers.

4 Drain wood chips. For a charcoal grill, arrange medium-hot coals around a drip pan. Test for medium heat above the drip pan. Sprinkle wood chips over coals. Place chicken, bone sides up, on grill rack over drip pan. Cover and grill for 50 to 60 minutes or until chicken is tender and juices run clear (170°F for breasts; 180°F for thighs and drumsticks). (For a gas grill, preheat grill. Reduce heat to medium. Adjust for indirect cooking. Add wood chips according to manufacturer's directions. Grill as at left.) Serve chicken with lime wedges.

Smoker Directions: Prepare chicken as directed. Substitute 6 to 8 fruit wood chunks for the wood chips. In a smoker arrange preheated coals, drained wood chunks, and water pan according to the manufacturer's directions. Pour water into pan. Place chicken on the grill rack over water pan. Cover and smoke for 1½ to 2 hours or until chicken is tender and juices run clear (170°F for breasts; 180°F for thighs and drumsticks). Add additional coals and water as needed to maintain temperature and moisture. Serve as directed.

Preparing the Grill

1 LIGHT THE CHARCOAL

Light the charcoal using one of the methods described on pages 22 to 23. Allow the charcoal to burn until it glows red-hot and is fully covered with a layer of white ash.

2 ADD THE DRIP PAN

Place a disposable aluminum drip pan in the middle of the charcoal grate. Arrange the hot coals in two equal piles on both sides of the drip pan. (If you light the charcoal with starter fluid or an electric starter, separate the charcoal into two piles with a long-handled tool such as a hoe and place the pan between the piles.)

3 ADD THE WOOD CHIPS

Soak the wood chips in water for at least 1 hour before using. Drain off the water and sprinkle the wet wood chips directly on the hot coals. Add enough hot water to the drip pan to fill it 1 or 2 inches deep and then insert the cooking rack in the grill.

Preparing the Chicken

1 PREPARE THE MARINADE

Mince the garlic, as shown, by first slicing each clove and then chopping the slices into tiny pieces with a steady up-and-down motion. Combine with the remaining marinade ingredients, pour over the chicken pieces, and marinate in the refrigerator for 1 to 4 hours.

2 APPLY THE RUB

Drain and discard the marinade. Arrange the chicken pieces, meat side up, in a shallow dish and sprinkle with the jerk seasoning. Rub the seasoning in with the tips of your fingers. Grill or smoke the chicken as directed.

Apple or cherry smoke will give the chicken an authentic jerk flavor.

Smoked Curried Chicken

With the right mix of spices and your smoker, you can transport the authentic taste of India from around the world to your backyard.

GRILLING DETAILS

PREP: 15 minutes
CHILL: 4 to 8 hours
SOAK: 1 hour
GRILL: 1¼ hours
STAND: 10 minutes
MAKES: 4 servings

INGREDIENTS

- 1 3- to 3½-pound whole broiler-fryer chicken
- 1 tablespoon olive oil
- 2 teaspoons curry powder
- 1 teaspoon garlic salt
- ½ teaspoon ground cardamom
- ½ teaspoon garam masala
- ½ teaspoon ground cumin
- ¼ teaspoon ground cinnamon
- 3 to 4 cups apple, orange, or cherry wood chips

REAL WORLD

CURRY VS. CURRY POWDER

Curry isn't a single spice but rather a general term referring to spicy, sauced dishes—usually served over rice—from south Asia, especially India. Most curries are seasoned with curry powder, which is an aromatic mixture of ground spices, and that's what you will buy at your local food store. There are an infinite number of curry powders, but most contain some mixture of cardamom, chiles, cinnamon, cloves, coriander, cumin, fennel seed, fenugreek, mace, nutmeg, pepper, saffron, tamarind, and turmeric.

1 Rinse the inside of the chicken; pat dry with paper towels. Brush the entire surface of the chicken with the oil. For the rub, in a small bowl combine curry powder, garlic salt, cardamom, garam masala, cumin, and cinnamon. Sprinkle rub evenly over chicken; pat in with your fingers. Skewer the neck skin to the back. Tie legs to tail. Twist wing tips under back. Place chicken in a shallow pan. Cover and refrigerate for 4 to 8 hours.

2 At least 1 hour before smoke cooking, soak wood chips in enough water to cover.

3 Insert a meat thermometer into the center of an inside thigh muscle, making sure tip does not touch bone.

4 Drain wood chips. For a charcoal grill, arrange medium-hot coals around a drip pan. Test for medium heat above the pan. Sprinkle wood chips over coals. Place chicken, breast side up, on grill rack over the drip pan. Cover and grill for 1¼ to 1½ hours or until thermometer registers 180°F. Add additional coals, wood chips, and water as needed to maintain temperature, smoke, and moisture. (For a gas grill, preheat grill. Reduce heat to medium. Adjust for indirect cooking. Add wood chips according to manufacturer's directions. Grill as at left.)

5 Remove chicken from grill. Cover with foil and let stand for 10 minutes before carving.

Smoker Directions: Prepare chicken as directed. Substitute 6 to 8 apple, orange, or cherry wood chunks for the wood chips. In a smoker arrange preheated coals, drained wood chunks, and water pan according to the manufacturer's directions. Pour water into pan. Place chicken, breast side up, on grill rack over water pan. Cover and smoke for 2½ to 3 hours or until thermometer registers 180°F. Add additional coals and water as needed to maintain temperature and moisture.

Preparing the Grill

1

LIGHT THE CHARCOAL

Light the charcoal using one of the methods described on pages 22 to 23. Allow the charcoal to burn until it glows red-hot and is fully covered with a layer of white ash.

2

ADD THE DRIP PAN

Place a disposable aluminum drip pan in the middle of the charcoal grate. Arrange the hot coals in two equal piles on both sides of the drip pan. (If you light the charcoal with starter fluid or an electric starter, separate the charcoal into two piles with a long-handled tool such as a hoe and place the pan between the piles.)

3

ADD THE WOOD CHIPS

Soak the wood chips in water for at least 1 hour before using. Drain off the water and sprinkle the wet wood chips directly on the hot coals. Add enough hot water to the drip pan to fill it 1 or 2 inches deep and then insert the cooking rack in the grill.

Preparing the Chicken

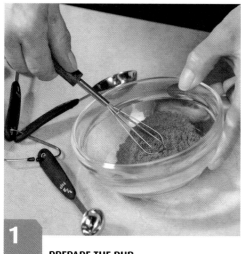

1

PREPARE THE RUB

In a small bowl, combine the curry powder, garlic salt, cardamom, garam masala, cumin, and cinnamon. Mix thoroughly, using a small wire whisk or a fork to break up any lumps and fully blend the spices.

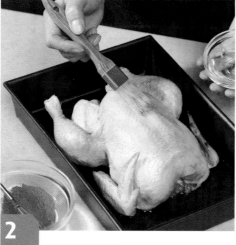

2

APPLY THE RUB

Place the rinsed and dried chicken in a shallow pan and brush its surface with olive oil. Sprinkle the rub evenly over the chicken and work it gently into the skin with your fingertips. Cover and refrigerate for 4 to 8 hours before smoking.

Serve with cooked rice and fresh fruit for an Indian-style meal.

Hickory-Smoked Turkey

The big bird in this recipe is going to take several hours to smoke—make sure you're ready to add fresh fuel to the fire and water to the pan throughout the cooking period.

INGREDIENTS

- 3 to 4 cups hickory wood chips
- 1 10-pound whole turkey
- 2 tablespoons olive oil
- 1½ to 2 tablespoons snipped fresh thyme or 1½ to 2 teaspoons dried thyme, crushed
- 1½ to 2 tablespoons snipped fresh sage or 1½ to 2 teaspoons dried sage, crushed
- 1 teaspoon salt
- ¼ teaspoon black pepper

SAFETY ALERT

Smoking cooks foods at low temperatures, and you run the risk of allowing your turkey to remain for long periods at temperatures that could encourage bacterial growth. Because of this, avoid trying to smoke large turkeys, especially those that are larger than 12 pounds. In addition, never stuff a turkey that is going to be smoked; it can take too long to reach a safe eating temperature. Finally, always use a meat thermometer to test your turkey for doneness. Do not remove the turkey from the smoker until the temperature of the meat on the inner thigh reaches 180°F.

1 At least 1 hour before smoke cooking, soak wood chips in enough water to cover.

2 Rinse the inside of the turkey, then pat dry with paper towels. Brush the entire surface of the turkey with the oil. For rub, combine thyme, sage, salt, and pepper. Sprinkle rub over the surface and cavity of the turkey; pat in with your fingers. Skewer the neck skin to the back. Tuck ends of drumsticks under the band of skin or tie to tail. Twist wing tips under back. Insert a meat thermometer into the center of an inside thigh muscle, making sure tip does not touch bone.

3 Drain wood chips. For a charcoal grill, arrange medium-hot coals around a drip pan. Test for medium heat above the drip pan. Sprinkle half of the wood chips over hot coals. Place turkey, breast side up, on grill rack over drip pan. Cover; grill for 2¾ to 3½ hours or until thermometer registers 180°F. Add additional coals, water, and wood chips as needed to maintain temperature, moisture, and smoke. Cut band of skin or string between legs after about 2 hours of cooking. (For a gas grill, preheat grill. Reduce heat to medium. Adjust for indirect cooking. Add wood chips according to manufacturer's directions. Grill as at left.) Remove turkey from grill and let stand for 15 minutes before carving.

Smoker Directions: Prepare turkey as at left. Substitute 6 to 8 hickory wood chunks for the wood chips. In a smoker arrange preheated coals, drained wood chunks, and water pan according to the manufacturer's directions. Pour water into pan. Place turkey, breast side up, on grill rack over water pan. Cover and smoke for 4½ to 5 hours or until thermometer registers 180°F. Add additional coals and water as needed to maintain temperature and moisture. Cut band of skin or string between legs after about 3½ hours of smoking. Remove turkey from smoker. Cover with foil and let stand for 15 minutes before carving.

Preparing the Grill

1 LIGHT THE CHARCOAL

Light the charcoal using one of the methods described on pages 22 to 23. Allow the charcoal to burn until it glows red-hot and is fully covered with a layer of white ash.

2 ADD THE DRIP PAN

Place a disposable aluminum drip pan in the middle of the charcoal grate. Arrange the hot coals in two equal piles on both sides of the drip pan. (If you light the charcoal with starter fluid or an electric starter, separate the charcoal into two piles with a long-handled tool such as a hoe and place the pan between the piles.)

3 ADD THE WOOD CHIPS

Soak the wood chips in water for at least 1 hour before using. Drain off the water and sprinkle the wet wood chips directly on the hot coals. Add enough hot water to the drip pan to fill it 1 or 2 inches deep and then insert the cooking rack in the grill.

5

SMOKING

Preparing the Turkey

1 MIX THE RUB

If using fresh thyme and sage leaves, snip the leaves into small pieces until you have 1½ to 2 tablespoons of each. Crush the herbs with your fingers to release extra flavor. Combine with the remaining rub ingredients, sprinkle the mixture over the turkey, and rub it in with your fingers.

2 SMOKE THE TURKEY

Smoke the turkey, breast side up, for 4½ to 5 hours, adding charcoal, water, and wood chips as needed. After 3½ hours, use scissors to cut the skin band or string, as shown, to free the drumsticks. Cook until the internal temperature of the thigh reaches 180°F.

Cover the turkey with foil and let it rest 15 minutes before carving.

Honey-Bourbon Salmon

Talk about bringing the world to your plate—juicy salmon steaks from the Pacific Ocean topped with a sauce boast hints of Asia and Kentucky, U.S.A.

GRILLING DETAILS

PREP: 10 minutes
SOAK: 1 hour
MARINATE: 1 hour
GRILL: 14 to 18 minutes
MAKES: 4 servings

INGREDIENTS

- 3 to 4 cups apple or alder wood chips
- 4 6-ounce fresh or frozen salmon steaks, cut 1 inch thick
- ¾ cup bourbon
- ½ cup packed brown sugar
- 2 tablespoons honey
- 2 teaspoons soy sauce
- ½ teaspoon ground ginger
- ¼ teaspoon pepper

GOOD IDEA

SALMON IS HEART-HEALTHY FOOD

Grill chefs have reason to celebrate whenever they can find a food that tastes great and is also really good for you. Salmon is one of those foods. The oils in salmon have been shown to contain high concentrations of omega-3 fatty acids, which have been proven to lower blood pressure, decrease the incidence of heart disease, and reduce the risk of heart attacks and stroke. There is also some evidence that omega-3 fatty acids can help reduce depression and relieve the pain of rheumatoid arthritis.

1 At least 1 hour before smoke cooking, soak wood chips in enough water to cover.

2 Thaw fish, if frozen. Rinse fish; pat dry with paper towels. Place fish in a resealable large plastic bag set in a shallow dish. For marinade, combine bourbon, brown sugar, honey, soy sauce, ginger, and pepper. Pour over fish; seal bag. Marinate in the refrigerator for 1 hour, turning bag occasionally. Drain fish, reserving marinade.

3 Drain wood chips. For a charcoal grill, arrange medium-hot coals around a drip pan. Test for medium heat above the drip pan. Sprinkle wood chips over coals. Place fish on greased grill rack over the drip pan. Cover; grill for 14 to 18 minutes or until fish flakes easily when tested with a fork. (For a gas grill, preheat grill. Reduce heat to medium. Adjust for indirect cooking. Add wood chips according to manufacturer's directions. Grill as above.)

4 Meanwhile, transfer marinade to a small saucepan. Bring to boiling; reduce heat. Simmer, uncovered, for 5 to 10 minutes or until slightly thickened. Before serving, brush marinade over fish.

Smoker Directions: Prepare salmon as at left. Substitute 6 to 8 apple or alder wood chunks for the wood chips. In a smoker arrange preheated coals, drained wood chunks, and water pan according to manufacturer's directions. Pour water into pan. Place fish on greased grill rack over water pan. Cover and smoke for 45 to 60 minutes or until fish flakes easily when tested with a fork.

5

SMOKING

Preparing the Grill

1 LIGHT THE CHARCOAL

Light the charcoal using one of the methods described on pages 22 to 23. Allow the charcoal to burn until it glows red-hot and is fully covered with a layer of white ash.

2 ADD THE DRIP PAN

Place a disposable aluminum drip pan in the middle of the charcoal grate. Arrange the hot coals in two equal piles on both sides of the drip pan. (If you light the charcoal with starter fluid or an electric starter, separate the charcoal into two piles with a long-handled tool such as a hoe and place the pan between the piles.)

3 ADD THE WOOD CHIPS

Soak the wood chips in water for at least 1 hour before using. Drain off the water and sprinkle the wet wood chips directly on the hot coals. Add enough hot water to the drip pan to fill it 1 or 2 inches deep and then insert the cooking rack in the grill.

Preparing the Salmon

1 MARINATE THE FISH

Rinse the salmon steaks and pat them dry with paper towels. Place the steaks in a resealable plastic bag, pour the marinade over the steaks, and place in the refrigerator for 1 hour. Drain the marinade and reserve it.

2 SMOKE THE FISH

Place the salmon on the grill rack and grill for 14 to 18 minutes or until the fish flakes easily. Meanwhile, heat the marinade to boiling in a small saucepan, reduce the heat, and simmer for 5 to 10 minutes. Brush the sauce on the salmon and serve.

Alder is the traditional wood for smoking salmon in the Pacific Northwest.

Fennel-Stuffed Trout

Because of its tradition as the main course in many shoreside or campfire meals, fresh whole trout tastes especially good cooked over a smoky fire.

GRILLING DETAILS

PREP: 30 minutes
SOAK: 1 hour
GRILL: 20 minutes
MAKES: 4 servings

INGREDIENTS

- 3 to 4 cups alder or pecan wood chips
- 4 10- to 12-ounce fresh or frozen dressed trout or other fish
- 2 fennel bulbs
- 1 clove garlic, minced
- 1/4 teaspoon salt
- 1/8 teaspoon black pepper
- 2 tablespoons butter or margarine
- 1 tablespoon snipped fresh parsley
- 3 tablespoons butter or margarine
- 1 tablespoon lemon juice
- 1/2 teaspoon dried rosemary, crushed
  Dash black pepper
  Lemon slices (optional)

CLOSER LOOK

TRIPLE-THREAT FENNEL

Fennel is a plant that is native to southern Europe but is now grown throughout the world. It has spread so much throughout the U.S. that some consider it a weed. In the kitchen, fennel has a better reputation and three distinct uses: The bulbs (which look like fat, plump bunches of celery) are used as a food, the leaves are used as an herb, and the seeds are used as a spice. Fennel has a mild anise, or licorice-like, flavor.

1 At least 1 hour before grilling, soak wood chips in enough water to cover.

2 Thaw fish, if frozen. For stuffing, cut off and discard upper stalks of fennel. Remove any wilted outer layers; cut off a thin slice from bases. Chop fennel bulbs (should have about 2 1/2 cups). In a medium saucepan cook and stir fennel, garlic, salt, and the 1/8 teaspoon pepper in the 2 tablespoons butter about 10 minutes or until fennel is tender. Stir in parsley; set aside.

3 For sauce, in a small saucepan combine the 3 tablespoons butter, the lemon juice, rosemary, and the dash pepper. Heat through.

4 Rinse fish; pat dry with paper towels. Spoon the stuffing into the fish cavities. Skewer the cavities closed with wooden toothpicks. Brush fish with some of the sauce.

5 Drain wood chips. For a charcoal grill, arrange medium-hot coals around a drip pan. Test for medium heat above the drip pan. Add drained wood chips to coals. Place fish on greased grill rack over drip pan. Cover; grill for 20 to 25 minutes or until fish flakes easily when tested with a fork, brushing once with sauce halfway through grilling. (For a gas grill, preheat grill. Reduce heat to medium. Adjust for indirect cooking. Add wood chips according to manufacturer's directions. Grill as above.)

6 Discard any remaining sauce. Remove the toothpicks from fish. If desired, serve fish with lemon wedges.

Smoker Directions: Prepare trout as at left. Substitute 6 to 8 alder or pecan wood chunks for the wood chips. In a smoker arrange preheated coals, drained wood chunks, and water pan according to the manufacturer's directions. Pour water into pan. Place fish on the greased grill rack over water pan. Cover and smoke for 1 1/2 to 2 hours or until fish flakes easily when tested with a fork, brushing once with sauce halfway through cooking. Add additional coals and water as needed to maintain temperature and moisture. Discard any remaining sauce.

Preparing the Grill

1 LIGHT THE CHARCOAL
Light the charcoal using one of the methods described on pages 22 to 23. Allow the charcoal to burn until it glows red-hot and is fully covered with a layer of white ash.

2 ADD THE DRIP PAN
Place a disposable aluminum drip pan in the middle of the charcoal grate. Arrange the hot coals in two equal piles on both sides of the drip pan. (If you light the charcoal with starter fluid or an electric starter, separate the charcoal into two piles with a long-handled tool such as a hoe and place the pan between the piles.)

3 ADD THE WOOD CHIPS
Soak the wood chips in water for at least 1 hour before using. Drain off the water and sprinkle the wet wood chips directly on the hot coals. Add enough hot water to the drip pan to fill it 1 or 2 inches deep and then insert the cooking rack in the grill.

Prepare the Stuffing

1 CHOP THE FENNEL
Trim the leaves and stems from two fresh fennel bulbs. Slice and chop the bulbs into small pieces, as shown. Cook the fennel and minced garlic, salt, and pepper in the butter about 10 minutes. Stir in the parsley.

2 STUFF THE TROUT
Rinse each fish, inside and out, with water and pat dry with paper towels. Using a spoon, stuff the cavity of each trout with the cooked fennel mixture, as shown. Close the cavity with toothpicks, brush the fish with sauce, and grill for 20 to 25 minutes.

Serve with fresh lemon wedges for a squeeze of extra flavor.

Frying

rying is the latest craze in outdoor cooking, and it's sweeping across the country. No, frying isn't grilling, but it does involve cooking over an open flame, and because it is propane-powered, gas grillers are comfortable with the fuel system. Most important, once you taste your first deep-fried turkey, you'll understand why frying has a well-earned place in the flavorful family of outdoor cooking, right alongside grilling and smoking.

The history of turkey fryers goes back about 50 years or so, and the tradition evolved alongside the Southern backyard barbecues. For years, fry enthusiasts rigged their own cooking setups—with very mixed results—but by the 1970s and 1980s companies started developing and selling backyard fryers that delivered great food every time. Soon the whole country, tired of the same old roasted (often dry) holiday bird, was embracing the turkey-frying phenomenon.

Backyard frying takes technique, but the results offer unique table fare. Two things jump to the forefront when you talk about deep-fried turkey: flavor and juiciness. While roasted turkey can be dry and a little flavorless, deep-frying solves these problems in a big way, especially the juicy part. Because it is a quicker cooking process than roasting and the turkey is enveloped in oil, the bird's juices are trapped inside, making for

Chapter 6 Recipes

a moist, tasty meal. And the flavor? We all know that fried foods are tasty, but add the right spices through rubs or even injection and the taste can be out of this world.

As outdoor cooks have embraced fryers and started to experiment with them, they've discovered that turkeys are only the tip of the frying iceberg. Chicken is a natural, and seafood, pork chops, and beef roasts are all candidates for the fryer. Plus, this cooking tool is versatile enough that you could use one to prepare an entire meal. Fried appetizers, vegetables, potatoes, even desserts can be cooked in a snap in a backyard fryer, and with memorable results.

As popular as fryers have become, they are not foolproof and require strict attention to safety. The hot oil can burn the chef, and it's a legitimate fire hazard—every holiday season you hear stories about people who set their deck or garage on fire with a turkey fryer. These horror stories are the exception; frying is safe if you purchase quality equipment, follow the instructions carefully, use the appropriate tools and safety gear, and focus your attention on the fryer and the food inside. With a little effort, you can turn out memorable meals that will make you wonder why you would cook a turkey any other way.

How to Fry in a Fryer

The first thing to remember about working with a turkey fryer is that it's outdoor cooking, and you need to select an appropriate, safe spot for the job. Garages are not safe for fryer cooking and neither are wooden decks—too much fire risk. Instead, look for a level dirt or grassy area at least 10 feet away from the nearest structure or brushy vegetation. A concrete patio is a safe surface, but you will probably stain it with spilled grease. If you must cook on concrete, cover the area with sand to absorb any oil spills.

Check the level in your propane tank and make sure you have enough fuel for approximately 1¹/₂ hours of cooking. Connect the propane to the fryer burner following the manufacturer's instructions. Before lighting the burner, place the cooking pot on the stand, make sure it is

stable, and then fill it with the oil of your choice. A number of oils are appropriate for deep-fryer cooking, but they have different smoking points. Peanut oil, recommended for the recipes in this chapter, has a smoking point of 410°F. Monitor the temperature carefully to ensure it never reaches the smoking point.

Fill the cooking pot with oil until there is about 6 inches of space at the top of the pot. When frying large items such as turkeys, determine how much oil you will need by placing the food in the pot and adding water to the correct depth; remove the turkey and mark the depth on the side of the pot. Fill the pot with oil to the line (see page 155). Insert a deep-fry thermometer into the oil. Light the burner, turn it to high, and heat the oil while you carefully watch the temperature rise. When the

temperature reaches the correct level for cooking, turn the burner off. Don the appropriate safety gear (mitts, apron, and goggles) and then very slowly lower your food into the hot oil. Relight the burner only after the food is safely in place. Monitor the temperature while the food cooks, adjusting the burner to keep the oil in the appropriate cooking range. Never place a lid on the pot while food is cooking.

When the cooking time is complete, turn the burner off, make sure all your safety gear is in place, and slowly lift the food out of the pot. Place the food and cooking rack on a heat-resistant surface and check the internal temperature with a quick-read thermometer. If the food needs additional cooking time, return it to the pot and relight the burner.

Fryer Safety and Cooking Tips

▲ Always remove the giblets and neck from the turkey body cavity—and never stuff it—before frying.

▲ The small twist knob to the right of the red regulator controls the burner level on the fryer.

◀ The vented lid (which stays off while food fries) prevents dangerous steam buildup while the oil heats.

▶ This view down into a fryer stand shows the propane-fueled burner and the triangle-shape brackets that support the cooking pot.

▲ Place the turkey in the cooking pot and start filling it with water to determine the amount of cooking oil you'll need.

▲ Add just enough water to cover the turkey. Lift it from the pot and let the excess water drain back in.

▲ Mark the water line with a waterproof marker. Empty the water and fill the pot with oil to the mark.

Cajun Deep-Fried Turkey

Turkey frying first gained popularity in Cajun country, so this spicy Louisiana-style bird is about as authentic—and as tasty—as deep-fried turkey gets.

GRILLING DETAILS

PREP: 30 minutes
FRY: 24 minutes
STAND: 15 minutes
MAKES: 10 to 12 servings

INGREDIENTS

1	8- to 10-pound turkey
	Peanut oil
1½	teaspoons salt
1½	teaspoons sweet paprika
¾	teaspoon dried thyme, crushed
¾	teaspoon black pepper
½	teaspoon garlic powder
½	teaspoon onion powder
¼	teaspoon cayenne pepper

GOOD IDEA

CHOOSING HEALTHIER OILS

Most dietary experts will tell you that frying is not the healthiest way to cook food, but if you choose to fry, you can make healthy choices with regards to your frying oil. When selecting an oil, use only pure unblended vegetable oils and choose one that is low in saturated fats, high in monounsaturated fats, and low in polyunsaturated fats. Among the oils commonly used for deep-frying, peanut and canola oils easily get the highest marks when evaluated on these criteria.

1 Remove neck and giblets from turkey. Rinse the inside of the turkey and pat dry with paper towels. If present, remove and discard plastic leg holder and pop-up timer.

2 Preheat oil to 350°F.

3 For the rub, in a small bowl combine salt, paprika, thyme, black pepper, garlic powder, onion powder, and cayenne pepper. Slip your fingers between the skin and the meat to loosen the skin over the breast and leg areas. Lift turkey skin and spread some of the rub directly over breast, thigh, and drumstick meat. Season body cavity with any remaining rub. Tuck the ends of the drumsticks under the band of skin across the tail or tie legs to tail with 100-percent-cotton string. Twist wing tips under back.

4 Place turkey on cooking rack as shown on page 157. Slowly lower turkey into hot oil, being cautious of splattering oil. Maintain oil temperature around 350°F. Fry turkey for 24 to 30 minutes (3 minutes per pound). Remove turkey from hot oil to check doneness. Insert a quick-read meat thermometer into the meaty part of the thigh. Turkey is done when the thermometer registers 180°F. (If the turkey hasn't reached 180°F when you check for doneness, remove the thermometer and slowly lower the turkey back into the oil. Fry 3 to 5 minutes more and check the temperature again.)

5 Remove turkey from hot oil and drain on a wire rack. Let stand for 15 minutes before carving.

Preparing the Fryer

1

ADD THE OIL

Pour the oil in a cool cooking pot, filling it to a pre-marked level that will cover your food but leave at least 6 inches from the top of the pot. Insert a deep-fry thermometer into the oil.

2

HEAT THE OIL

Turn on the propane and light the burner. Turn the burner to its highest setting and carefully monitor the oil temperature as it heats. When the cooking temperature is reached (usually 350°F), turn off the burner.

3

ADD THE FOOD

While wearing cooking mitts, goggles, and an apron, carefully and slowly lower the turkey or cooking basket into the hot oil. Relight the burner, carefully monitor the thermometer, and adjust the burner to maintain the appropriate cooking temperature.

Preparing the Turkey

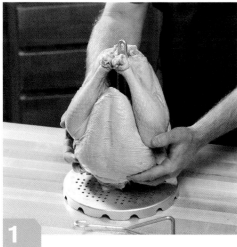

1

PLACE TURKEY ON RACK

Apply the rub to the turkey under the skin on the breast, thigh, and drumstick areas and in the body cavity. Tie the legs to the tail with kitchen string and tuck the wing tips under the back. Place the turkey with legs up on the cooking rack and with the lifting rod centered in the body cavity, as shown.

2

FRY THE TURKEY

Fry the turkey in 350°F oil for 3 minutes per pound. Carefully remove the turkey from the cooking pot and check the thigh meat temperature. The turkey is ready at 180°F. If it needs more cooking, return it to the oil, fry 3 to 5 minutes more, and check again.

Let the turkey stand and drain for 15 minutes before carving.

Garlic-Rosemary Turkey

This seasoned and deep-fried turkey breast just may be the simplest, juiciest, and tastiest white meat that you've ever eaten.

INGREDIENTS

Peanut oil
1 boneless turkey breast half
   (about 3 pounds)
3 cloves garlic
1 teaspoon dried rosemary, crushed
½ teaspoon salt
¼ teaspoon black pepper
1 lemon, halved
1 recipe Fried Garlic on Toast
   (see recipe, below)

6

FRYING

CLOSER LOOK

SO MUCH TO LOVE ABOUT GARLIC

Garlic is closely related to the onion and is one of our most popular food flavorings. Though you can buy garlic powder or jars of minced garlic, use fresh, whole garlic to get the best flavor. Whole garlic is called a bulb or a head and is covered with a papery skin. Peel off the skin and you'll find a number of individual cloves. In addition to its great taste, garlic is often touted as a "wonder food" and has been credited with everything from preventing colds to managing cholesterol to repelling mosquitoes. Although some of these claims are questionable, recent research indicates that, in fact, garlic is a mild antibiotic and provides some powerful antioxidant properties.

1 Preheat oil to 350°F. Remove skin from turkey breast. Cut garlic cloves into slivers. Using a small knife, make ½-inch slits on surface of turkey. Slide a sliver of garlic into each slit.

2 For rub, in a small bowl combine rosemary, salt, and pepper. Rub onto turkey.

3 Place turkey in basket. Slowly lower basket into hot oil, being cautious of splattering oil. Maintain oil temperature around 350°F. Fry turkey 30 minutes (10 minutes per pound). Remove turkey from hot oil to check doneness. Be cautious of splattering oil. Insert a quick-read meat thermometer into the center of the turkey. Turkey is done when thermometer registers 170°F. (If the turkey hasn't reached 170°F when you check for doneness, remove the thermometer and slowly lower the turkey back into the oil. Fry for 3 to 5 minutes more and check the temperature again.)

4 Squeeze lemon halves over turkey. Serve with Fried Garlic on Toast.

Fried Garlic on Toast: Place 1 whole unpeeled head of garlic in basket. Slowly lower basket into hot oil, being cautious of splattering oil. Fry for 5 to 7 minutes or until golden. Remove garlic from hot oil. Drain on paper towels. Squeeze paste from garlic cloves. Serve with 12 to 16 slices of toasted baguette bread.

1 **ADD THE OIL**
Pour the oil in a cool cooking pot, filling it to a pre-marked level that will cover your food but leave at least six inches from the top of the pot. Insert a deep-fry thermometer into the oil.

2 **HEAT THE OIL**
Turn on the propane and light the burner. Turn the burner to its highest setting and carefully monitor the oil temperature as it heats. When the cooking temperature is reached (usually 350°F), turn off the burner.

3 **ADD THE FOOD**
While wearing cooking mitts, goggles, and an apron, carefully and slowly lower the turkey or cooking basket into the hot oil. Relight the burner, carefully monitor the thermometer, and adjust the burner to maintain the appropriate cooking temperature.

Preparing the Turkey

Drain the turkey on several layers of paper towels before serving.

1 **REMOVE THE SKIN**
Using a sharp knife, detach the edges of the skin from the turkey breast and then peel the skin free with your fingers, as shown. Using the same knife, cut several shallow ½-inch slits in the top of the turkey breast.

2 **SEASON THE TURKEY**
Cut three garlic cloves into narrow slices and insert a slice into each slit in the turkey breast, as shown. Apply the rub, place the turkey in a cooking basket, and fry it for 10 minutes per pound until the internal temperature is 170°F.

Chicken Po' Boys with Chipotle Mayonnaise

Deep-fried chicken tenders combine with a spicy sauce to create a Southwestern-style sandwich that's the perfect centerpiece for your next backyard party.

GRILLING DETAILS

PREP: 45 minutes
FRY: 2 minutes per batch
MAKES: 8 to 10 servings

INGREDIENTS

Peanut oil
2 eggs, slightly beaten
½ cup milk
2 teaspoons salt
½ teaspoon black pepper
1 cup cornmeal
1 cup all-purpose flour
2 pounds skinless, boneless chicken breast halves, cut into 1½- to 2-inch strips
1 recipe Chipotle Mayonnaise (see recipe, below)
8 to 10 hoagie buns, split and, if desired, toasted (see tip, page 139)
2 cups shredded lettuce

TOOL SAVVY

THE ESSENTIAL FRY BASKET

A quick scan of the recipes in this book will reveal that most fryer dishes, other than a whole turkey, are best cooked in a basket. A fry basket is a simple perforated container that fits inside your cooking pot and makes it easy to cook and remove smaller foods. Just lift the basket with the food out of the pot and let the hot oil drain safely away. Most complete turkey fryer kits come with at least one basket, but some basic outfits don't. Either buy the complete kit or invest in a separate basket to fit your cooking pot—it will greatly expand your frying options.

1 Preheat oil to 350°F.

2 In a shallow bowl combine eggs, milk, salt, and pepper. In another shallow bowl combine cornmeal and flour. Dip chicken into the egg mixture, then coat with the cornmeal mixture.

3 Fry chicken, in six batches, for 2 to 3 minutes each or until crisp and golden. Do not crowd. Be cautious of splattering oil. Maintain oil temperature around 350°F. Remove chicken from hot oil and drain on wire racks.

4 Spread the Chipotle Mayonnaise on the bottom half of each bun. Top with lettuce, tomatoes, and the chicken. Add bun tops.

Chipotle Mayonnaise: Combine 1 cup mayonnaise or salad dressing and 2 to 3 teaspoons very finely chopped canned chipotle peppers in adobo sauce. Season to taste with salt and black pepper.

6

FRYING

1 **ADD THE OIL**
Pour the oil in a cool cooking pot, filling it to a pre-marked level that will cover your food but leave at least 6 inches from the top of the pot. Insert a deep-fry thermometer into the oil.

2 **HEAT THE OIL**
Turn on the propane and light the burner. Turn the burner to its highest setting and carefully monitor the oil temperature as it heats. When the cooking temperature is reached (usually 350°F), turn off the burner.

3 **ADD THE FOOD**
While wearing cooking mitts, goggles, and an apron, carefully and slowly lower the turkey or cooking basket into the hot oil. Relight the burner, carefully monitor the thermometer, and adjust the burner to maintain the appropriate cooking temperature.

Preparing the Chicken

1 **BREAD THE CHICKEN**
Dip the chicken pieces in the egg mixture and let the excess drip off. Next, thoroughly coat all sides of each piece in the cornmeal mixture and then set aside on a cooking tray.

2 **FRY THE CHICKEN**
Heat the oil to 350°F, insert a cooking basket into the pot, and carefully add 2 or 3 chicken pieces to the basket with long-handled tongs. Fry for 2 to 3 minutes, lift the basket, and empty the cooked chicken onto paper towels to drain. Replace the basket and repeat with the remaining chicken.

Serve with a cold salad or side dish to cool the spicy chipotle.

6

FRYING

Pork Chops on a Stick

Thanks to deep-fryer technology, anybody can enjoy this timeless state fair treat all year long, right in his or her own backyard.

GRILLING DETAILS

PREP: 15 minutes
MARINATE: 1 hour
FRY: 5 minutes per batch
MAKES: 8 servings

INGREDIENTS

- 8 boneless pork loin chops, 1 inch thick (about 2½ pounds)
- ½ cup bottled Italian salad dressing
  Peanut oil
- 8 8×¼-inch wooden skewers or dowels
  Honey mustard or bottled barbecue sauce

BUYER'S GUIDE

PORK CHOP PRIMER

Chops are a popular cut from the pork loin, the strip of meat that runs from a pig's shoulder to its hip. A chop's name identifies what part it came from:

Loin: Lower back. Have a T-bone shape, but often sold boneless.

Rib: Center of the rib area.

Sirloin: Hip area.

Top loin: Area toward the head.

Blade: Shoulder area. Sometimes sold as country-style ribs.

No matter where they came from, all chops cook the same. The required cooking time will depend on their thickness (which varies from ½ inch to 2 inches).

1 Place chops in a resealable large plastic bag. Pour salad dressing over chops. Seal bag. Marinate in the refrigerator for 1 hour, turning bag occasionally.

2 Preheat oil to 350°F.

3 Drain chops, discarding the marinade. Insert a wooden skewer into a short side of each chop.

4 Fry the chops, half at a time, for 5 to 8 minutes or until 160°F. (To test for doneness, carefully remove one chop from the hot oil.) Be cautious of splattering oil. Maintain oil temperature around 350°F. Remove chops from hot oil and drain on wire racks. Serve chops with honey mustard.

1 ADD THE OIL

Pour the oil in a cool cooking pot, filling it to a pre-marked level that will cover your food but leave at least 6 inches from the top of the pot. Insert a deep-fry thermometer into the oil.

2 HEAT THE OIL

Turn on the propane and light the burner. Turn the burner to its highest setting and carefully monitor the oil temperature as it heats. When the cooking temperature is reached (usually 350°F), turn off the burner.

3 ADD THE FOOD

While wearing cooking mitts, goggles, and an apron, carefully and slowly lower the turkey or cooking basket into the hot oil. Relight the burner, carefully monitor the thermometer, and adjust the burner to maintain the appropriate cooking temperature.

Preparing the Pork Chops

1 SKEWER THE CHOPS

Marinate the chops in Italian dressing for 1 hour. Drain the chops and discard the dressing. Insert a wooden skewer through the center of each chop, pushing it most of the way through the longest portion of the meat.

2 FRY THE CHOPS

Heat the oil to 350°F and add a cooking basket to the pot. Fry, 4 chops at a time, for 5 to 8 minutes. Remove one of the chops and check its internal temperature with a quick-read thermometer. The chops are done when the temperature is 160°F.

The sticks make these finger foods perfect for a picnic or backyard party.

6

FRYING

Cornmeal Catfish and Hush Puppies

The cornmeal coating authenticates the Southern-fried goodness of this popular freshwater fish. "Old Whiskers" may be funny to look at, but he sure tastes good!

GRILLING DETAILS

START TO FINISH: 50 Minutes
MAKES: 8 servings

INGREDIENTS

- 8 fresh or frozen skinless catfish fillets (about 3 to 3½ pounds)
- Peanut oil
- 3 cups cornmeal
- ½ cup all-purpose flour
- 2 teaspoons baking powder
- 1¾ teaspoons salt
- ⅛ teaspoon cayenne pepper (optional)
- 2 eggs, slightly beaten
- ¾ to 1 cup buttermilk
- 2 tablespoons finely chopped onion
- 2 cloves garlic, minced (optional)
- 1 teaspoon paprika or chili powder (optional)
- Salt
- Purchased coleslaw (optional)

CLOSER LOOK

CATFISH: FROM THE POND TO THE PLATE

The catfish that most people eat is channel catfish, a species that occurs naturally in rivers and lakes across the U.S. Some people are turned off by the idea of eating fish that lived in a muddy river, but that really shouldn't be a concern. Most of the catfish sold in the U.S. has been commercially raised in ponds in the South. You can buy the frozen fillets year-round in supermarkets across the country, and you can store them in the freezer for up to 2 months. Catfish is very high in protein, relatively low in fat, and a good source of selenium, vitamin B_{12}, potassium, and niacin.

1 Thaw catfish, if frozen. Rinse catfish and pat dry. Cover and chill catfish until needed.

2 Preheat oil to 350°F.

3 To make the hush puppies, in a medium bowl combine 1½ cups of the cornmeal, flour, baking powder, ¾ teaspoon of the salt, and, if desired, the cayenne pepper. Make a well in the center of the cornmeal mixture. In a small bowl combine eggs, buttermilk, onion, and, if desired, garlic. Add the buttermilk mixture all at once to the cornmeal mixture. Stir just until moistened. (If batter seems stiff, gradually add additional buttermilk as needed.)

4 Drop the batter by rounded tablespoons into the hot oil. Fry hush puppies, 8 to 10 at a time, for 2 to 3 minutes or until golden brown on both sides, turning once. Do not crowd. Be cautious of splattering oil. Maintain oil temperature around 350°F. Remove hush puppies from hot oil and drain on wire racks. Keep warm in a 300°F oven while frying the catfish.

5 Combine the remaining 1½ cups cornmeal, the remaining 1 teaspoon salt, and, if desired, the paprika. Coat the catfish fillets with the cornmeal mixture.

6 Fry fillets, 2 or 3 at a time, for 4 to 6 minutes or until golden and fish flakes easily with a fork, carefully turning once or twice to prevent sticking. Do not crowd. Be cautious of splattering oil. Maintain oil temperature around 350°F. Remove fish from hot oil and drain on wire racks. Season to taste with salt. Serve catfish with hush puppies and, if desired, coleslaw.

6

FRYING

1 ADD THE OIL

Pour the oil in a cool cooking pot, filling it to a pre-marked level that will cover your food but leave at least six inches from the top of the pot. Insert a deep-fry thermometer into the oil.

2 HEAT THE OIL

Turn on the propane and light the burner. Turn the burner to its highest setting and carefully monitor the oil temperature as it heats. When the cooking temperature is reached (usually 350°F), turn off the burner.

3 ADD THE FOOD

While wearing cooking mitts, goggles, and an apron, carefully and slowly lower the turkey or cooking basket into the hot oil. Relight the burner, carefully monitor the thermometer, and adjust the burner to maintain the appropriate cooking temperature.

Preparing the Catfish and Hush Puppies

Peanut oil is both a traditional and healthier choice for frying this meal.

1 FRY THE HUSH PUPPIES

For each hush puppy, carefully drop a tablespoonful of batter into the fry basket. Fry, 8 to 10 hush puppies at a time, for 2 to 3 minutes, turning once. Remove the basket and deposit the fried hush puppies on a wire rack or paper towels to drain. Repeat with the remaining batter.

2 FRY THE CATFISH

Coat the catfish fillets in the cornmeal mixture and place them, 1 at a time, in the fry basket. Fry 2 or 3 fillets together for 4 to 6 minutes or until the fish flakes easily. Drain on racks or paper towels and repeat with the remaining fillets.

6

FRYING

Shrimp and Vegetable Tempura

Choose light, not dark, beer for the batter to ensure that the tempura has a traditional light texture and color.

PREP: 25 minutes
FRY: 3 minutes per batch
MAKES: 4 servings

INGREDIENTS

- 12 large fresh or frozen shrimp in shells (about 6 ounces)
  Peanut oil
- 1½ cups all-purpose flour
- 1½ teaspoons salt
- 1 teaspoon black pepper
- ½ teaspoon cayenne pepper
- 1 12-ounce can beer
- 3 medium red, yellow, and/or orange sweet peppers, cut into ½-inch-thick rings
- 3 cups broccoli florets
- 1 recipe Soy Dipping Sauce (see recipe, below)

6

FRYING

REAL WORLD

COOKING WITH BEER

Most people prefer to consume beer in liquid form, but cooks are discovering that beer is a great ingredient in foods. In addition to providing a wonderful flavor, beer can help tenderize meat, add moisture to baked goods, and help batter—such as in this recipe—to puff up nicely when fried. Researchers are even showing that beer consumed in moderation offers some health benefits. It is important to note that contrary to popular belief not all the alcohol is removed by cooking, so chefs should be considerate of dinner guests that prefer an alcohol-free lifestyle.

1. Thaw shrimp, if frozen. Peel and devein shrimp and, if desired, remove the tails. Rinse shrimp and pat dry.

2. Preheat oil to 350°F.

3. For the batter, in a medium bowl combine flour, salt, black pepper, and cayenne pepper. Slowly whisk in the beer until smooth. Dip the shrimp and the vegetables into the batter and let the excess drip off.

4. Fry shrimp and vegetables, 5 or 6 pieces at a time, for 3 to 4 minutes or until crisp and golden. Do not crowd. Be cautious of splattering oil. Maintain oil temperature around 350°F. Remove shrimp and vegetables from hot oil and drain on wire racks. Serve shrimp and vegetables with Soy Dipping Sauce.

Soy Dipping Sauce: In a small bowl stir together ¼ cup soy sauce, 3 tablespoons rice vinegar, 2 tablespoons honey, 1 tablespoon sliced green onion, and 2 teaspoons lime juice.

1

ADD THE OIL

Pour the oil in a cool cooking pot, filling it to a pre-marked level that will cover your food but leave at least 6 inches from the top of the pot. Insert a deep-fry thermometer into the oil.

2

HEAT THE OIL

Turn on the propane and light the burner. Turn the burner to its highest setting and carefully monitor the oil temperature as it heats. When the cooking temperature is reached (usually 350°F), turn off the burner.

3

ADD THE FOOD

While wearing cooking mitts, goggles, and an apron, carefully and slowly lower the turkey or cooking basket into the hot oil. Relight the burner, carefully monitor the thermometer, and adjust the burner to maintain the appropriate cooking temperature.

Preparing the Shrimp

1

MIX THE BATTER

Combine the flour, salt, black pepper, and cayenne pepper in a bowl. Slowly blend in the beer with a whisk, as shown, and mix until the batter is smooth.

2

COAT WITH THE BATTER

Peel and devein the shrimp (see tip, page 65). Individually dip the shrimp and vegetable pieces in the batter, let the excess batter drip off, and set on a plate. Fry, 5 or 6 pieces of the batter-coated food at a time, in a fry basket for 3 to 4 minutes. Drain well before serving.

Serve with Soy Dipping Sauce for taste and chopsticks for authenticity and fun.

6

FRYING

Fried Cheese Ravioli with Marinara Sauce

Deep-fried pasta is a taste sensation that will generate fans from here to Napoli, and you can travel as near as your backyard to enjoy this easy-to-make treat.

GRILLING DETAILS

PREP: 20 minutes
FRY: 2 minutes per batch
MAKES: 4 servings

INGREDIENTS

Peanut oil
- 1   28-ounce package frozen cheese-filled ravioli
- 1   cup yellow cornmeal
- ¼   cup grated Romano or Parmesan cheese
- ½   teaspoon black pepper
- ⅓   cup milk
- 1   26-ounce jar marinara sauce, warmed

CLOSER LOOK

RAPPING ABOUT RAVIOLI

Ravioli is a popular type of pasta that is made up of two layers of dough—usually round or rectangular in shape—encasing a meat, vegetable, or cheese filling. Not surprisingly, the name ravioli is derived from the Italian verb "*ravvolgere,*" which means "to wrap." Stuffed pastas like ravioli have been around for hundreds of years. Some traditions used leftover meat or fish from big meals to fill ravioli. During Lent, vegetables or cheese replaced the meat. Today, some chefs still like to make their own ravioli, but if you want to minimize the work and maximize your eating pleasure, turn to the quick-cooking, premade varieties that you'll find in your supermarket's frozen foods department.

1 Preheat oil to 350°F.

2 Meanwhile, cook ravioli according to package directions and drain well. Rinse with cold water and drain again.

3 In a shallow bowl combine cornmeal, cheese, and pepper. Dip the cooked ravioli in the milk, then coat with the cornmeal mixture.

4 Fry ravioli, about one-third at a time, for 2 to 3 minutes or until crisp and golden brown. (Ravioli will rise to the top of the oil when cooked through.) Do not crowd. Be cautious of splattering oil. Maintain oil temperature around 350°F. Remove ravioli from hot oil and drain on wire racks. Serve ravioli with warm marinara sauce.

6

FRYING

ADD THE OIL

Pour the oil in a cool cooking pot, filling it to a pre-marked level that will cover your food but leave at least 6 inches from the top of the pot. Insert a deep-fry thermometer into the oil.

HEAT THE OIL

Turn on the propane and light the burner. Turn the burner to its highest setting and carefully monitor the oil temperature as it heats. When the cooking temperature is reached (usually 350°F), turn off the burner.

ADD THE FOOD

While wearing cooking mitts, goggles, and an apron, carefully and slowly lower the turkey or cooking basket into the hot oil. Relight the burner, carefully monitor the thermometer, and adjust the burner to maintain the appropriate cooking temperature.

Preparing the Ravioli

Serve with your favorite brand of marinara-style spaghetti sauce.

COOK THE RAVIOLI

Boil the frozen ravioli according to the directions on the package. Drain the ravioli, rinse it in cold water, and let it drain again. Meanwhile, combine the cornmeal, Parmesan cheese, and pepper in a shallow bowl.

COAT IN CORNMEAL

Dip each ravioli into the cornmeal mixture and set aside on a cooking tray. Heat the oil in the fryer to 350°F. Use a basket to fry one-third of the ravioli at a time for 2 to 3 minutes. Drain well before serving.

Peppered Onion Rings

This spicy, crispy treat will upgrade an old classic that you probably thought was next to impossible to improve.

6

FRYING

GRILLING DETAILS

PREP: 15 minutes
STAND: 15 minutes
FRY: 2 minutes per batch
MAKES: 6 servings

INGREDIENTS

	Peanut oil
1	pound yellow onions (about 3 medium)
1	cup buttermilk
1½	cups all-purpose flour
2	teaspoons salt
1	teaspoon black pepper
½	to 1 teaspoon cayenne pepper

WORK SMARTER

CRYING OVER CUT ONIONS

Crying while cutting onions has kind of become a cliché, but it's true that some people are very sensitive and their eyes water. There's a good reason for this—cut onions actually release a chemical into the air that is converted into a very mild form of sulfuric acid. There are lots of folk remedies for preventing the tears, but the best solution is to avoid cutting off the bottom of an onion until the very last minute: Most of the cells that release the offending compounds are concentrated in an onion's base.

1 Preheat oil to 350°F.

2 Cut the onions into ½-inch slices and separate into rings. Pour the buttermilk into a bowl, then gently stir in the onion rings.

3 In a resealable plastic bag combine flour, salt, black pepper, and cayenne pepper. Remove the onion rings from the buttermilk and add them to the plastic bag, half at a time, shaking to coat. Let stand for 15 minutes to allow the coating to set.

4 Fry onion rings, a few at a time, for 2 to 4 minutes or until crisp and golden brown. Do not crowd. Be cautious of splattering oil. Maintain oil temperature around 350°F. Remove onion rings from the hot oil and drain on wire racks. Keep warm in a 300°F oven while frying the remaining onion rings. If desired, season to taste with additional salt.

1

ADD THE OIL

Pour the oil in a cool cooking pot, filling it to a pre-marked level that will cover your food but leave at least 6 inches from the top of the pot. Insert a deep-fry thermometer into the oil.

2

HEAT THE OIL

Turn on the propane and light the burner. Turn the burner to its highest setting and carefully monitor the oil temperature as it heats. When the cooking temperature is reached (usually 350°F), turn off the burner.

3

ADD THE FOOD

While wearing cooking mitts, goggles, and an apron, carefully and slowly lower the turkey or cooking basket into the hot oil. Relight the burner, carefully monitor the thermometer, and adjust the burner to maintain the appropriate cooking temperature.

Preparing the Onion Rings

Serve with a cool dipping sauce to temper the spicy cayenne pepper.

1

SLICE THE ONIONS

Using a sharp knife, trim the tops and the bottoms off the onions and peel off the outer skin. Cut the onions into 1/2-inch slices. With your fingers, separate the slices into individual rings, as shown.

2

COAT THE RINGS

Place the rings in a bowl and cover with buttermilk. Lift the rings from the buttermilk and add them, half at a time, to a resealable plastic bag containing the flour mixture. Shake the bag to coat. Place the rings on a tray and allow them to stand for 15 minutes before frying.

6

FRYING

Mozzarella Cheese Sticks

Crispy fried on the outside and melted cheesy-good on the inside, these appetizers served with a selection of warm dipping sauces are sure to be the hit of any get-together.

GRILLING DETAILS

PREP: 20 minutes
FREEZE: 1 hour to 2 days
FRY: 2 minutes per batch
MAKES: 4 servings

INGREDIENTS

- ¾ cup all-purpose flour
- ½ teaspoon salt
- ½ teaspoon black pepper
- 2 eggs, slightly beaten
- 2 tablespoons water
- 12 mozzarella cheese sticks or one 16-ounce block mozzarella cheese, cut into twelve 4×½-inch sticks
- 1 cup fine dry Italian bread crumbs
   Peanut oil
- 1 cup warm marinara sauce or bottled buttermilk ranch salad dressing

GOOD IDEA

MAKE YOUR OWN BREAD CRUMBS

So you find yourself with half a loaf of stale bread or some old hamburger buns—do you toss them? Why not make bread crumbs with them? Lay the bread slices on a cookie sheet and bake them in a 200°F oven until they are dry. Cool the slices and process them in a food processor—use a grating blade for fine crumbs and a cutting blade for coarse crumbs. Add Italian seasoning or other flavorings while they process. You'll find that you need about four slices of bread to make 1 cup of fine bread crumbs.

1 Combine flour, salt, and pepper. Combine eggs and water. Dip the cheese sticks in the egg mixture, then coat with the flour mixture. Repeat, dipping the cheese sticks in the egg mixture, then coating with the bread crumbs. Place the cheese sticks on a baking sheet. Cover and freeze for 1 hour or up to 2 days.*

2 Preheat oil to 350°F. Preheat the basket in the hot oil.

3 Fry the cheese sticks, half at a time, in basket for 2 to 2½ minutes or until crisp and golden. Do not crowd. Be cautious of splattering oil. Maintain oil temperature around 350°F. Remove cheese sticks from the hot oil and drain on wire racks. Serve cheese sticks with marinara sauce.

*****Note:** If the cheese sticks are frozen for 1 or 2 days, let them stand at room temperature for 15 minutes before frying.

6

FRYING

1

ADD THE OIL

Pour the oil in a cool cooking pot, filling it to a pre-marked level that will cover your food but leave at least 6 inches from the top of the pot. Insert a deep-fry thermometer into the oil.

2

HEAT THE OIL

Turn on the propane and light the burner. Turn the burner to its highest setting and carefully monitor the oil temperature as it heats. When the cooking temperature is reached (usually 350°F), turn off the burner.

3

ADD THE FOOD

While wearing cooking mitts, goggles, and an apron, carefully and slowly lower the turkey or cooking basket into the hot oil. Relight the burner, carefully monitor the thermometer, and adjust the burner to maintain the appropriate cooking temperature.

Preparing the Cheese Sticks

1

SLICE THE CHEESE

Use a knife to cut a 1-pound block of mozzarella cheese across the short side to make 6 thick slices. Cut each of the slices in half to make 12 mozzarella sticks.

2

COAT THE STICKS

Dip each stick in the egg mixture and then dip in the flour mixture. Dip each stick a second time in the egg mixture, coat with bread crumbs, and set on a baking sheet. Place in the freezer for at least 1 hour before frying.

Warm your dipping sauces before serving for optimum flavor.

6

FRYING

Spicy Cheddar Corn Fritters

You might not know exactly what a "fritter" is, but these spicy-cheesy treats need little analysis; they are guaranteed to be a hit as an appetizer at your next cookout.

GRILLING DETAILS

PREP: 20 minutes
FRY: 3 minutes per batch
MAKES: 6 appetizer servings

INGREDIENTS

Peanut oil
½	cup yellow cornmeal
½	cup all-purpose flour
1	teaspoon baking powder
¾	teaspoon salt
¼	teaspoon cayenne pepper
1	egg, slightly beaten
½	cup milk
1	cup frozen whole kernel corn, thawed
1	cup shredded cheddar cheese (4 ounces)
¼	cup thinly sliced green onions (2)

TOOL SAVVY

DOWNSIZE YOUR FRY POT

Many turkey fryer kits only include a single turkey-size cooking pot (usually 30 quarts), which provides far too much volume for many fryer entrées. To make frying small-size foods simpler and more fun, invest in (or buy a fryer kit that includes) what is often called a "fish fry" pot. Typically, these are about 10 quarts in size, and they come with a custom-fitted fry basket. These smaller setups are much easier to handle, and you'll use less oil and cook foods more quickly.

1 Preheat oil to 350°F.

2 To make the batter, in a medium bowl combine cornmeal, flour, baking powder, salt, and cayenne pepper. Stir in egg and milk just until moistened. Stir in corn, cheese, and green onions (batter will be thick).

3 Drop the batter by rounded tablespoons into the hot oil. Fry fritters, 8 to 10 at a time, for 3 to 4 minutes or until golden brown on both sides, turning once. Do not crowd. Be cautious of splattering oil. Maintain oil temperature around 350°F. Remove fritters from the hot oil and drain on wire racks.

FRYING

6

1 ADD THE OIL

Pour the oil in a cool cooking pot, filling it to a pre-marked level that will cover your food but leave at least 6 inches from the top of the pot. Insert a deep-fry thermometer into the oil.

2 HEAT THE OIL

Turn on the propane and light the burner. Turn the burner to its highest setting and carefully monitor the oil temperature as it heats. When the cooking temperature is reached (usually 350°F), turn off the burner.

3 ADD THE FOOD

While wearing cooking mitts, goggles, and an apron, carefully and slowly lower the turkey or cooking basket into the hot oil. Relight the burner, carefully monitor the thermometer, and adjust the burner to maintain the appropriate cooking temperature.

Preparing the Fritters

1 MIX THE BATTER

Combine the dry ingredients in a medium bowl. Add the egg and milk and stir just until the mixture is moistened. Add the corn, cheese, and green onions. Stir well to form a thick batter.

2 FRY THE FRITTERS

Drop tablespoons of the batter into a basket, as shown, and fry in 350°F oil. Fry 8 to 10 fritters at a time for 3 to 4 minutes, turning once. Remove the fritters with the basket and drain well before serving.

Drain well on racks or paper towels before serving.

6

FRYING

Crab Cakes with Lemon Mayonnaise

For an extra-crispy, flaky crust use Japanese panko bread crumbs, available at specialty and ethnic grocers or at many supermarkets.

GRILLING DETAILS

PREP: 35 minutes
CHILL: 1 to 24 hours
FRY: 4½ minutes per batch
MAKES: 12 appetizer servings

INGREDIENTS

- 1 egg, slightly beaten
- 1 cup fine dry bread crumbs
- ¼ cup mayonnaise
- ¼ cup finely chopped green onions (2)
- ¼ cup chopped roasted red sweet peppers
- 2 teaspoons Dijon-style mustard
- 1 teaspoon seafood seasoning
- ¼ teaspoon black pepper
- 1 pound lump crabmeat
  Peanut Oil
- 1 recipe Lemon-Mayonnaise (see recipe, below)

CLOSER LOOK

WHY CAKES FOR CRAB?

Crab cakes are a treat most closely associated with Maryland and the Chesapeake Bay, which has a long history of producing large populations of the tasty crustaceans. The idea for turning the crab and other minced meat into "cakes" (actually meat patties) traces back to England. Part of the reason was economy—mixing the more expensive meat with cheaper bread made it go further. Today, using frozen lump (body) meat allows us to serve this tasty seafood treat year-round and with a lot less mess than cracking open crab legs.

1 In a large bowl combine egg, ½ cup of the bread crumbs, mayonnaise, green onions, roasted peppers, mustard, seafood seasoning, and black pepper. Stir in crabmeat. Place the remaining ½ cup bread crumbs in a shallow dish. Divide the crab mixture into 12 portions. Pat each portion into a ¾-inch-thick patty. Gently press each crab cake into the bread crumbs, turning to coat. Place crab cakes on a waxed paper-lined baking sheet. Cover and refrigerate for 1 to 24 hours.

2 Preheat oil to 325°F. Preheat the basket in the oil.

3 Fry crab cakes, half at a time, in the basket for 4½ to 5 minutes or until 160°F. (To test for doneness, carefully remove 1 crab cake from the hot oil and insert a quick-read thermometer into the crab cake.) Do not crowd. Be cautious of splattering oil. Maintain oil temperature around 325°F. Remove crab cakes from hot oil and drain on wire racks. Serve crab cakes with Lemon-Mayonnaise.

Lemon-Mayonnaise: In a small bowl stir together ½ cup mayonnaise, 2 tablespoons snipped fresh parsley or 2 teaspoons dried parsley, 1 tablespoon lemon juice, and, if desired, 1 tablespoon drained capers. Season to taste with salt and black pepper.

6

FRYING

1

ADD THE OIL

Pour the oil in a cool cooking pot, filling it to a pre-marked level that will cover your food but leave at least 6 inches from the top of the pot. Insert a deep-fry thermometer into the oil.

2

HEAT THE OIL

Turn on the propane and light the burner. Turn the burner to its highest setting and carefully monitor the oil temperature as it heats. When the cooking temperature is reached (usually 350°F), turn off the burner.

3

ADD THE FOOD

While wearing cooking mitts, goggles, and an apron, carefully and slowly lower the turkey or cooking basket into the hot oil. Relight the burner, carefully monitor the thermometer, and adjust the burner to maintain the appropriate cooking temperature.

Preparing the Crab Cakes

1

MIX THE CRABMEAT

Set aside ½ cup of bread crumbs in a shallow dish. Combine all the ingredients except the crabmeat in a large bowl and mix well. Add the crabmeat and stir the mixture until well blended.

2

MAKE THE CAKES

Divide the crab mixture into 12 equal portions and pat each portion into a small patty. Dip each patty into the bread crumbs until they are well coated. Place the patties on a waxed paper-lined baking sheet and refrigerate for 1 to 24 hours before frying.

These can be served as a dinner entrée or as an appetizer.

6

FRYING

Grill Gadgets

Thanks to a proliferation of new gear, your backyard grill has evolved from a simple outdoor cooker into a versatile culinary machine. Where in the past you were limited to cooking things that could sit safely on the cooking rack, today there are very few limits to the type of food that you can expose to the glory of the open flame. A variety of devices have emerged for holding and cooking food that is small enough to slip through the grate or is too delicate for traditional grilling treatment. Buying and trying out these new gadgets add a whole new dimension of fun to backyard cooking—and a new variety of great-tasting grilled food to share with family and friends.

Some of the gadgets to consider adding to your grilling arsenal are traditional favorites that every griller should have—skewers are a good example. The metal rod or wood stick on which you thread meat and vegetables isn't a new concept; most grillers are familiar with shish kabobs. What is interesting to consider is the wide range of skewers that is available and the variety of foods with which they can be matched—all kinds of meat, seafood, and vegetables can be grilled on this versatile tool. Most grill chefs will probably want to invest in a quality set of metal skewers, plus keep a supply of disposable wooden ones around.

Chapter 7 Recipes

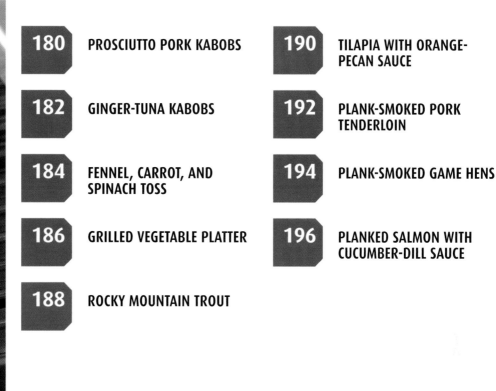

Grill baskets are a broad family of cooking tools that share a similar purpose: To safely hold small or delicate items that normally would end up falling into a grill fire rather than getting cooked by it. Some baskets are simply meant to loosely hold pieces of food—for example, vegetable chunks. Other types employ fold-together grates that secure larger items such as fish fillets that could fall apart as they cook. Either style makes it easier to add, remove, and turn the items on the grill and fully expose them to the open flame and smoky goodness.

The latest generation of grill gadgets is the perforated cooking pan—including skillets and woks—that allows grill chefs to cook stove-top-style on the grill grate. The advantage is that the perforations allow the items to be enveloped in the smoke as they cook giving foods like stir-fried vegetables authentic grilled taste.

Finally, for people who like the idea of smoked flavor, but don't like the idea of investing all that time in smoke cooking, there is the plank. Planks are hardwood pieces that are soaked in water and placed on the cooking grate. When the plank gets hot and starts to smoke, on go the fish, poultry, vegetables, or even your favorite cut of beef or pork. As the food grills indirect-heat style, it gets a savory hardwood-smoke flavor that some people swear is as good as what the top-quality smokers deliver.

Prosciutto Pork Kabobs

Prosciutto is a dry-cured, thin-sliced Italian ham that you wrap around the pork cubes before grilling to give them a delicate salty-smoked flavor

GRILLING DETAILS

PREP: 20 minutes
GRILL: 18 minutes
MAKES: 4 servings

INGREDIENTS

- ¼ cup garlic-flavor olive oil
- 2 tablespoons lemon juice
- ¼ teaspoon crushed red pepper
- 1 pound pork tenderloin
- 3 to 4 ounces thinly sliced prosciutto
- 8 ounces fresh mushrooms, stems removed
- 2 small zucchini and/or yellow summer squash, cut into ¾-inch slices
- 2 tablespoons grated Parmesan or Romano cheese

TOOL SAVVY

SKEWER SUCCESS

The skewer is a dangerously simple tool—which means that it's easy to do things the wrong way and make cooking more difficult than it needs to be. To make skewer cooking successful, follow these tips:

- Soak wooden skewers in water for 30 minutes before adding the food to prevent them from burning.
- Keep metal skewers clean and rub with oil before using to keep food from sticking.
- Cut food pieces to a uniform size to ensure even cooking.
- Use two skewers (or two-pronged metal skewers) on large pieces of food to prevent food from spinning when you're trying to turn them.

1 In a small bowl combine oil, lemon juice, and crushed red pepper; set aside.

2 Trim fat from pork. Cut pork into 1½-inch cubes. Cut prosciutto into 1½-inch-wide strips. Wrap a strip of prosciutto around each pork cube. On 4 long skewers, alternately thread pork cubes, mushrooms, and zucchini, leaving a ¼-inch space between pieces.

3 Lightly grease an unheated grill rack. For a charcoal grill, grill kabobs, uncovered, directly over medium coals for 18 to 20 minutes or until pork is no longer pink and juices run clear, turning once halfway through grilling. Brushing with the oil mixture during the last 4 minutes of grilling. (For a gas grill, preheat grill. Reduce heat to medium. Place kabobs on greased grill rack over heat. Cover; grill as above.)

4 Just before serving, sprinkle kabobs with Parmesan cheese.

Preparing the Grill

1

LIGHT THE CHARCOAL

Light the charcoal using one of the methods described on pages 22 to 23. Allow the charcoal to burn until it glows red-hot and is fully covered with a layer of white ash

2

SPREAD OUT THE COALS

Using a sturdy, long-handled tool such as a pair of tongs, a garden rake, or a hoe, spread the coals so that they evenly cover the charcoal grate. Put the cooking rack in place, and when it has heated, give it a quick cleaning with a wire grill brush.

3

CHECK THE TEMPERATURE

Using a thermometer or your hand (see pages 24 to 25), check the temperature of the cooking rack. Start cooking when the heat is medium (about 350°F). If the heat is too high, wait for the coals to burn down and cool on their own or adjust the grill vents to reduce air flow.

Preparing the Kabobs

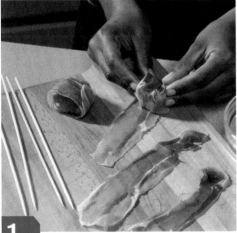

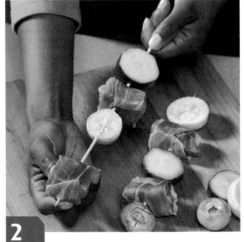

Sprinkle with grated cheese and serve with a salad on the side.

1

ROLL THE PORK CUBES

Soak the skewers in water for 30 minutes. Cut the pork into 1¹/₂-inch cubes and the prosciutto into 1¹/₂-inch-wide strips. Place a pork cube on the end of each strip and roll the prosciutto around the cube, as shown.

2

SKEWER THE FOOD

Alternately thread the pork between pieces of vegetable. To keep the wrap in place, thread the skewer through each cube near the end of the prosciutto strip. Grill over direct heat for 18 to 20 minutes, turning once and basting during the last 4 minutes of grilling.

7

GRILL GADGETS

Ginger-Tuna Kabobs

This easy-to-make, Asian-inspired dish will provide mouthwatering proof that grilled tuna is every bit as tasty as a grilled beefsteak.

GRILLING DETAILS

PREP: 20 minutes
MARINATE: 20 minutes
GRILL: 6 minutes
MAKES: 4 servings

INGREDIENTS

12	ounces skinless tuna steaks
3	tablespoons reduced-sodium soy sauce
3	tablespoons water
1	tablespoon snipped green onion tops or snipped fresh chives
2	teaspoons grated fresh ginger
½	medium pineapple, cored and cut into 1-inch cubes
1	medium red or green sweet pepper, cut into 1-inch squares
6	green onions, cut into 2-inch pieces
¼	cup honey

CLOSER LOOK

TUNA: STEAK FROM THE SEA?

Lay raw tuna steak side by side with raw beefsteak, and it takes your mind a second to figure out that they are different foods. Both are rich red meats that look tantalizingly ready for the grill. Cook them both and you'll end up with two equally flavorful dinner entrées. That's where the similarities end—the tuna has a big advantage when you analyze what's inside. A serving of tuna has fewer than half the calories as a serving of beef, just a fraction of the fat, and roughly the same amount of protein. Plus, tuna is a great source of the heart-healthy omega-3 fatty acids.

1 Cut tuna into 1-inch cubes. Place in a resealable large plastic bag set in a shallow dish. Add soy sauce, water, snipped green onion tops, and ginger. Seal bag and turn gently to coat cubes. Marinate at room temperature for 20 minutes. Drain fish, reserving marinade.

2 Thread tuna, pineapple, sweet pepper, and green onion pieces onto 4 long metal skewers.

3 Lightly grease an unheated grill rack. For a charcoal grill, grill kabobs, uncovered, directly over medium coals for 6 to 9 minutes or until fish flakes easily when tested with a fork, turning kabobs once halfway through grilling. (For a gas grill, preheat grill. Reduce heat to medium. Place skewers on greased grill rack over heat. Cover; grill as above.)

4 Meanwhile, in a small saucepan bring reserved marinade to boiling; strain. Discard any solids. Stir honey into hot marinade. Brush kabobs generously with honey-soy mixture just before serving.

Preparing the Grill

1 LIGHT THE CHARCOAL
Light the charcoal using one of the methods described on pages 22 to 23. Allow the charcoal to burn until it glows red-hot and is fully covered with a layer of white ash

2 SPREAD OUT THE COALS
Using a sturdy, long-handled tool such as a pair of tongs, a garden rake, or a hoe, spread the coals so that they evenly cover the charcoal grate. Put the cooking rack in place, and when it has heated, give it a quick cleaning with a wire grill brush.

3 CHECK THE TEMPERATURE
Using a thermometer or your hand (see pages 24 to 25), check the temperature of the cooking rack. Start cooking when the heat is medium (about 350°F). If the heat is too high, wait for the coals to burn down and cool on their own or adjust the grill vents to reduce air flow.

Preparing the Tuna Kabobs

Serve with steamed rice and the leftover honey-soy sauce.

1 PREPARE THE SAUCE
Heat the reserved marinade in a saucepan until it boils. Pour the hot liquid through a strainer into a small bowl. Add the honey to the liquid in the bowl and stir it well to combine.

2 GRILL THE KABOBS
Thread the meat, vegetables, and pineapple on skewers, alternating pieces as you add them. Place the skewers on the cooking rack directly over medium coals. Grill for 6 to 9 minutes, turning once, until the tuna flakes easily. Brush with the sauce and serve.

Fennel, Carrot, and Spinach Toss

After grilling the fennel and carrot until they're tender, add the spinach and cook just until it wilts—usually in a minute or two.

INGREDIENTS

1½	cups packaged peeled baby carrots
1	medium fennel bulb, trimmed and cut into thin wedges
2	tablespoons olive oil
½	teaspoon salt
½	teaspoon cracked black pepper
	Nonstick cooking spray
1	10-ounce package prewashed spinach
½	cup grated Parmesan cheese
	Lemon wedges (optional)

TOOL SAVVY

GRILL WOK BASICS

The grill wok is a cooking tool that offers big bang for relatively few bucks. Most are simple square or circular perforated cooking pans with a nonstick black surface. They sit atop your cooking grate and require no special tools. The perforations allow smoke to circulate around and flavor the food. Grill woks should be coated with oil before using to help season them and maintain their nonstick properties. Some charcoal grill models feature custom-fit woks that sit on the cooking grate support brackets. These woks are pricey, but some grillers swear by them because they are very large and get very hot, allowing an authentic wok-cooking experience.

1 In a large bowl combine carrots and fennel. Add oil, salt, and pepper; toss to coat.

2 Lightly coat an unheated grill wok with nonstick cooking spray. For a charcoal grill, preheat the grill wok on the rack of an uncovered grill directly over medium coals for 15 seconds. Add the vegetable mixture to the grill wok. Grill vegetables in the wok for 15 to 20 minutes or until tender, stirring occasionally. Add spinach to grill wok (gradually, if necessary). Cook until spinach is wilted, stirring occasionally. (For a gas grill, preheat grill. Reduce heat to medium. Preheat the grill wok on grill rack over heat for 15 seconds. Add vegetable mixture to grill wok. Cover; grill as at left.)

3 Transfer vegetable mixture to a serving plate. Sprinkle with Parmesan cheese. If desired, serve with lemon wedges.

Preparing the Grill

1 LIGHT THE CHARCOAL
Light the charcoal using one of the methods described on pages 22 to 23. Allow the charcoal to burn until it glows red-hot and is fully covered with a layer of white ash

2 SPREAD OUT THE COALS
Using a sturdy, long-handled tool such as a pair of tongs, a garden rake, or a hoe, spread the coals so that they evenly cover the charcoal grate. Put the cooking rack in place, and when it has heated, give it a quick cleaning with a wire grill brush.

3 CHECK THE TEMPERATURE
Using a thermometer or your hand (see pages 24 to 25), check the temperature of the cooking rack. Start cooking when the heat is medium (about 350°F). If the heat is too high, wait for the coals to burn down and cool on their own, or adjust the grill vents to reduce air flow.

Preparing the Vegetables

Never spray your wok with cooking spray while it's on the grill.

1 SPRAY THE WOK
Before placing on the grill, coat the surface of the wok with nonstick cooking spray. Place a piece of absorbent paper under the wok to catch the overspray. Never spray the wok while it is on the grill.

2 GRILL THE VEGETABLES
Briefly preheat the wok on the cooking grate. Add the carrot and fennel mixture to the wok and grill for 15 to 20 minutes, stirring occasionally. Add the spinach to the wok, stir, and cook just until the spinach is wilted.

Grilled Vegetable Platter

This colorful and good-tasting side dish is a breeze to cook in a grill wok. Cook the vegetables on one side of the grill over direct heat while the main entrée slow grills with indirect heat.

GRILLING DETAILS

PREP: 25 minutes
GRILL: 30 minutes
MAKES: 8 to 10 side-dish servings

INGREDIENTS

- 1 pound yellow summer squash, cut into ½-inch slices, or baby pattypan squash (about 3 cups)
- 2 medium yellow, orange, and/or red sweet peppers, seeded and cut into strips or squares
- 12 ounces fresh green beans, trimmed (3 cups)
- 15 baby carrots with tops, trimmed
- 10 cherry sweet peppers
- 2 tablespoons olive oil or cooking oil
- ½ teaspoon salt
- ¼ teaspoon black pepper
- 2 teaspoons finely shredded lemon peel
- 2 teaspoons lemon juice
- 2 cloves garlic, minced
  Nonstick cooking spray

WORK SMARTER

GETTING THE MOST FROM YOUR LEMON
Turn to fresh lemons, which provide flavor from both their juice and their shredded peel—also called the zest—when grilling recipes call for lemon juice. A medium-size lemon will yield 2 to 3 tablespoons of juice and ½ to 1 tablespoon of finely shredded peel. Before you juice a lemon, roll the fruit on a hard surface, pressing firmly to encourage the pulp to release the juice. Zest the lemon with the finest edge of a box grater or use a microplane zester made specifically for the job

1 In an extra-large bowl combine squash, sweet peppers, green beans, carrots, cherry peppers, oil, salt, and black pepper; toss to coat. In a small bowl combine lemon peel, lemon juice, and garlic; set aside.

2 Lightly coat an unheated grill wok with nonstick cooking spray. Add vegetables to the wok.

3 For a charcoal grill, place the wok on the rack of an uncovered grill directly over medium coals. Grill for 30 to 35 minutes or just until vegetables are tender and light brown, stirring occasionally. (For a gas grill, preheat grill. Reduce heat to medium. Place the wok on grill rack over heat. Cover; grill as above.)

4 Return cooked vegetables to the extra-large bowl. Add the lemon mixture; toss well to coat. To serve, arrange vegetables on a platter.

Preparing the Grill

1 LIGHT THE CHARCOAL

Light the charcoal using one of the methods described on pages 22 to 23. Allow the charcoal to burn until it glows red-hot and is fully covered with a layer of white ash.

2 SPREAD OUT THE COALS

Using a sturdy, long-handled tool such as a pair of tongs, a garden rake, or a hoe, spread the coals so that they evenly cover the charcoal grate. Put the cooking rack in place, and when it has heated, give it a quick cleaning with a wire grill brush.

3 CHECK THE TEMPERATURE

Using a thermometer or your hand (see pages 24 to 25), check the temperature of the cooking rack. Start cooking when the heat is medium (about 350°F). If the heat is too high, wait for the coals to burn down and cool on their own or adjust the grill vents to reduce air flow.

Preparing the Vegetables

1 COAT THE VEGETABLES

Combine the vegetables in an extra-large bowl with the oil, salt, and pepper. Toss to coat. Lightly coat the cooking surface of a grill wok with cooking spray. Place the vegetables in the oiled wok.

2 GRILL THE VEGETABLES

Place the wok and vegetables on your grill, directly over the heat. Cook the vegetables for 30 to 35 minutes, stirring them a few times while they cook. Return the vegetables to the bowl and pour the lemon juice mixture over them. Stir and serve.

Try canola oil in this recipe to reduce the amount of saturated fat.

7

GRILL GADGETS

Rocky Mountain Trout

Bring the taste of the mountains to your backyard—and while cooking these fish over an open fire, you'll swear you can smell pine needles and hear the sound of water gurgling over rocks.

GRILLING DETAILS

PREP: 15 minutes
GRILL: 6 minutes
MAKES: 2 servings

INGREDIENTS

- 2   8- to 10-ounce fresh or frozen dressed rainbow trout
- 2   tablespoons finely chopped red onion
- 2   tablespoons finely chopped green sweet pepper
- 1   tablespoon snipped fresh cilantro or basil
- ¼   teaspoon ground cumin
- ⅛   teaspoon salt
- ⅛   teaspoon black pepper
-     Cooking oil
-     Lemon slices (optional)

WORK SMARTER

DRESSED FOR DINNER

If you see a recipe that calls for "dressed" trout, this means that the fish is whole—including its head and tail—but its entrails and gills have been removed. This is the traditional way to cook and serve trout (complete with eyes that turn white during cooking). Some people are a little squeamish about their fish, which is where "pan-dressed" trout come into play. These fish also have had both their head and tail removed. Of course, there is no rule that says you can't simply cut off the heads and tails of dressed trout before serving them to guests with a more delicate constitution.

1 Thaw fish, if frozen. In a bowl combine onion, sweet pepper, cilantro, cumin, salt, and black pepper. Brush each entire fish with oil. Spoon onion mixture into fish.

2 Brush a small wire grill basket with oil. Place fish in basket.

3 For a charcoal grill, place grill basket on the rack of an uncovered grill directly over medium-hot coals. Grill for 6 to 9 minutes or until fish flakes easily when tested with a fork, turning the grill basket over once halfway through grilling. (For a gas grill, preheat grill. Reduce heat to medium high. Place grill basket on grill rack over heat. Cover; grill as above.)

4 If desired, serve with lemon slices.

Preparing the Grill

1
LIGHT THE CHARCOAL
Light the charcoal using one of the methods described on pages 22 to 23. Allow the charcoal to burn until it glows red-hot and is fully covered with a layer of white ash

2
SPREAD OUT THE COALS
Using a sturdy, long-handled tool such as a pair of tongs, a garden rake, or a hoe, spread the coals so that they evenly cover the charcoal grate. Put the cooking rack in place, and when it has heated, give it a quick cleaning with a wire grill brush.

3
CHECK THE TEMPERATURE
Using a thermometer or your hand (see pages 24 to 25), check the temperature of the cooking rack. Start cooking when the heat is medium (about 350°F). If the heat is too high, wait for the coals to burn down and cool on their own or adjust the grill vents to reduce air flow.

Preparing the Fish

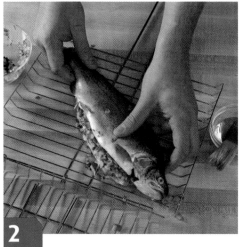

The trout is fully cooked when the flesh flakes easily with a fork.

1
OIL THE TROUT
Use whole, dressed trout for this meal; keep the head on the fish. Use a basting brush to generously coat both sides of each fish with cooking oil.

2
STUFF THE TROUT
Spoon half the onion-pepper stuffing into the body cavity of each fish. Place the fish inside a lightly oiled grill basket, close the basket, and place it on the cooking rack over direct heat. Grill for 6 to 9 minutes, carefully turning the basket once during this time.

Tilapia with Orange-Pecan Sauce

Put your grill basket to work cooking this quick and tasty dish, which will change your attitude about fish.

GRILLING DETAILS

PREP: 25 minutes
GRILL: 4 minutes per ½-inch thickness
MAKES: 4 servings

INGREDIENTS

- 4 4-ounce fresh or frozen tilapia or other fish fillets, cut ¾ inch thick
- ½ cup parsley, finely chopped
- 4 teaspoons finely shredded orange peel
- 1 clove garlic, minced
- ¼ teaspoon salt
- 1 tablespoon cooking oil
- ⅓ cup pecan pieces
- 2 tablespoons butter
- 2 medium oranges, peeled and sectioned
- ⅓ cup orange juice

CLOSER LOOK

WHAT THE HECK IS A TILAPIA?

Tilapia is a type of freshwater fish—and a very tasty one at that. Native to Africa, tilapia is becoming very popular in the U.S. and is the second most popular farm-raised fish in the world. Tilapia is sometimes known as "St. Peter's fish" and often sold in stores or restaurants as perch or whitefish. Tilapia is high in protein and low in fat and it tastes good. The white flesh has a fine texture and a mildly sweet flavor that is a good base for citrus or spicy sauces.

1 Thaw fish, if frozen. Rinse fish; pat dry with paper towels.

2 In a small bowl stir together parsley, orange peel, garlic, and salt. Divide parsley mixture in half. Set half of parsley mixture aside. Add oil to the remaining half of the parsley mixture; spread over fish.

3 Place fish, parsley sides up, in a well-greased grill basket, tucking under any thin edges. For a charcoal grill, grill fish on the rack of an uncovered grill directly over medium coals for 4 to 6 minutes per ½-inch thickness of fish or until fish flakes easily when tested with a fork, turning basket once halfway through grilling. (For a gas grill, preheat grill. Reduce heat to medium. Place fish on grill rack over heat. Cover; grill as above.)

4 For sauce, in a medium skillet cook pecans in hot butter for 3 minutes or until golden. Remove from heat. Stir in orange sections and orange juice; return to heat. Cook and gently stir until sauce is heated through. Gently stir in reserved parsley mixture.

5 To serve, place fish on platter and spoon sauce over fillets.

7

GRILL GADGETS

1 **LIGHT THE CHARCOAL**
Light the charcoal using one of the methods described on pages 22 to 23. Allow the charcoal to burn until it glows red-hot and is fully covered with a layer of white ash.

2 **SPREAD OUT THE COALS**
Using a sturdy, long-handled tool such as a pair of tongs, a garden rake, or a hoe, spread the coals so that they evenly cover the charcoal grate. Put the cooking rack in place, and when it has heated, give it a quick cleaning with a wire grill brush.

3 **CHECK THE TEMPERATURE**
Using a thermometer or your hand (see pages 24 to 25), check the temperature of the cooking rack. Start cooking when the heat is medium (about 350°F). If the heat is too high, wait for the coals to burn down and cool on their own or adjust the grill vents to reduce air flow.

Preparing the Fish

Pour the orange sauce over the grilled fillets before serving.

1 **PLACE FISH ON THE RACK**
Thaw the fish and pat dry with paper towels. Top each fillet with the oil and seasoning mixture and place in a well-oiled grilling basket. Tuck under the thin tail section of each fish, as shown, to prevent overcooking. Grill for 4 to 6 minutes per 1/2-inch thickness of fish over direct heat, turning once.

2 **PREPARE THE SAUCE**
Peel 2 oranges and, using a sharp, thin knife, slice out the individual sections, as shown, removing the skin. In a saucepan cook the pecans in hot butter for 3 minutes. Stir in the orange sections and orange juice, heat through, and stir in the parsley seasoning mixture.

7

GRILL GADGETS

Plank-Smoked Pork Tenderloin

On pirate ships sailing the high seas of old the plank was for walking, but for the backyards of today the plank is for grilling—and this hardwood-smoked pork is good enough to quiet any mutiny.

GRILLING DETAILS

PREP: 30 minutes
SOAK: 1 hour
GRILL: 30 minutes
MAKES: 4 servings

INGREDIENTS

- 1 12×6×³/₄-inch cedar or alder plank
- 2 12-ounce pork tenderloins
- 2 tablespoons Dijon-style mustard
- Salt and black pepper
- 2 tablespoons snipped fresh sage
- 2 tablespoons snipped fresh thyme
- 1 tablespoon snipped fresh rosemary
- 1 recipe Apple-Cherry Salad
  (see recipe, below)

TOOL SAVVY

PLANK PARTICULARS
The concept of the grilling plank is amazingly simple, but there are a few things to keep in mind to get the best possible meal from your hardwood slab:

- Match-making meat to wood to is essential—turn to pages 124 to 125 for more information.
- Submerge (holding down with a weight, if necessary) your plank in water for a full hour before grilling.
- Coat the top with a layer of oil before adding the food.
- Place the plank directly over the heat source and preheat it until it smokes.
- Fill a spray bottle with water and keep it handy during cooking to extinguish any flames on the plank.

1 At least 1 hour before grilling, soak plank in enough water to cover. Place a weight on the plank so it stays submerged during soaking.

2 Trim fat from pork. Brush tenderloins with mustard; sprinkle generously with salt and pepper. In a small bowl combine sage, thyme, and rosemary. Sprinkle herb mixture evenly over each tenderloin; pat in with your fingers.

3 Remove plank from water. For a charcoal grill, place plank on the rack of an uncovered grill directly over medium coals about 5 minutes or until plank begins to crackle and smoke. Place tenderloins on plank. Cover; grill for 30 to 40 minutes or until

a meat thermometer registers 160°F. (For a gas grill, preheat grill. Reduce heat to medium. Place tenderloins on plank over heat. Cover; grill as above.) Serve with Apple-Cherry Salad.

Apple-Cherry Salad: In a medium bowl combine 2 Granny Smith apples, chopped; ¹/₄ cup coarsely chopped walnuts, toasted; 1 ounce crumbled blue cheese; 2 tablespoons snipped dried tart red cherries; 2 tablespoons Calvados or applejack; and 1 tablespoon olive oil. Just before serving, stir in 3 slices bacon, cooked, drained, and crumbled. Makes about ³/₄ cups.

Preparing the Grill

1 LIGHT THE CHARCOAL

Light the charcoal using one of the methods described on pages 22 to 23. Allow the charcoal to burn until it glows red-hot and is fully covered with a layer of white ash.

2 SPREAD OUT THE COALS

Using a sturdy, long-handled tool such as a pair of tongs, a garden rake, or a hoe, spread the coals so that they evenly cover the charcoal grate. Put the cooking rack in place, and when it has heated, give it a quick cleaning with a wire grill brush.

3 CHECK THE TEMPERATURE

Using a thermometer or your hand (see pages 24 to 25), check the temperature of the cooking rack. Start cooking when the heat is medium (about 350°F). If the heat is too high, wait for the coals to burn down and cool on their own or adjust the grill vents to reduce air flow.

Preparing the Pork

Cedar or alder planks are a good flavor match for smoking pork.

1 SOAK THE PLANK

Place the plank in a pan filled with water. Make sure the plank is completely submerged; weight it down if necessary. Allow the plank to soak for 1 hour. Drain the water and brush the top of the plank with a light coating of oil.

2 GRILL THE PORK

Place the plank directly on the cooking rack over a medium fire and preheat it until it starts to smoke. Place the meat on the plank and grill for 30 to 40 minutes or until a meat thermometer reaches 160°F.

Plank-Smoked Game Hens

Plank cooking can be traced back to Native Americans in the Pacific Northwest, an area where alder and cedar trees grow in abundance and have been used for generations to give food a wonderful smoky flavor.

GRILLING DETAILS

PREP: 30 minutes
SOAK: 1 hour
GRILL: 50 minutes
MAKES: 4 servings

INGREDIENTS

1   cedar or alder plank
¼   cup finely chopped onion
1   clove garlic, minced
2   teaspoons cooking oil
½   cup apricot spreadable fruit
1   serrano chile pepper, seeded and finely chopped (see tip, page 52)
½   teaspoon finely shredded lime peel
1   tablespoon lime juice
2   1¼- to 1½-pound Cornish game hens, halved
    Salt and black pepper
1   recipe Tipsy Fruit salad (see recipe, below)

REAL WORLD

AMERICA'S OWN MINI-CHICKENS
Though they sound like some kind of exotic import from the Old World, Cornish game hens are a very American food and they arrived on the scene relatively recently, in the mid-1960s. The folks at Tyson (the largest chicken supplier in the U.S.) developed the small-size chickens as a gourmet item with the hopes of selling them at a much higher price than regular chicken. The little birds have been a modest hit, but they are very affordable and a good substitute when you want something a little different than grilled chicken.

1 At least one hour before grilling, soak the plank in enough water to cover.

2 In a medium skillet cook onion and garlic in hot oil over medium heat until tender. In a small bowl combine onion mixture, spreadable fruit, chile pepper, lime peel, and lime juice. Set aside.

3 For a charcoal grill, place a plank on the rack of an uncovered grill directly over medium coals until plank begins to crackle and smoke. Place hens, cut sides down, on the plank. Sprinkle lightly with salt and pepper. Cover; grill for 25 minutes. Carefully spoon glaze on hens. Cover; grill 25 to 35 minutes more or until no longer pink (180°F in a thigh muscle). (For a gas grill, preheat grill. Reduce heat to medium. Adjust for indirect cooking. Grill as above.)

4 Transfer plank with Cornish game hens to a serving platter. Serve with Tipsy Fruit Salad.

Tipsy Fruit Salad: In a medium bowl combine 1 large nectarine, pitted and chopped; 1½ cups cubed honeydew melon; 1 cup halved red seedless grapes; ½ cup blueberries; 2 tablespoons rum or pineapple juice; 1 tablespoon honey; ½ teaspoon finely shredded lime peel; and 1 tablespoon lime juice. Cover and chill for up to 24 hours.

Preparing the Grill

1 LIGHT THE CHARCOAL
Light the charcoal using one of the methods described on pages 22 to 23. Allow the charcoal to burn until it glows red-hot and is fully covered with a layer of white ash.

2 SPREAD OUT THE COALS
Using a sturdy, long-handled tool such as a pair of tongs, a garden rake, or a hoe, spread the coals so that they evenly cover the charcoal grate. Put the cooking rack in place, and when it has heated, give it a quick cleaning with a wire grill brush.

3 CHECK THE TEMPERATURE
Using a thermometer or your hand (see pages 24 to 25), check the temperature of the cooking rack. Start cooking when the heat is medium (about 350°F). If the heat is too high, wait for the coals to burn down and cool on their own or adjust the grill vents to reduce air flow.

Preparing the Game Hens

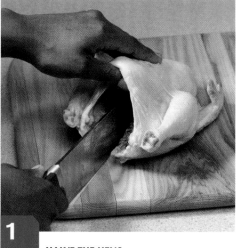

Each of these mini-sized chickens will yield two servings.

1 HALVE THE HENS
Lay a game hen, breast side up, on a cutting board. Grasp the bird firmly and insert a large, sharp knife into the body cavity. Slice completely through the center of the back, as shown (above left). Turn the bird over and finish cutting the game hen in half by slicing through the center of the breast, as shown (above right).

2 GRILL THE HENS
Lay the hen halves, cut sides down, on the preheated, smoking plank and grill them for 25 minutes. Spoon the glaze on the game hens and grill them for an additional 25 to 30 minutes. The bird is done when the thigh meat temperature reaches 180°F.

Planked Salmon with Cucumber-Dill Sauce

Thank Native Americans from the Pacific Northwest for this great idea—they cooked salmon by nailing fillets to wood planks set up around a smoky fire.

GRILLING DETAILS

PREP: 10 minutes
CHILL: 8 to 24 hours
SOAK: 1 hour
GRILL: 18 minutes
MAKES: 4 servings

INGREDIENTS

- 1   1½-pound fresh or frozen salmon fillet, 1 inch thick
- 1   tablespoon packed brown sugar
- 1   teaspoon salt
- ¼   teaspoon black pepper
- 1   cedar grill plank
- 1   recipe Cucumber-Dill Sauce (see recipe, below)

BUYER'S GUIDE

SELECTING QUALITY FISH

When it's time to choose a fish fillet like the one called for in this recipe, there are some things to keep an eye open for to get the best quality. If you are choosing fresh fish, give it a sniff; it should smell like the sea, not fishy. The flesh should be firm and elastic, not squishy, and should have no blemishes. If you are looking at frozen fillets, choose those with slightly shiny skin and flesh and even color and texture throughout. Put the fish back if you see white spots—a sign of freezer burn—or if the packaging is damaged in any way.

1 Thaw salmon, if frozen. Rinse salmon; pat dry with paper towels. Place salmon, skin side down, in a shallow dish. For rub, in a small bowl stir together brown sugar, salt, and black pepper. Sprinkle rub evenly over salmon (not on skin side); pat in with your fingers. Cover and refrigerate for 8 to 24 hours.

2 At least 1 hour before grilling, soak plank in enough water to cover. Place a weight on the plank so it stays submerged during soaking.

3 For a charcoal grill, arrange medium-hot coals around edge of grill. Place salmon, skin side down, on grill plank. Place plank in center of grill rack. Cover; grill for 18 to 22 minutes or until fish flakes easily when tested with a fork. (For a gas grill, preheat grill. Reduce heat to medium. Adjust heat for indirect cooking. Grill as above.)

4 To serve, cut salmon into 4 or 6 pieces. Slide a spatula between the fish and skin to release pieces from plank. Serve with Cucumber-Dill Sauce.

Cucumber-Dill Sauce: In a small bowl combine ⅓ cup finely chopped cucumber, 3 tablespoons plain yogurt, 2 tablespoons mayonnaise or salad dressing, 2 teaspoons snipped fresh dill, and 2 teaspoons prepared horseradish. Cover and chill until serving time or for up to 4 hours. Makes ⅔ cup.

Preparing the Grill

1
LIGHT THE CHARCOAL
Light the charcoal using one of the methods described on pages 22 to 23. Allow the charcoal to burn until it glows red-hot and is fully covered with a layer of white ash.

2
SPREAD OUT THE COALS
Using a sturdy, long-handled tool such as a pair of tongs, a garden rake, or a hoe, spread the coals so that they evenly cover the charcoal grate. Put the cooking rack in place, and when it has heated, give it a quick cleaning with a wire grill brush.

3
CHECK THE TEMPERATURE
Using a thermometer or your hand (see pages 24 to 25), check the temperature of the cooking rack. Start cooking when the heat is medium (about 350°F). If the heat is too high, wait for the coals to burn down and cool on their own or adjust the grill vents to reduce air flow.

Preparing the Salmon

Apply the rub a day in advance to free up your time during a cookout.

1
GRILL THE FISH
Soak the cedar plank in water for 1 hour and then place on the cooking rack directly over medium coals. Preheat the plank until it starts to smoke and then place the salmon on the plank, skin side down. Cover the grill.

2
REMOVE THE FISH
Grill the salmon for 18 to 22 minutes until the fish flakes easily with a fork. Gently slide a spatula under the cooked fish, but above the skin, and lift the salmon fillet off the skin. Cut into serving-size portions.

Brining

 ne of the pitfalls of long, slow grilling is that sometimes you end up drying out the meat. Few things are more frustrating than investing a lot of time into cooking a meal and having your main entrée about as palatable as an old sneaker. Is there some kind of insurance policy against dried-out meat? Other than keeping the number for the local barbecue shack on speed dial, there is one technique that you should consider adding to your repertoire: brining. Brining is the age-old tradition of soaking meats in a salt-and-water solution, except that it has been updated with 21st-century ideas for giving your entrées fantastic flavors that are enhanced on the grill.

Most important, brining is a secret weapon for keeping some types of slow-grilled foods juicier and more tender, no matter how long you have to leave them on the cooking rack.

Soaking meat in a strong salt solution has long been used as a preservation method, though in the modern era salt curing has become less popular (and less necessary), thanks to refrigeration and freezing. Brining for grillers is really a type of marinating using less-concentrated salt solutions along with flavoring ingredients such as fruit juice, beer, sugar, onion, garlic, and any number of herbs and spices. Not all meats are good candidates for brining. Mild-flavored, lean meats such as poultry,

Chapter 8 Recipes

pork, and seafood—all of which tend to dry out on the grill—are perfect for brining, while beef and lamb aren't really improved by the saltwater marinade.

How does brining work? Food scientists disagree about exactly what happens on the cellular level when you soak meat in a saltwater solution, but they do agree on the results. The high concentrations of salt inside brined meats cause proteins to "denature"—that is, unwind—and during cooking these denatured proteins trap water and the flavorings from the brine solution and hold them tightly. The result is a flavorful and juicy dish—as long as you don't overcook it.

There are a few things to keep in mind when brining food. Some people aren't crazy about the salty flavor and think they can get away with a lower concentration of salt in the brine or a shorter brining time—neither adjustment works. Follow the recipes carefully and use the amount of salt and the brining time recommended or you won't get enough—or even any—of the benefit of the brining and you might as well skip it altogether. Conversely, avoid the "more is better" concept—add extra salt or brine for too long and you'll end up with food that's just too salty. In addition, brining must be done in the refrigerator. Some people mistakenly think that the salt solution will kill bacteria, but you need to treat this like any other meat to ensure the safety of your meal. Along the same lines, always discard your brine after you are finished with it because it can't be safely reused.

Spicy Beer-Brined Ribs

Instead of liquid smoke, try sprinkling some water-soaked hardwood chips or chunks on the hot coals to give the ribs an honest-to-goodness smoked flavor.

GRILLING DETAILS

PREP: 20 minutes
MARINATE: 6 hours
GRILL: 1½ hours
MAKES: 4 servings

INGREDIENTS

- 3   12-ounce cans beer
- 3   tablespoons kosher salt
- 3   tablespoons packed brown sugar
- 1   tablespoon celery seeds
- 1   tablespoon cayenne pepper
- 1½ teaspoons black pepper
- 1   teaspoon liquid smoke (optional)
- 4   pounds meaty pork spareribs or loin back ribs
- ½   cup Honey-Beer Barbecue Sauce (see recipe, below) or bottled barbecue sauce

8

BRINING

WORK SMARTER

KOSHER SALT VERSUS TABLE SALT
Kosher salt—which has much larger crystals than table salt but is still plain old sodium chloride—is a popular choice among professional chefs because of its "cleaner" taste. In reality, there probably isn't much difference between the flavor of kosher and table salts once you dissolve them in a brine solution, but there is an important difference in the amount of saltiness they supply. Because it has coarser crystals, 1 cup of kosher salt has less salt (and more air) than 1 cup of table salt. All the brining recipes in this chapter specify kosher salt, which is what you should use for better results. If you are forced to use table salt, reduce the amount specified for kosher salt by about one-third.

1 For brine, in a large bowl combine beer, salt, brown sugar, celery seeds, cayenne pepper, black pepper, and, if desired, liquid smoke; stir until salt and brown sugar are dissolved. Cut ribs into 2-rib portions; place in a resealable large plastic bag set in a shallow dish. Pour brine over ribs; seal bag. Marinate in the refrigerator for 6 hours, turning bag occasionally.

2 Remove ribs from bag; discard brine. Pat ribs dry with paper towels.

3 For a charcoal grill, arrange medium-hot coals around a drip pan. Test for medium heat above the drip pan. Place ribs, bone sides down, on the grill rack over the drip pan. (Or place ribs in a rib rack; place rib rack on the grill rack over the drip pan.) Cover; grill for 1½ to 1¾ hours or until ribs are tender, brushing with Honey-Beer Barbecue Sauce during the last 5 minutes of grilling. Add fresh coals as needed to maintain temperature. (For a gas grill, preheat grill. Reduce heat to medium. Adjust for indirect cooking. Grill as above.)

Honey-Beer Barbecue Sauce: In a medium saucepan cook ⅓ cup chopped onion and 1 minced clove garlic in 1 tablespoon cooking oil until tender. Stir in ¾ cup chili sauce, ½ cup beer, ¼ cup honey, 2 tablespoons Worcestershire sauce, and 1 tablespoon yellow mustard. Bring to boiling; reduce heat. Simmer, uncovered, about 20 minutes or until desired consistency, stirring occasionally.

Make-ahead directions: Prepare as directed through step 2. Cover and refrigerate ribs up to 24 hours. Grill as directed in step 3.

Preparing the Grill

1 LIGHT THE CHARCOAL

Light the charcoal using one of the methods described on pages 22 to 23. Allow the charcoal to burn until it glows red-hot and is fully covered with a layer of white ash.

2 SEPARATE THE COALS

Using a sturdy, long-handled tool such as a pair of tongs, a garden rake, or a hoe, separate the coals into two equal piles about 10 inches apart. The space between the piles should be wide enough to accommodate a disposable aluminum drip pan.

3 ADD A DRIP PAN

Place an aluminum drip pan in the area between the coals and pour enough hot water into the pan to fill it about $\frac{1}{2}$ inch deep. Replace the grill's cooking grate and allow it to heat up before adding the food.

Preparing the Ribs

1 TRIM THE RIBS

Trim any excess fat from the pork ribs. Cut the racks into two-rib, serving-size portions, as shown. Place the ribs in a resealable large plastic bag and set the bag in a shallow dish.

2 ADD THE BRINE

Mix the brine ingredients in a large bowl until the salt and sugar are dissolved. Pour the brine into the plastic bag, seal the bag, and place in the refrigerator for 6 hours. Drain the brine and grill the ribs using indirect heat for $1\frac{1}{2}$ to $1\frac{3}{4}$ hours.

Coat generously with the Honey-Beer Barbecue Sauce or your favorite bottled barbecue sauce.

Beer and Caraway Pork Chops

Use your favorite beer when brining these chops. A dark ale will give fuller flavor than a lighter-color beer.

GRILLING DETAILS

PREP: 20 minutes
MARINATE: 4 to 6 hours
GRILL: 30 minutes
MAKES: 4 servings

INGREDIENTS

1	12-ounce can or bottle ale or beer
½	cup cider vinegar
3	tablespoons kosher salt
2	tablespoons packed brown sugar
1	tablespoon caraway seeds, crushed
1	tablespoon dried thyme, crushed
½	teaspoon black pepper
4	boneless pork loin chops,* cut 1 to 1¼ inches thick
3	tablespoons apple jelly, melted
¼	teaspoon caraway seeds, crushed

GOOD IDEA

RINSE AND DRY CYCLE

Some grill chefs may be surprised to see brining recipes that instruct them to rinse their food in water after brining and before cooking—go ahead, it's okay. Rinsing is helpful after marinating in brines that have very high salt or sugar concentrations. Rinsing salt off the surface reduces unnecessary salty flavoring, and some sugars tend to burn during grilling. Whether you rinse or not, always dab your brined meat dry with paper towels before you put it on the grill.

1 For brine, pour ale slowly to avoid foaming into a large bowl. Stir in vinegar, salt, brown sugar, the 1 tablespoon caraway seeds, the thyme, and pepper. Stir until salt and brown sugar are dissolved. Place chops in a resealable large plastic bag set in a shallow dish. Pour brine over chops; seal bag. Marinate in the refrigerator for 4 to 6 hours, turning bag occasionally.

2 Remove chops from bag; discard brine. Rinse chops and pat dry with paper towels. In a small bowl stir together melted apple jelly and the ¼ teaspoon caraway seeds; set aside.

3 For a charcoal grill, arrange medium-hot coals around a drip pan. Test for medium heat above the drip pan. Place chops on the grill rack over the drip pan. Cover; grill for 30 to 35 minutes or until done (160°F), turning once halfway through grilling and brushing with apple jelly mixture during the last 5 minutes of grilling. (For a gas grill, preheat grill. Reduce heat to medium. Adjust for indirect cooking. Grill as above.)

*Note: For chops that will be brined, be sure to purchase chops that have not been enhanced with additional moisture.

Preparing the Grill

1
LIGHT THE CHARCOAL
Light the charcoal using one of the methods described on pages 22 to 23. Allow the charcoal to burn until it glows red-hot and is fully covered with a layer of white ash.

2
SEPARATE THE COALS
Using a sturdy, long-handled tool such as a pair of tongs, a garden rake, or a hoe, separate the coals into two equal piles about 10 inches apart. The space between the piles should be wide enough to accommodate a disposable aluminum drip pan.

3
ADD A DRIP PAN
Place an aluminum drip pan in the area between the coals and pour enough hot water into the pan to fill it about ½ inch deep. Replace the grill's cooking grate and allow it to heat up before adding the food.

Preparing the Pork Chops

Dark beer is the perfect beverage companion when serving these pork chops.

1
BRINE THE CHOPS
Marinate the pork chops in the brine mixture in a refrigerator for 4 to 6 hours. Drain the brine off the chops and discard it. Rinse the chops with water, then dry the chops with paper towels.

2
GRILL THE CHOPS
Place the chops over a drip pan and close the grill cover. Grill the chops using indirect heat (about 350°F) for 30 to 35 minutes or until the internal temperature is 160°F. Brush the chops with the apple jelly mixture during the last 5 minutes of grilling.

New England Grilled Turkey

If you prefer, omit the drip pan and grill the turkey on a rack in a roasting pan, which will work better to hold the large amount of drippings.

⟡ GRILLING DETAILS

PREP: 50 minutes
MARINATE: Overnight
GRILL: 2½ hours
STAND: 15 minutes
MAKES: 10 to 12 servings

✓ INGREDIENTS

- 4 cups hot water
- 1¼ cups kosher salt
- 1 cup pure maple syrup
- 1 6-ounce can apple juice concentrate, thawed
- 3 cloves garlic, crushed
- 4 whole cloves
- ¼ teaspoon whole black peppercorns
- 16 cups cold water
- 1 8- to 10-pound whole turkey
- ¼ cup butter, softened
- 1 teaspoon ground sage
  Salt and black pepper
- 1 recipe Gingered Cranberry Sauce (see recipe, right)

📖 WORK SMARTER

MATCH GRILLING TIME TO TURKEY SIZE
As one of the largest things you'll cook on your grill, a whole turkey is going to take a relatively long time to cook—and the larger the bird the longer the time. Using indirect heat and maintaining a constant temperature of 325°F to 350°F, grill birds according to these guidelines:

6 to 8 pounds—1¾ to 2¼ hours
8 to 12 pounds—2½ to 3½ hours
12 to 16 pounds—3½ to 4 hours

The ultimate measurement of doneness for a whole turkey is the internal temperature of the thigh meat, which should register 180°F.

1 For brine, in a deep stockpot combine hot water, the 1¼ cups kosher salt, the maple syrup, and juice concentrate. Stir until salt is dissolved. Add garlic, cloves, peppercorns, and the cold water.

2 Rinse inside of turkey; remove any excess fat from the cavity. Add turkey to brine and weight to keep turkey covered in brine. Cover and marinate in the refrigerator overnight. Remove turkey from pot; discard brine. Pat turkey dry with paper towels.

3 In a small bowl combine butter and sage; set aside. Starting at the neck on one side of the breast, slip your fingers between skin and meat, loosening the skin as you work toward the tail end. Once your entire hand is under the skin, free the skin around the thigh and leg area up to, but not around, the tip of the drumstick. Repeat on the other side of the breast. Rub sage butter under the skin directly on meat. Skewer the neck skin to the back. Twist wing tips behind back. Sprinkle surface and cavity of turkey with salt and pepper. Tuck drumsticks under band of skin or tie to tail with 100-percent-cotton string.

4 For a charcoal grill, arrange medium-hot coals around a drip pan. Test for medium heat above the drip pan.* Place turkey, breast side up, on grill rack over drip pan. Cover; grill for 2½ to 3 hours or until drumsticks move easily in their sockets and turkey is no longer pink (180°F in inside thigh muscle), adding fresh coals every 45 to 60 minutes and cutting band of skin or string the last hour of grilling. (For a gas grill, preheat grill. Reduce heat to medium. Adjust for indirect cooking. Grill as above.)

5 Remove turkey from grill. Cover with foil; let stand for 15 minutes before carving. Serve with Gingered Cranberry Sauce.

Gingered Cranberry Sauce: In a medium saucepan combine 1 cup sugar and 1 cup water. Bring to boiling, stirring to dissolve sugar. Boil rapidly for 5 minutes. Add 2 cups fresh cranberries, ½ cup snipped dried apples, 1½ teaspoons grated fresh ginger, and 1 teaspoon finely shredded lemon peel. Return to boiling; reduce heat. Boil gently, uncovered, over medium heat for 3 to 4 minutes or until skins pop, stirring occasionally. Remove from heat. Serve warm or chilled.

*Note: Due to the large amount of turkey drippings, you may prefer to omit the drip pan and place the turkey on a rack in a roasting pan. Place the pan in the center of the grill, not directly over the heat source.

8

BRINING

Preparing the Grill

1 LIGHT THE CHARCOAL
Light the charcoal using one of the methods described on pages 22 to 23. Allow the charcoal to burn until it glows red-hot and is fully covered with a layer of white ash.

2 SEPARATE THE COALS
Using a sturdy, long-handled tool such as a pair of tongs, a garden rake, or a hoe, separate the coals into two equal piles about 10 inches apart. The space between the piles should be wide enough to accommodate a disposable aluminum drip pan.

3 ADD A DRIP PAN
Place an aluminum drip pan in the area between the coals and pour enough hot water into the pan to fill it about ½ inch deep. Replace the grill's cooking grate and allow it to heat up before adding the food.

Preparing the Turkey

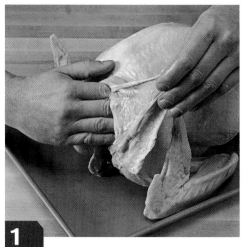

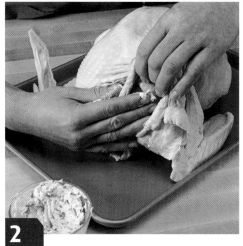

Add fresh charcoal briquettes to keep the cooking temperature constant.

1 LOOSEN THE SKIN
Remove the turkey from the brine, drain it well, and pat it dry. Starting at the neck end, slide your fingers under the skin on the breast, as shown, and loosen it from the meat. Keep working until you've loosened the skin around the thigh and most of the drumstick.

2 ADD THE BUTTER
Use your fingers to apply the sage butter to the entire surface of the meat under the loosened skin. Skewer the neck skin to the back, tuck the wing tips under the back, and secure the drumsticks to the tail. Grill using indirect heat for 2½ to 3 hours.

Asian-Spiced Chicken

The key to this chicken's flavor is star anise, the pod of a small evergreen tree native to China. Look for this in your supermarket's spice section or in Asian specialty stores.

GRILLING DETAILS

PREP: 15 minutes
MARINATE: 6 to 8 hours
GRILL: 1¼ hours
STAND: 10 minutes
MAKES: 4 servings

INGREDIENTS

- 8 cups water
- ⅓ cup kosher salt
- ¼ cup soy sauce
- ¼ cup rice vinegar or white vinegar
- 8 star anise, crushed
- 2 3-inch pieces stick cinnamon, broken
- 1 tablespoon sugar
- 2 teaspoons fennel seeds, crushed
- 1 3- to 3½-pound whole broiler-fryer chicken

WORK SMARTER

WHOLE CHICKEN GRILLING GUIDELINES

Whole chickens are a less formidable grilling project than whole turkeys, but they take some time to cook and it's essential to cook them to a safe internal temperature. Using indirect heat and maintaining a constant temperature of 325°F to 350°F, grill whole chickens according to these guidelines:
2½ to 3 pounds—1 to 1¼ hours
3 to 4 pounds—1¼ to 1¾ hours
4 to 5 pounds—1¾ to 2 hours
Always test the internal temperature of the thigh meat to determine doneness; it should register 180°F.

1 For brine, in a stainless-steel or enamel stockpot or plastic container large enough to hold the chicken combine water, salt, soy sauce, vinegar, star anise, cinnamon, sugar, and fennel seeds. Stir until salt is dissolved.

2 Rinse inside of chicken. Carefully add chicken to brine. Cover and marinate in the refrigerator for 6 to 8 hours, turning the chicken occasionally. Remove chicken from pot; discard brine. Rinse chicken and pat dry with paper towels. Twist wing tips under the back. Skewer the neck skin to the back. Tie legs to tail with 100-percent-cotton string.

3 For a charcoal grill, arrange medium-hot coals around a drip pan. Test for medium heat above the drip pan. Place chicken, breast side up, on grill rack over the drip pan. Cover; grill for 1¼ to 1½ hours or until drumsticks move easily in their sockets and chicken is no longer pink (180°F in inside thigh muscle). Add fresh coals as needed to maintain temperature. (For a gas grill, preheat grill. Reduce heat to medium. Adjust for indirect cooking. Grill as above.)

4 Remove chicken from grill. Cover chicken with foil; let stand for 10 minutes before carving.

Preparing the Grill

1
LIGHT THE CHARCOAL
Light the charcoal using one of the methods described on pages 22 to 23. Allow the charcoal to burn until it glows red-hot and is fully covered with a layer of white ash.

2
SEPARATE THE COALS
Using a sturdy, long-handled tool such as a pair of tongs, a garden rake, or a hoe, separate the coals into two equal piles about 10 inches apart. The space between the piles should be wide enough to accommodate a disposable aluminum drip pan.

3
ADD A DRIP PAN
Place an aluminum drip pan in the area between the coals and pour enough hot water into the pan to fill it about ½ inch deep. Replace the grill's cooking grate and allow it to heat up before adding the food.

Preparing the Chicken

1
BREAK THE STAR ANISE
Place eight star anise pods on a clean, stable work surface. Tap the pods with a wooden cooking mallet to crush them into small pieces, as shown. Combine the star anise with the other brine ingredients in a container large enough to hold the whole chicken.

2
GRILL THE CHICKEN
Place the chicken over a drip pan and grill using indirect medium (350°F) heat for 1¼ to 1½ hours. Insert a quick-read thermometer into the thigh meat, as shown, taking care to not touch a bone. The chicken is done when the temperature registers 180°F.

Rinse the chicken thoroughly after brining and pat dry with paper towels.

8

BRINING

Tandoori Spiced Chicken

This buttermilk-bathed chicken borrows seasonings used in traditional Indian tandoori cooking and employs a tasty cucumber sauce to cool the heat.

8

BRINING

REAL WORLD

TANDOORI: GRILLING INDIAN STYLE

Tandoori is not a spice, but rather a popular style of cooking that gets its name from a type of oven that is common in India and Pakistan. A tandoor is a clay, often-cylindrical oven that is traditionally fired by charcoal. Tandoors cook food at very high temperatures—usually 500°F or higher—and are most often used for cooking marinated meats (especially chicken) and some types of bread.

1 For brine, in a large bowl combine buttermilk, salt, sugar, and garlic; set aside. In a small bowl combine ginger, curry powder, onion powder, and cayenne pepper; set aside 2 teaspoons of the ginger mixture. Add remaining ginger mixture to brine mixture, stirring until salt and sugar are dissolved. Place chicken in a resealable large plastic bag set in a shallow dish. Pour brine mixture over chicken to coat; seal bag. Marinate in the refrigerator for 2 to 4 hours, turning bag occasionally.

2 Remove chicken from bag; discard brine. Sprinkle chicken evenly with the reserved 2 teaspoons ginger mixture.

3 For a charcoal grill, arrange medium-hot coals around a drip pan. Test for medium heat above the drip pan. Place chicken pieces, bone sides down, on a greased grill rack over the drip pan. Cover; grill for 50 to 60 minutes or until chicken is tender and no longer pink (170°F for breast halves, 180°F for thighs and drumsticks). (For a gas grill, preheat grill. Reduce heat to medium. Adjust for indirect cooking. Grill as above.)

4 Serve chicken with Curry-Cucumber Sauce. If desired, garnish with carrot and parsley.

Curry-Cucumber Sauce: In a medium bowl stir together 1 cup chopped, seeded cucumber; 1/2 cup mayonnaise or salad dressing; 1/3 cup buttermilk; 1/2 teaspoon curry powder; and 1/4 teaspoon ground ginger. Cover and chill until serving. Makes about 1 1/2 cups.

Preparing the Grill

1

LIGHT THE CHARCOAL

Light the charcoal using one of the methods described on pages 22 to 23. Allow the charcoal to burn until it glows red-hot and is fully covered with a layer of white ash.

2

SEPARATE THE COALS

Using a sturdy, long-handled tool such as a pair of tongs, a garden rake, or a hoe, separate the coals into two equal piles about 10 inches apart. The space between the piles should be wide enough to accommodate a disposable aluminum drip pan.

3

ADD A DRIP PAN

Place an aluminum drip pan in the area between the coals and pour enough hot water into the pan to fill it about ½ inch deep. Replace the grill's cooking grate and allow it to heat up before adding the food.

Preparing the Chicken and Sauce

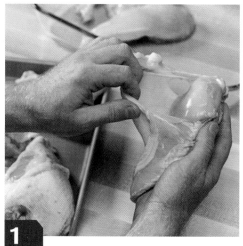

1

SKIN THE CHICKEN

Remove the skin from the chicken pieces with your fingers, as shown. Keep a knife nearby to loosen the skin edges or cut any stubborn membranes. Place the chicken in a resealable plastic bag and cover with the brine. Marinate for 2 to 4 hours and then grill with indirect heat.

2

SEED THE CUCUMBER

Slice a cucumber in half lengthwise and scoop out the seeds with a spoon, as shown. Chop the cucumber into small pieces and combine with the other sauce ingredients. Mix well and serve with the grilled chicken.

Use chicken legs, thighs, and/or breasts for this traditional Indian-style dish.

Sauces, Marinades, Rubs, and Mops

Harnessing the amazing cooking powers of fire and smoke is only half the equation for grilling success. All budding outdoor cooks owe it to themselves to learn about the Four Pillars of Even More Grilling Flavor: Sauces, Marinades, Rubs, and Mops. There are a variety of ways to enhance the flavor of grilled entrées, everything from a simple sprinkle of salt and pepper to elaborate seasoning-and-saucing programs that have been custom-fitted to a certain cut of meat. Yet, as you expand your grilling repertoire, you will quickly discover that you don't necessarily have to follow a formal plan every time you fire up the grill. This chapter's recipes offer you a variety of ways to flavor grilled meals that can be successfully married to a number of different foods.

In a grilling sense, it's important to understand the difference between the three styles of sauces you'll encounter in this section; each type has a specific use. Just plain "sauces" are liquids that are applied to foods after cooking or are served with foods. Barbecue sauce, on the other hand, is brushed on food during cooking. It also can be served with food or used as a condiment, but the benefit of its flavor-adding abilities is spending time on the food at grilling temperatures. Mops are specialized barbecue sauces that are extra watery.

While you are sure to find several great recipes in the pages that follow, you will quickly discover that flavorings offer one of the great creative outlets for grill chefs. All kinds of great flavors mix well with grilling and the only limit is your imagination as you experiment with your own sauces, rubs, mops, and marinades. Remember that grilling imparts its own smoky flavor, and your seasonings and sauces should work well with this flavor, not cover it up. Ultimately the best part of experimenting is that every new creation you concoct gives you another reason to fire up the grill.

Chapter 9 Recipes

Blue Cheese Steak Toppers

Some purists think it's wrong to put anything on a grilled steak—those purists are missing out on a fantastic-tasting piece of beef.

DETAILS

START TO FINISH: 10 minutes
MAKES: ½ cup

INGREDIENTS

- ¼ cup crumbled blue cheese
- ¼ cup butter, softened
- 1 tablespoon snipped fresh parsley or 1 teaspoon dried parsley flakes
- ½ teaspoon dried basil, crushed
- ½ teaspoon bottled minced garlic

1 CRUMBLE THE BLUE CHEESE
Use a fork to break a block of blue cheese into small crumbles. In a small bowl combine ¼ cup of the blue cheese crumbles with the butter, parsley, basil, and garlic. Mix well and serve on top of grilled steaks.

Mustard-Horseradish Sauce

Spread this cool, creamy topping with just the right bite on sandwiches made with grilled meats.

DETAILS

START TO FINISH: 10 minutes
MAKES: about ½ cup

INGREDIENTS

- 2 tablespoons finely chopped green onion (1)
- ⅓ cup dairy sour cream
- 1 tablespoon Dijon-style mustard
- 1 to 2 teaspoons prepared horseradish

1 CHOP THE GREEN ONION
Slice the green onion bulb and then chop the slices into tiny pieces. In a small bowl combine 2 tablespoons of the green onion with the sour cream, mustard, and horseradish. Mix the sauce well and serve immediately with beef, pork, lamb, or poultry or cover and refrigerate for up to 4 hours.

Cajun Beer Sauce

Beer tastes good right out of the bottle, but you will be amazed at what a great cooking ingredient it is, especially in this spicy Louisiana-style sauce

DETAILS

START TO FINISH: 15 minutes
MAKES: about 1¼ cups

INGREDIENTS

- ¼ cup chopped onion
- ¼ cup chopped green or red sweet pepper
- 1 tablespoon cooking oil
- ½ cup beer
- ½ cup water
- 1 tablespoon cornstarch
- 1 tablespoon Cajun seasoning

1 COOK THE SAUCE
In a saucepan cook the onion and sweet pepper in oil until tender. In a bowl combine beer, water, cornstarch, and Cajun seasoning; add to the cooked onion mixture. Stir and heat until the mixture is thickened and bubbly. Cook for another 2 minutes and serve with beef or lamb.

Bordelaise Sauce

This classic French sauce is made with red wine and is a popular choice for serving with roast beef.

DETAILS

PREP: 10 minutes
COOK: 15 minutes
MAKES: 1 cup

INGREDIENTS

- ¼ cup chopped green onion (2)
- 2 tablespoons butter or margarine
- 1 tablespoon all-purpose flour
- ½ teaspoon dried thyme, crushed
- 1 14-ounce can beef broth
- ¼ cup dry red wine

1 STIR IN THE FLOUR
In a saucepan cook the green onions in butter until they are tender. Stir in the flour and thyme. Add the broth and wine and heat the mixture to boiling, stirring occasionally. Reduce the heat and boil gently, uncovered, for 15 to 20 minutes. Serve with grilled beef or lamb.

Rich Brown Sauce

This sauce—like souped-up gravy—is great for serving over beef, pork, lamb, or poultry.

DETAILS

PREP: 10 minutes
COOK: 25 minutes
MAKES: about 1 cup

INGREDIENTS

½	cup chopped onion (1 medium)
½	cup sliced carrot (1 medium)
2	tablespoons butter or margarine
2	teaspoons sugar
4	teaspoons all-purpose flour
1½	cups beef broth
2	tablespoons tomato paste
½	teaspoon dried thyme, crushed
⅛	teaspoon black pepper
1	bay leaf

STRAIN THE SAUCE

1 In a saucepan cook the onion and carrot in butter until tender. Stir in the sugar and cook for 5 minutes. Stir in the flour and cook for 6 to 8 minutes until the flour is brown. Stir in the remaining ingredients and heat to boiling. Reduce the heat and simmer, uncovered, for 10 minutes. Strain the sauce and serve.

Brandy Cream Sauce

Grilled beef, pork, lamb, or poultry becomes a gourmet treat when served with this rich sauce.

DETAILS

PREP: 15 minutes
COOK: 14 minutes
MAKES: about 1 cup

INGREDIENTS

½	cup chicken broth
2	tablespoons chopped shallot or green onion
⅓	cup whipping cream
3	tablespoons brandy or cognac
¾	cup butter, cut into small pieces and softened
4	teaspoons lemon juice
¼	teaspoon white pepper

ADD THE BUTTER

1 In a saucepan heat the broth and shallot to boiling. Reduce the heat and simmer, covered, for 2 minutes. Stir in the cream and brandy. Simmer, uncovered, for 12 to 14 minutes. Strain the sauce and return it to the pan. Add tablespoon-size pats of butter and stir until each melts. Add the lemon juice and pepper and serve.

Fresh Herb Sauce

With a delicate flavor, this white sauce is a good companion for poultry, pork, or fish.

DETAILS

START TO FINISH: 15 minutes
MAKES: about 3/4 cup

INGREDIENTS

- 1 cup dry white wine
- 2 tablespoons hazelnut liqueur (optional)
- 1/4 cup thinly sliced leek
- 2 teaspoons snipped fresh rosemary
- 1/2 teaspoon snipped fresh tarragon
- 1/8 teaspoon salt
- 1/8 teaspoon ground white pepper
- 1/2 cup whipping cream

1 ADD THE WHIPPING CREAM

In a saucepan heat the wine and, if desired, liqueur to boiling. Reduce the heat and simmer, uncovered, 10 minutes. Add the leek, rosemary, tarragon, salt, and pepper. Simmer 5 minutes more. Add whipping cream and stir well. Heat to boiling, stirring constantly, and cook over low heat for 2 to 3 minutes until thickened..

Tangy Coconut Sauce

Wasabi, a green fiery-flavored Japanese condiment that's a favorite with fish, flavors a coconut milk sauce.

DETAILS

PREP: 10 minutes
COOK: 3 minutes
CHILL: 2 to 24 hours
MAKES: 1 cup

INGREDIENTS

- 1 teaspoon cornstarch
- 1/3 cup coconut milk
- 2 to 4 teaspoons wasabi paste
- 2 teaspoons grated fresh ginger
- 1 teaspoon lime juice

1 ADD THE CORNSTARCH

In a saucepan mix the coconut milk and cornstarch with a wire whisk. Cook over low heat, stirring constantly, for 3 to 5 minutes. Set aside. In a bowl, combine the wasabi paste, ginger, and lime juice. Stir into the cooled coconut milk mixture. Cover and refrigerate for 2 to 24 hours before serving.

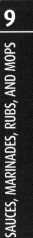

9

SAUCES, MARINADES, RUBS, AND MOPS

Sweet-Hot Barbecue Sauce

Sugar and spice will make all your grilled meats taste nice.

DETAILS

PREP: 15 minutes
COOK: 45 minutes
MAKES: about 2 cups

INGREDIENTS

- 1¼ cups water
- 1 6-ounce can tomato paste
- ½ cup mild-flavor molasses
- ½ cup dark-color corn syrup
- ¼ cup vinegar
- ¼ cup honey
- 1 tablespoon whiskey or bourbon
- 1 tablespoon Worcestershire sauce
- 2 teaspoons paprika
- 1 teaspoon garlic salt
- 1 teaspoon liquid smoke
- 1 teaspoon bottled hot pepper sauce
- ½ teaspoon chili powder
- ¼ teaspoon onion powder
- ¼ to ½ teaspoon cayenne pepper

1 BRUSH ON THE SAUCE
In a saucepan combine all the ingredients and heat to boiling. Reduce the heat and simmer, uncovered, for 45 minutes, stirring frequently. Generously brush the sauce on beef, pork, or poultry during the last 10 minutes of grilling. Reheat any remaining sauce until bubbly and serve with the meat.

Shirt-Staining Barbecue Sauce

Cranberries provide a tart North Country accent to your choice of bottled sauce.

DETAILS

PREP: 10 minutes
COOK: 10 minutes
MAKES: about 3½ cups

INGREDIENTS

- 1 18-ounce bottle (1¾ cups) barbecue sauce
- 1 16-ounce can jellied cranberry sauce
- ¼ cup water
- 2 tablespoons chili powder
- 2 tablespoons packed brown sugar
- ¼ teaspoon garlic powder
- ¼ teaspoon ground cloves

1 SIMMER THE SAUCE
In a medium saucepan combine all the ingredients and heat to boiling. Reduce the heat and simmer the sauce, uncovered, for 10 minutes. Brush on pork or poultry during the last 5 minutes of grilling. Reheat any remaining sauce until bubbly and serve with the meat.

Hot, Hot, Hot Sauce

Three times the heat, thanks to chili powder, black pepper, and cayenne pepper.

DETAILS

START TO FINISH: 15 minutes
MAKES: about 2½ cups

INGREDIENTS

- 2 cups ketchup
- ½ cup dark-color corn syrup
- 2 tablespoons packed brown sugar
- 1 tablespoon lemon juice
- 2½ teaspoons hot chili powder
- 2 teaspoons dried minced onion
- ½ teaspoon black pepper
- ¼ to ½ teaspoon cayenne pepper
- ¼ teaspoon salt

1 ADD THE SAUCE

In a small saucepan combine all the ingredients and mix well. Heat just to boiling, stirring occasionally. Reduce the heat and simmer, uncovered, for 8 minutes. Top grilled chops, ribs, or burgers with some of the sauce before serving and pass the remainder at the table.

Everything-But-the-Kitchen-Sink Sauce

Empty the cupboards for this barbecue brush-on with its own complex palette of great flavors.

DETAILS

PREP: 20 minutes
COOK: 10 minutes
MAKES: about 2 cups

INGREDIENTS

- ¼ cup finely chopped onion
- 6 cloves garlic, minced
- ½ teaspoon paprika
- ½ teaspoon crushed red pepper
- 1 tablespoon cooking oil
- 2 tablespoons packed brown sugar
- 1 15-ounce can tomato puree, undrained
- 3 tablespoons cider vinegar
- 3 tablespoons mild-flavor molasses
- 2 tablespoons stone-ground mustard
- ½ teaspoon salt
- ½ teaspoon dried oregano, crushed
- ½ teaspoon liquid smoke (optional)

1 MEASURE THE SUGAR

In a saucepan cook the onion, garlic, paprika, and red pepper in oil until the onion is tender. Measure brown sugar, as shown, and add with the remaining ingredients to the onion mixture. Heat to boiling; reduce heat. Simmer, uncovered, for 10 minutes. Brush on beef, pork, or poultry during the last 10 minutes of grilling.

Molasses Barbecue Sauce

Molasses adds both sweetness and a unique, rich flavor that complements grilled meat.

DETAILS

START TO FINISH: 10 minutes
MAKES: about 1½ cups

INGREDIENTS

- 1 cup ketchup
- ¼ cup full-flavor molasses
- ¼ cup water
- ½ teaspoon finely shredded lemon peel (optional)
- 1 tablespoon lemon juice
- 2 teaspoons Worcestershire sauce
- ½ teaspoon black pepper
- ⅛ teaspoon salt

1 COMBINE THE INGREDIENTS
In a small bowl combine all the ingredients and stir the mixture thoroughly to dissolve the molasses. Brush the sauce on beef, pork, or poultry during the last 5 to 10 minutes of grilling. Heat any remaining sauce until bubbly and serve with the meat.

Smoky Barbecue Sauce

Out of hardwood chips? This recipe will give meat the smoked flavor you want.

DETAILS

PREP: 10 minutes
COOK: 20 minutes
MAKES: about 2 cups

INGREDIENTS

- 1 15-ounce can tomato sauce
- ½ cup cider vinegar
- ½ cup packed brown sugar
- 2 tablespoons finely chopped onion
- 2 tablespoons liquid smoke
- 1 tablespoon Worcestershire sauce
- 1 teaspoon chili powder
- 1 clove garlic, minced
- ¼ teaspoon celery salt
- ⅛ to ¼ teaspoon cayenne pepper
- ⅛ teaspoon ground allspice
- 3 drops bottled hot pepper sauce

1 COOK THE SAUCE
In a saucepan combine all the ingredients and heat to boiling. Reduce the heat and simmer the sauce, uncovered, for 30 minutes, stirring frequently. Brush the sauce on pork or poultry during the last 10 minutes of grilling. Reheat any remaining sauce until bubbly and serve with the meat.

Bourbon-Peach Barbecue Sauce

A simple upgrade to your favorite bottled sauce results in a memorable topping for grilled chicken or pork.

DETAILS

START TO FINISH: 10 minutes
MAKES: about 3 cups

INGREDIENTS

- 2½ cups bottled barbecue sauce
- ½ cup peach preserves
- ½ cup bourbon
- ¼ teaspoon ground cloves
- ¼ teaspoon cayenne pepper

1 MEASURE THE SAUCE

Measure 2½ cups of your favorite bottled barbecue sauce. In a medium bowl combine the sauce with the remaining ingredients and mix thoroughly. Brush the sauce on meat during the last 10 minutes of grilling. Heat any remaining sauce until bubbly and serve with the meat.

Fire-Breathin' BBQ Ketchup

It starts off as your favorite condiment and ends up as a sauce that packs a serious punch.

DETAILS

START TO FINISH: 20 minutes
MAKES: about 2 cups

INGREDIENTS

- 1 cup coarsely chopped onion (1 large)
- 1 to 2 tablespoons chipotle peppers in adobo sauce
- 1 fresh jalapeño chile pepper, seeded and cut up (see tip, page 52)
- 2 cloves garlic, minced
- 1 teaspoon dried oregano, crushed
- ½ teaspoon salt
- 1 cup ketchup
- ¼ cup red wine vinegar or cider vinegar
- 2 tablespoons cooking oil

1 PROCESS THE SAUCE

In a food processor combine the onion, chipotle and jalapeño peppers, garlic, oregano, and salt. Cover and process until combined. Add the remaining ingredients and process until smooth. Brush on beef or pork during the last 10 minutes of grilling. Heat any remaining sauce until bubbly and serve with the meat.

How to Marinate

Marinades are seasoned liquids in which you soak foods prior to cooking. In addition to flavoring meats, marinades—especially those with acidic liquids such as vinegar or wine—can also tenderize them, which is great when you're grilling inexpensive, tougher cuts. Tenderizing marinades need some time to work, anywhere from 4 to 24 hours, but tender cuts can be flavored by marinating for a relatively short period of time— as little as 15 minutes and up to 2 hours. It's important not to "overmarinate" food—highly acidic marinades can work too well and make your food mushy if you leave it in the liquid for more than 24 hours.

Working with marinades is a pretty simple process, though there are a couple of things that you can do to make the job easier and the marinade more effective. The resealable plastic kitchen bag is an invaluable tool when it comes to working with marinades. Buy yourself a generous supply of large resealable bags with a capacity of at least one gallon. Also, make sure you have a large kitchen casserole dish or some type of flat-bottom container with fairly tall sides.

Mix your marinade in a generous-size mixing bowl. Cut your meat or vegetables into serving-size pieces and place them in a clean resealable bag. Don't overfill the bag. If you have more food than will fit in a single bag, use multiple bags (which may require mixing additional marinade). The food pieces should have room to move around, you should be able to easily seal the bag, and the food should be generously bathed in the liquid.

Place the bag in the bottom of the casserole, which serves as a catch basin in the event of a spill or leak. Pour the marinade into the bag and carefully seal it. Turn the bag gently to make sure all the food pieces are covered in marinade. Place the bag—safely sitting in the casserole—in a refrigerator and leave it there for the specified amount of time. It is essential that food marinate at cold temperatures to prevent bacterial contamination.

As the food marinates, occasionally turn the bag to re-coat and immerse different parts of the meat or vegetables in the liquid. When the food is finished marinating, remove the pieces from the bag with tongs, allowing the marinade to drain off. Discard the marinade when you're done using it. If a recipe calls for adding some of the marinade to a sauce or basting grilling meat with it, the marinade must first be heated to a full boil.

▲ Large resealable kitchen bags help keep liquids sealed inside and they can be turned easily to coat marinating food. Setting them in a casserole dish while in the refrigerator provides extra insurance in case of a leak.

▲ Handle marinated food with tongs to minimize mess and the chance of bacterial contamination in your food prep area.

Best Beef Marinade

Whether you need flavoring, tenderizing, or both, this versatile marinade does the trick.

⊘ DETAILS

PREP: 10 minutes
MARINATE: 30 minutes or 3 to 24 hours
MAKES: enough for 1 to 1½ pounds of beef

✓ INGREDIENTS

- ¼ cup finely chopped onion
- 3 tablespoons soy sauce
- 2 tablespoons cooking oil
- 2 tablespoons balsamic vinegar or cider vinegar
- 1 teaspoon dried thyme, crushed
- 1 clove garlic, minced
- ½ teaspoon black pepper

1 ADD THE MARINADE
In a bowl combine all the ingredients and mix well. Pour the marinade over meat in a resealable plastic bag. Seal the bag, turn to coat the meat, and place in a refrigerator. Marinate tender cuts for 30 minutes and tougher cuts for 3 to 24 hours. Drain the marinade and discard..

Jalapeño Marinade

Give your food some serious heat with just 1 hour in this marinade.

⊘ DETAILS

PREP: 10 minutes
MARINATE: 1 hour
MAKES: enough for 2 pounds of meat

✓ INGREDIENTS

- ¼ cup cooking oil
- 3 tablespoons white wine vinegar
- 2 tablespoons lime juice
- 1 tablespoon honey
- 2 teaspoons Jamaican jerk seasoning
- 1 fresh jalapeño chile pepper, seeded and finely chopped (see tip, page 52)

1 MIX THE MARINADE
In a screw-top jar combine all the ingredients, add the lid, and tighten carefully. Shake the jar vigorously to mix. Pour the marinade over pork, poultry, fish, or seafood in a resealable plastic bag. Refrigerate for 1 hour, turning the bag occasionally. Drain the marinade and discard.

9

SAUCES, MARINADES, RUBS, AND MOPS

Teriyaki-Ginger Marinade

This Japanese-inspired marinade is a flavorful match for almost any kind of meat.

🚫 DETAILS

PREP: 5 minutes
MARINATE: 30 minutes
MAKES: enough for 2 pounds of meat

✓ INGREDIENTS

- 1 teaspoon grated fresh ginger or
  ¼ teaspoon ground ginger
- 2 tablespoons teriyaki sauce
- 4 teaspoons toasted sesame oil
- 2 cloves garlic, minced
- 1 teaspoon sugar

1 GRATE THE GINGER
Use a kitchen grater to finely shred a piece of fresh ginger, as shown. In a small bowl combine 1 teaspoon of the ginger with the remaining ingredients and mix well. Pour over beef, pork, poultry, or fish in a resealable plastic bag. Refrigerate for 30 minutes. Drain the marinade and discard.

Balsamic-Mustard Marinade

The vinegar used in this marinade has been aged in wood casks to give it a unique Old-World flavor.

🚫 DETAILS

PREP: 5 minutes
MARINATE: 2 to 4 hours
MAKES: enough for 3 pounds of beef, pork, or poultry

✓ INGREDIENTS

- ¼ cup Dijon-style mustard
- ¼ cup balsamic vinegar
- 2 teaspoons cracked black pepper
- ¼ teaspoon white pepper

1 ADD MARINADE TO BAG
In a small bowl combine the ingredients; set aside 2 or 3 tablespoons of the mixture. Add the remaining marinade and beef, pork, or poultry to a resealable plastic bag and refrigerate for 2 to 4 hours. Drain the marinade and discard. Brush the reserved marinade on the meat during the last 10 minutes of grilling.

Beer Marinade

The beer adds great flavor, while the fresh lime juice helps tenderize meat.

PREP: 15 minutes
MARINATE: 6 to 24 hours
MAKES: enough for 1 pound of meat

✓ **INGREDIENTS**

- ½ cup lime juice
- 1 cup beer
- ½ cup chopped onion (1 medium)
- 3 tablespoons cooking oil
- 2 tablespoons steak sauce
- 1 tablespoon chili powder
- 4 cloves garlic, minced
- 1 teaspoon ground cumin

1 **JUICE THE LIMES**
Cut a couple of fresh limes in half and squeeze the halves, as shown, to juice them. In a bowl combine ½ cup of the lime juice with the remaining ingredients. Pour the marinade over beef or lamb in a resealable bag. Refrigerate for 6 to 24 hours, turning the bag occasionally. Drain and discard the marinade.

Whiskey-Mustard Marinade

Add some "spirit" and spice to your favorite grilled fish or seafood.

⬤ **DETAILS**

PREP: 10 minutes
MARINATE: 2 to 4 hours
MAKES: enough for 2½ pounds of fish or
            seafood

✓ **INGREDIENTS**

- ¼ cup cooking oil
- ¼ cup whiskey or bourbon
- ¼ cup stone-ground mustard
- 2 tablespoons honey
- 2 tablespoons vinegar
- 1 tablespoon soy sauce
- ½ teaspoon bottled hot pepper sauce
- ¼ teaspoon salt

1 **WHISK THE INGREDIENTS**
In a small bowl combine the ingredients and mix well with a kitchen whisk to dissolve the honey and the salt. Pour the marinade over fish or seafood in a resealable plastic bag and refrigerate for 2 to 4 hours. Drain and discard the marinade.

9

SAUCES, MARINADES, RUBS, AND MOPS

Rubs

When it comes to seasoning meat on the grill, many outdoor cooks are content to shake on some salt, pepper, or spices after the meat is on the grill rack. The trouble is that while they might add a hint of flavor with these basic efforts, they probably won't get the full advantage of the seasonings and spices. Many new grill chefs are hesitant to "overseason" their food and don't use nearly enough to add any discernable flavor. Furthermore, some flavors need time to work—often more than the time it takes for meat to cook. Plus grilling is an active style of cooking, and most seasonings simply fall off when meat is turned or run off with juices before they can work. These reasons are why serious grillers turn to rubs when they want serious flavor.

Rubs are mixtures of spices, herbs, and seasonings that you apply to the surface of meat and then rub in with your fingers—hence the name. Most rubs are dry, but some may incorporate some type of liquid ingredient such as oil or mustard. Rubs use ample portions of various flavorings, ensuring that the tastes imparted by the spices and herbs stand out and complement the smoky grilling flavor. Rubs are especially great for grilling because they stick better to the surface of the meat. Many recipes will call for applying the rub, then allowing the meat to sit in the refrigerator for a while to give the spices and seasonings more time to work their flavoring magic.

When using a rub, don't make the mistake of thinking you can save time by applying the individual ingredients to the meat and then rubbing. This can result in inconsistent flavoring and disappointing results. Mix your rub ingredients thoroughly in a bowl or other container before applying them. Most dry rub recipes will yield a quantity of seasoning for a specified amount of meat. If your cut of meat is smaller, make sure you use an appropriate portion of the rub—it's easy to "overseason" meat with a rub. If you end up with extra dry rub, place it in an airtight container and store it in the cupboard for up to six months.

When it's time to use the rub, sprinkle the mixture over the entire cut of meat and gently work the spices into the surface of the meat with your fingertips. Cover the meat and set it aside in the refrigerator until you're ready to grill. Some recipes will specify a certain "resting" time after cooking. If no time is specified, a good rule of thumb is to apply your rub and place the meat in the refrigerator while you start your fire. This will give the rub spices and seasonings ample time to flavor the meat.

▲ Dry rubs are simple to apply. Sprinkle a generous amount of the seasoning mixture on all surfaces of the meat and then work it in with your fingertips to help the spices stick and the flavor penetrate more deeply.

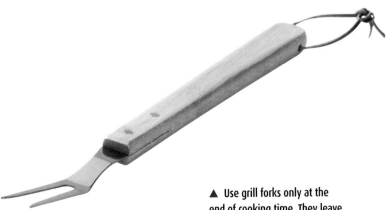

▲ Use grill forks only at the end of cooking time. They leave holes that allow juices and flavor to escape from meat.

Kansas City Barbecue Rub

This spicy-sweet mixture is perfect for seasoning slow-cooked smoked foods.

DETAILS

START TO FINISH: 10 minutes
MAKES: enough for 6 to 8 pounds of meat

INGREDIENTS

¼	cup sugar
1	tablespoon seasoned salt
1	tablespoon garlic salt
1	tablespoon paprika
1	tablespoon barbecue seasoning
1½	teaspoons onion salt
1½	teaspoons celery salt
1½	teaspoons chili powder
1½	teaspoons black pepper
¾	teaspoon ground ginger
¾	teaspoon lemon-pepper seasoning
¼	teaspoon ground thyme
⅛	teaspoon cayenne pepper

1 COMBINE THE INGREDIENTS
In a bowl combine all the ingredients and blend them thoroughly with a kitchen whisk. Sprinkle the mixture evenly on the surface of beef, pork, or poultry and pat it in with your fingers. Set the meat aside in the refrigerator until grilling time.

Chipotle Rub

Wake up your steaks or chops with this peppery seasoning.

DETAILS

START TO FINISH: 5 minutes
MAKES: enough for 2½ pounds of meat

INGREDIENTS

1	teaspoon ground coriander
¼	teaspoon paprika
¼	to ½ teaspoon black pepper
1	small dried chipotle chile pepper, seeded and crushed, or ⅛ to ¼ teaspoon cayenne pepper

1 RUB IN THOROUGHLY
In a bowl combine the ingredients and mix well. Sprinkle the mixture evenly on beef, pork, or poultry and gently pat it into the surface with your fingers, as shown. Turn the meat over and apply the rub to the other side. Set the meat aside in the refrigerator until grilling time.

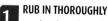

9

SAUCES, MARINADES, RUBS, AND MOPS

Mustard-and-Pepper Rub

This wet rub packs a peppery pop that complements flavorful meats such as beef, lamb, and pork.

DETAILS

PREP: 10 minutes
CHILL: 15 minutes
MAKES: enough for 3 pounds of meat

INGREDIENTS

- 2 teaspoons coarsely cracked black pepper
- 1 tablespoon coarse-grain brown mustard
- 2 teaspoons olive oil
- 1 teaspoon coarse salt or salt
- ½ teaspoon dried tarragon, crushed

1 CRACK THE PEPPERS
Use a rolling pin to coarsely crack whole black peppercorns, as shown. In a small bowl combine 2 teaspoons of the cracked pepper with the remaining ingredients. Apply the mixture to the meat and pat in with your fingers. Cover and refrigerate the meat for 15 minutes to 4 hours before grilling.

Jamaican Jerk Rub

A traditional Caribbean spice mixture is now a favorite seasoning for pork and chicken everywhere.

DETAILS

PREP: 5 minutes
MAKES: enough for 2 pounds of pork or poultry

INGREDIENTS

- 1 tablespoon onion powder
- 1 tablespoon packed brown sugar
- 1 tablespoon dried thyme, crushed
- 1½ teaspoons allspice
- 1½ teaspoons salt
- 1 teaspoon cracked black pepper
- ½ teaspoon ground nutmeg
- ½ teaspoon ground cinnamon
- ½ teaspoon ground cloves
- ¼ teaspoon cayenne pepper

1 RUB IN THE SEASONINGS
In a bowl combine all the ingredients and mix well. Place the meat in a pan and sprinkle evenly with the rub mixture. Work the seasonings into the surface of the meat with your fingers. Place the meat in the refrigerator for 30 minutes before grilling.

Cajun Rub

Straight out of Louisiana, this medley of spices puts three different kinds of pepper to work on your food.

DETAILS

START TO FINISH: 5 minutes
MAKES: enough for 3½ pounds of meat

INGREDIENTS

1½	teaspoons white pepper
1½	teaspoons black pepper
1	teaspoon cayenne pepper
1	teaspoon dried thyme, crushed
1	teaspoon onion powder
1	teaspoon garlic powder
½	teaspoon salt

1 SPRINKLE ON THE RUB
In a small bowl combine all the ingredients and mix well. Sprinkle the mixture evenly on pork, poultry, or fish and work the seasonings in, gently rubbing with the tips of your fingers, as shown. Turn the meat over and repeat the process. Refrigerate the meat until you're ready to grill.

Herb Rub

Flavor just about any type of grill-friendly food with this versatile rub.

DETAILS

START TO FINISH: 10 minutes
MAKES: enough for 5 pounds of beef, pork, poultry, or seafood

INGREDIENTS

2	teaspoons dried rosemary
2	teaspoons dried thyme
2	teaspoons dried minced onion
2	teaspoons dried minced garlic
1	teaspoon salt
¾	teaspoon black pepper

1 PROCESS THE RUB
In a food processor combine all the ingredients. Cover and process the mixture until it's coarsely ground and well blended. Sprinkle the mixture evenly on beef, pork, poultry, or seafood and pat it in with your fingers. Set the meat aside in the refrigerator until you're ready to grill.

Mops

Mops have their roots in the famed large-scale pit barbecues of Texas. Traditional mops are thin, watery sauces that are applied during cooking with an actual cotton kitchen mop (remember, they do things in a big way in the Lone Star State). As the meat cooks (in Texas it's usually beef), the mop sauce adds flavor along with moisture to keep meat from drying out during a slow cooking process.

Don't worry; you don't have to dig a giant pit in the backyard and fill it with a whole cow's worth of meat to get in on the mopping fun. Mops are especially great sauces for smoking or for long, slow indirect cooking on your standard backyard charcoal or gas grill. You can mix up your own mop sauces and slop them on the meat with the aid of a nifty grilling tool called a basting mop, which is usually outfitted with a foot-long handle and looks like a mini kitchen mop. The tool is important when applying authentic mop sauces which are supposed to be runny.

Mops are fun to work with because they can be made with a wide variety of ingredients and, most important, all sorts of interesting liquids. You can easily create a mop-style sauce by simply diluting your favorite barbecue sauce with water or vinegar, but creativity rules for serious moppers. Possible mop sauce liquids include beer, orange juice, coffee, bourbon, wine, apple cider—whatever sounds tasty. Flavor your sauces with spices, seasonings, herbs, and condiments that you use in your favorite barbecue sauce or marinade.

Some mop sauces include a significant amount of sugar or sugary liquids among their ingredients, and you will need to take some care in using them. If you are using a sweet mop sauce on meat smoking at low temperatures, no problem—apply the mop liberally throughout the cooking process. If you are grilling (over either indirect or, especially, direct heat), you will be cooking the meat at temperatures above the burning point of the sugar. To avoid an excessive burnt flavor, either use a mop with little or no sugar or limit the sauce application to the last 10 minutes of grilling to keep the sugar in the sauce from burning.

▲ Basting mops look like miniature kitchen mops. To use, soak the mop in the sauce and generously slather the liquid on meats during cooking. Like all grilling tools, choose a long-handled model to minimize the risk of burns.

▲ A good basting brush is a decent substitute if you don't have a mop. Select one with natural bristles and a long handle.

Basic Moppin' Sauce

This coffee-powered mop will give your grilled meats a serious wake-up call.

⟩ DETAILS

PREP: 15 minutes
COOK: 30 minutes
MAKES: 2 cups

✓ INGREDIENTS

1	cup strong coffee
1	cup ketchup
½	cup Worcestershire sauce
¼	cup butter or margarine
1	tablespoon sugar
1	to 2 teaspoons black pepper
½	teaspoon salt (optional)

1 MOP ON THE SAUCE

In a medium saucepan combine all the ingredients. Heat to boiling, stirring occasionally. Reduce the heat and simmer, uncovered, for 30 minutes, stirring occasionally. During the last 10 minutes of grilling, dunk your basting mop in the sauce and generously coat beef, pork, or poultry, as shown.

Texas-Style Mop

In the Lone Star State, grill chefs use this sauce on beef, but you can put it to work on any meat.

⟩ DETAILS

PREP: 10 minutes
COOK: 10 minutes
MAKES: about 1¾ cups

✓ INGREDIENTS

1	4-ounce can diced green chile peppers, drained
1	cup finely chopped onion (1 large)
½	cup honey
½	cup ketchup
1	tablespoon chili powder
1	clove garlic, minced
½	teaspoon dry mustard

1 DRAIN THE CHILE PEPPERS

Drain the diced chiles in a basket strainer, as shown. In a saucepan stir the chiles together with the remaining ingredients and cook over low heat for 10 minutes. Mop on beef, pork, lamb, or poultry during the last 10 minutes of grilling.

9

SAUCES, MARINADES, RUBS, AND MOPS

Chili Mop

Add real chili flavor to any kind of grilled meat with this hearty sauce.

DETAILS

PREP: 10 minutes
COOK: 5 minutes
MAKES: about 1¾ cups

INGREDIENTS

1	cup chopped onion (1 large)
½	cup water
4	cloves garlic, minced
2	teaspoons chili powder
1	8-ounce can tomato sauce
⅓	cup vinegar
2	tablespoons honey
½	teaspoon salt
¼	teaspoon black pepper

1 COOK THE ONION MIXTURE
In a saucepan combine onion, water, garlic, and chili powder. Cook, stirring occasionally, until the onion is tender. Add the remaining ingredients and heat the mixture to boiling, stirring constantly. Boil for 5 minutes until the sauce is slightly thickened. Mop on beef, pork, or poultry during the last 10 minutes of grilling.

Bourbon-Mustard Mop

Use orange juice as an alternative liquid in this spicy-sweet sauce.

DETAILS

START TO FINISH: 10 minutes
MAKES: about 1 cup

INGREDIENTS

¼	cup brown mustard
¼	cup bourbon or orange juice
¼	cup mild-flavored molasses
2	tablespoons packed brown sugar
2	tablespoons soy sauce
1	teaspoon cooking oil

1 MEASURE THE INGREDIENTS
In a small saucepan combine all the ingredients. Stir the mixture and cook over low heat just until heated through. Mop the sauce on beef or pork during the last 10 minutes of grilling. Reheat any remaining sauce until it's bubbly and serve with the meat.

Mustard-Black Pepper Mop

Cracked pepper and minced garlic give the mustard a memorable zing.

⏱ DETAILS

START TO FINISH: 5 minutes
MAKES: enough for 1 pound of meat

✓ INGREDIENTS

- 1 clove garlic, minced
- 2 tablespoons Dijon-style mustard
- 1 teaspoon packed brown sugar
- ½ teaspoon coarsely cracked black pepper

1 MINCE THE GARLIC
Peel the skin off a garlic clove and mince the garlic by chopping it into tiny pieces, as shown. In a small bowl combine the minced garlic with the other ingredients and mix well. Mop the sauce on beef, pork, or poultry during the last 10 minutes of grilling.

Jalapeño-Mustard Mop

This seafood-friendly sauce features the tasty partnership of Mexican and French flavors.

⏱ DETAILS

START TO FINISH: 10 minutes
MAKES: enough for 1 pound of meat

✓ INGREDIENTS

- 3 tablespoons Dijon-style mustard
- 3 canned jalapeño chile peppers, seeded (if desired) and finely chopped
- 1 tablespoon frozen orange juice concentrate, thawed
- 1 tablespoon light-color corn syrup
- ½ teaspoon lemon-pepper seasoning

1 MOP ON THE SAUCE
In a small bowl combine all the ingredients and mix until well blended. With a basting mop generously apply the sauce, as shown, to fish or seafood during the last 2 or 3 minutes of grilling.

9

SAUCES, MARINADES, RUBS, AND MOPS

Index

▲ Drip pan on Ducane Gas Grill

INDEX

▼ **Toasting buns for Carolina Pulled Pork BBQ (see recipe, page 138)**

INDEX

▲ Brushing on sauce for Honey-Herb Glazed Chicken (see recipe, page 58)

INDEX

INDEX

▲ **Bias-slicing meat**

▼ **Ginger-Orange Beef Ribs (see recipe, page 130)**

Metric Information

The charts on this page provide a guide for converting measurements from the U.S. customary system, which is used throughout this book, to the metric system.

Product Differences

Most of the ingredients called for in the recipes in this book are available in most countries. However, some are known by different names. Here are some common American ingredients and their possible counterparts:

■ All-purpose flour is enriched, bleached or unbleached white household flour. When self-rising flour is used in place of all-purpose flour in a recipe that calls for leavening, omit the leavening agent (baking soda or baking powder) and salt.
■ Baking soda is bicarbonate of soda.
■ Cornstarch is cornflour.
■ Golden raisins are sultanas.
■ Green, red, or yellow sweet peppers are capsicums or bell peppers.
■ Light-colored corn syrup is golden syrup.
■ Powdered sugar is icing sugar.
■ Sugar (white) is granulated, fine granulated, or castor sugar.
■ Vanilla or vanilla extract is vanilla essence.

Volume and Weight

The United States traditionally uses cup measures for liquid and solid ingredients. The chart below shows the approximate imperial and metric equivalents. If you are accustomed to weighing solid ingredients, the following approximate equivalents will be helpful.

■ 1 cup butter, castor sugar, or rice = 8 ounces = $1/2$ pound = 250 grams
■ 1 cup flour = 4 ounces = $1/4$ pound = 125 grams
■ 1 cup icing sugar = 5 ounces = 150 grams

Canadian and U.S. volume for a cup measure is 8 fluid ounces (237 ml), but the standard metric equivalent is 250 ml.

1 British imperial cup is 10 fluid ounces.

In Australia, 1 tablespoon equals 20 ml, and there are 4 teaspoons in the Australian tablespoon.

Spoon measures are used for smaller amounts of ingredients. Although the size of the tablespoon varies slightly in different countries, for practical purposes and for recipes in this book, a straight substitution is all that's necessary. Measurements made using cups or spoons always should be level unless stated otherwise.

Common Weight Range Replacements

Imperial / U.S.	Metric
$1/2$ ounce	15 g
1 ounce	25 g or 30 g
4 ounces ($1/4$ pound)	115 g or 125 g
8 ounces ($1/2$ pound)	225 g or 250 g
16 ounces (1 pound)	450 g or 500 g
$1^1/4$ pounds	625 g
$1^1/2$ pounds	750 g
2 or $2^1/4$ pounds	1,000 g

Baking Pan Sizes

Imperial / U.S.	Metric
$9\times1^1/2$-inch round cake pan	22- or 23×4-cm (1.5 L)
$9\times1^1/2$-inch pie plate	22- or 23×4-cm (1 L)
8×8×2-inch square cake pan	20×5-cm (2 L)
9×9×2-inch square cake pan	22- or 23×4.5-cm (2.5 L)
$11\times7\times1^1/2$-inch baking pan	28×17×4-cm (2 L)
2-quart rectangular baking pan	30×19×4.5-cm (3 L)
13×9×2-inch baking pan	34×22×4.5-cm (3.5 L)
15×10×1-inch jelly roll pan	40×25×2-cm
9×5×3-inch loaf pan	23×13×8-cm (2 L)
2-quart casserole	2 L

Oven Temperature Equivalents

Fahrenheit Setting	Celsius Setting*	Gas Setting
300°F	150°C	Gas Mark 2 (very low)
325°F	160°C	Gas Mark 3 (low)
350°F	180°C	Gas Mark 4 (moderate)
375°F	190°C	Gas Mark 5 (moderate)
400°F	200°C	Gas Mark 6 (hot)
425°F	220°C	Gas Mark 7 (hot)
450°F	230°C	Gas Mark 8 (very hot)
475°F	240°C	Gas Mark 9 (very hot)
500°F	260°C	Gas Mark 10 (extremely hot)
Broil	Broil	Grill

U.S. / Standard Metric Equivalents

$1/8$ teaspoon = 0.5 ml	2 tablespoons = 25 ml	$1/2$ cup = 4 fluid ounces = 125 ml	2 cups = 1 pint = 500 ml
$1/4$ teaspoon = 1 ml	$1/4$ cup = 2 fluid ounces = 50 ml	$2/3$ cup = 5 fluid ounces = 150 ml	1 quart = 1 litre
$1/2$ teaspoon = 2 ml	$1/3$ cup = 3 fluid ounces = 75 ml	$3/4$ cup = 6 fluid ounces = 175 ml	
1 teaspoon = 5 ml	$1/3$ cup = 3 fluid ounces = 75 ml	1 cup = 8 fluid ounces = 250 ml	

Toolbox essentials: nuts-and-bolts books for do-it-yourself success.

Save money, get great results, and take the guesswork out of home improvement projects with a growing library of step-by-step books from the experts at The Home Depot.

Packed with lots of projects and practical tips, these books help you design, remodel, decorate, and repair your home or garden. Easy-to-follow, step-by-step instructions and colorful photographs ensure success. Projects even estimate time, skills, materials needed, and tools required.

**You can do it.
We can help.**

Look for the books that help you say "I can do that!" at The Home Depot®, www.meredithbooks.com, or wherever quality books are sold.